CONFESSIONS OF A
BIBLE THUMPER

Confessions of a Bible Thumper

My Homebrewed Quest for a Reasoned Faith

MICHAEL CAMP

"Every significant breakthrough comes from a break with traditional ways of thinking."

—*Stephen Covey*

ENGAGE
FAITH

ENGAGE FAITH PRESS • SEATTLE, WA

Published 2012

Printed in the United States of America

16 15 14 13 12   1 2 3 4

ISBN 978-1-936672-27-1

For information, address Engage Faith Press, PO Box 2222, Poulsbo WA 98370.

To Mom and Dad,
with love and gratitude

CONTENTS

ACKNOWLEDGEMENTS

When I first embarked on this project, I didn't know it takes a village—or in my case, a small city—to write a decent book. Soon I learned how many people I needed to help me with research, critique, encouragement, and promotion. I am grateful for every one.

Many friends pointed me in the right direction and a few gave me a gentle shove. Thank you Darwin Chandler, Roger MacNicol, John Paul, Jan Paul, Tim Cowley, and Rich Slimbach for your honest assessment of early and not-so-early drafts. Thanks Karen Ferris for your fabulous input and for convincing me I could actually pull this project off. I'm grateful for my wonderful Kitsap County Writer's Group. You all launched me into serious writing territory with your ongoing assistance and honest critiques. Special thanks to Randy Henderson, Larry Keeton, Juliet Nordeen, Gary Ley, and Beverly Lionberger.

The Pacific Northwest Writers Association was an incredible resource. Thanks to my fellow members Paul Hartman, Karen Alaniz, and Jennie Spohr for your inspiration and advice. For those who helped me promote the lessons of the book or just gave me advice, I'm grateful to Tripp Fuller, Chad Crawford, Brenda Michaels, Rob Spears, Rob Steiner, and Leslie Hazelton.

I really appreciate Jessica Maxwell who gave me valuable input on sample chapters. Thanks so much Julie and Steve Ferwerda for your encouragement and Julie for your feedback on a later draft. To my amazing Book Doctor Jason Black, I'm especially grateful. Thanks for your thoughtful evaluation and recommendations. Also Cherie

Tucker, my line (and more) editor extraordinaire, your input and suggested improvements worked wonders! Melinda Mendoza, thanks for your meticulous final edits. And Randy Kuckuck of PublishNext, you were an incredible resource. Thanks for all your advice.

To my wife, Lori, thank you for your love and support and for putting up with my writing weekends and understanding my vision. Thanks Joel, Jordan, Nathan, and Bethany for your patience with me "off writing" or chained to my office desk.

Finally, there are those who indirectly inspired and informed my writing through their outstanding ideas and extraordinary books. Thanks to Ayaan Hirsi Ali, David Berlinski, Marcus Borg, Tony Campolo, William Countryman, Harvey Cox, Gary DeMar, Bart Ehrman, Wendy Francisco, Anne Lamott, Raymond Lawrence, Brian McLaren, Mark Noll, Frank Schaeffer, Thomas Talbott, Mel White, Garry Wills, N. T. Wright, Philip Yancey, and many more too numerous to mention.

Author's Note

This book is based on my personal recollections and academic research. In so far as the book describes my inner spiritual journey and the conclusions I came to, it is one hundred percent true. With the exception of public personalities, the names and some descriptions of people in the book have been changed to protect their privacy.

I took creative license in portions of the book by enhancing scenes, creating dialogue, and making a composite of multiple real-life conversations, and sometimes people, into one. Although these are not altogether factual, they are based on my life experience. Most, but not all, are the scenes where I have conversations with Dan, Gina, Lori, and Steve at Silver City Brewery and Restaurant.

CONFESSIONS OF A BIBLE THUMPER

An Invitation

Religion. Some atheists think it poisons everything. I think that notion has merit.

In this book, I differentiate between religion and spiritual inspiration. If you join me on my journey, this distinction will become crystal clear. For now, understand I define religion as a man-made, human construct—an institutionalized system created to control people's attitudes, beliefs, and behaviors. This doesn't prove there isn't a God or that a belief in God poisons everything. It merely means humans often screw up how to relate to God. It also means religion can taint more than belief in a Higher Power. It can infect any philosophy. Even atheism.

Parts of this book were difficult for me to write. I critique a religious tradition—evangelicalism—that has certain values I cherish: a focus on God's love for the individual, personal spirituality, and faith communities where people actually know and care for each other. Compared to my experience in staid and stuffy mainline churches, these values were a refreshing change. It's what drew me into evangelicalism. (I have since learned many mainline churches aren't so staid and stuffy after all.)

Nevertheless, in time I discovered a deceptive paradox. Many of these positives in evangelicalism were one side of a half-truth. On the flipside were subtle falsehoods—the deception of exclusive faith, biblical literalism, and performance-oriented religion. A religion obsessed with individual piety and doctrine over and above concern for social justice. These attributes turn loving and caring for each

1

other into spiritual manipulation and abuse. They are what drove me to leave the movement.

Today, evangelicalism is deeply divided. This is a welcome trend. On the one side are traditionalists who are enmeshed in a fundamentalist paradigm and refuse to question long-held beliefs. They are committed to their religion. On the other side are progressives—the "emergent" church and post-evangelicals[1]—who are re-evaluating tradition in a post-modern society. Liberal readers may be surprised, but, yes, there is a progressive side to evangelicalism.[2] Their conclusions make traditionalists extremely nervous. They are questioning their religion. Because of them, I stayed in the movement as long as I did.

Meanwhile, a new spirituality has arisen in America—inclusive faith that is spiritual-but-not-religious. It claims everyday people outside churches and religious institutions can access a living God. They admire Christian mystics, Jesus, the Dalai Lama, Deepak Chopra, Rumi, Don Miguel Ruiz, and teachings that draw on a combination of Eastern, Western, and native spiritual traditions. They seek to relate to God outside organized religion. To the extent that they go where the historical and spiritual evidence leads, I think this is good. There was a time when I thought these folks were loony. Today, I feel very comfortable among them.

Confessions of a Bible Thumper is the story of my 25-years-plus spiritual journey into and out of evangelicalism. If you ever wondered how someone could buy into conservative religion, my story gives you the answer. More importantly, it tells why I remained for so long and how I overcame deep psychological and theological obstacles to finally leave and land on the soft ground of a progressive[3] Christianity—not a religion based on the certainty of doctrine, but a form of spiritual inspiration. Despite rejecting the falsehoods I mention above, I didn't run into the arms of angry secularists (who have their own form of closed-mindedness). While keeping my own faith, I found peace with unbelievers, agnostics, and atheists, many of whom, I discovered, are honest seekers. Ironically, I still consider myself an orthodox Christian, albeit one that unpacks religious and biblical concepts in a most unorthodox way.

I invite you to join me on my tenacious quest to make sense of faith and then live it devoid of religion. Observe the lessons I learned born out of my insatiable urge to know God, my ethereal spiritual experiences, and the gnawing feeling in my gut that something was amiss. Learn what drew me into the 1970s Jesus Movement at the age of fifteen. Relive my conversion to a God called Jesus. Come with me deep inside the evangelical movement: into a place within its bowels where I put my faith into practice, joined church movements, became a pro-life activist, and moved to Africa to serve the poor and save the world. Trouble was, the world had other plans.

What was the world teaching me about my faith? At first I couldn't put my finger on it. Then the fog cleared and it became obvious. My faith was full of religious baggage—the stuff of religion. Items the evangelical church told me I had to carry. Practices and beliefs I hadn't bargained for. Heavy luggage, like those old-fashioned bags you have to lift because there are no wheels or extendable handles. They were packed with myths, half-truths, and a dogmatic approach to life—stuff having to do with worshiping the Bible, idolizing church, canonizing doctrine, controlling behavior, and other paraphernalia, such as imposed religious disciplines, spiritual manipulation, resisting reason, and judging outsiders.

Gradually, my inquisitive mind caused me to unpack this baggage. That's when I uncovered a variety of startling revelations that turned my conservative Christian theology on its head. And when I eventually concluded we evangelicals—although correct about many things, like the importance of Divine connection, the wisdom of Christ, and charitable service and giving—are largely wrong on a host of other issues. You will learn what these are in nine of my confessions. As I wrote these words, bestselling novelist Anne Rice, known for her vampire novels and rediscovery of Christian faith, announced, "I quit being a Christian. I'm out. I remain committed to Christ as always, but not to being... part of Christianity." Although I feel she overlooks a progressive Christian option, I know how she feels. She is rejecting Christianity as a religion, not as a personal faith. Imagine that for a moment.

My story is also about the reaction of my evangelical friends and family. Most were not happy campers. I was walking on thin ice, they told me. A small minority thought I was onto something. What's more, the journey includes those I met along the path who helped me realign my theological worldview and see things in a new light. Ultimately, they helped me find a place to quench my spiritual yearnings, love God, and love others free from the poison of religion.

I should warn you: whether your faith is conservative, liberal, or non-existent, you might be surprised at some of my discoveries. In fact, you may love, hate, or doubt my revelations. Regardless, I promise you these four things: they are not stereotypical, I will keep you guessing, I won't shove them down your throat, and I'll respect you in the morning.

To readers outside of evangelicalism, twenty-five years sounds like a long time to uncover legalistic religion. I confess, I'm slow. But restless evangelical readers and those in the emergent church will know that the cult of evangelicalism is subtle. And as I said, not everything is negative. Evangelicalism has some positive things going for it. This is why it is so enticing for many. And why I took a few lightweight spiritual carry-ons with me on the way out the door. Moreover, I maintain respect for many within the movement, even while critiquing their positions. I hope they see it is loving, constructive criticism.

Can a former evangelical find lasting peace and a spiritual home? If God is not into exclusivist, organized religion, how the hell does the Divine work in the world? Join me, and let's see what we can discover together.

CONFESSION 1

BEER AND JESUS

"Beer is proof that God loves us and wants us to be happy."

– Benjamin Franklin

Silverdale, Washington 2010

My first confession is that I unashamedly love beer...*and* Jesus. The roots of this dual affection grew in my formative years on a memorable trip to the Bible Belt during the 1970s Jesus Movement— an evangelical phenomenon that appealed to spiritual seekers and burned-out hippies. That's an experience I would soon recount in my mind's eye. But at this moment, as I walked into my favorite watering hole, Silver City Brewery and Restaurant, I had two immediate goals: one, see a glass of an award-winning cold microbrew in my hand and two, get lucky—but not in the usual sense. I made a beeline for the bar.

As was typical, the whole place was packed and buzzing with noise and laughter from a variety of people—families and couples in the restaurant and groups of men, women, and couples in the bar area—it's one of the community's most popular pubs in this small Navy town west of Seattle. I looked around a bit. The pub area with its row of tall oak tables surrounding the actual bar is open, so you could see most of the art-deco-style restaurant beyond. You could also see the adjacent small but state-of-the-art brewery through towering windows with its four, massive, silver brew kettles.

5

Scanning the area, I quickly saw how promising things appeared. Right in the middle of the bar, next to an attractive, bright-eyed, thirty-something woman with short auburn hair sitting with a female friend, were two unoccupied stools. I recognized my good fortune. It wasn't the ladies, it was the seats. Immediately finding a place to sit in Silver City's pub on a Friday night was about as unlikely as winning the Washington State lottery.

I better nab those babies fast. I threw my coat on the seat next to the woman and sat down on the other. My second desire was to get that beer. I got a bartender's attention, and he walked over. "Hey, bro, what'll you have tonight?"

"Ah, let's see; give me a Ridgetop," I said, referring to their Ridgetop Red Amber Ale. "Oh, and, Brett, I'll start a tab, since I'm waiting for a table for dinner."

Now I felt better. My beer was being poured, and I had a seat for myself and my fellow middle-aged friend Dan, who was due to meet me. Dan and I frequent Silver City to shoot the breeze. While most patrons talk about sports, work, and their personal lives, and singles try to meet interesting people of the opposite sex, we have an obsession. We talk about religion and spirituality and how they influence politics, public policy, and popular culture. Sports come in a distant second.

Dan is a semi-retired dentist who served in the Navy. He and his wife Gina, a dental hygienist, regularly put their Christian faith into practice by volunteering on a dental relief team that goes to Senegal, West Africa, every year, a practice I deeply admire. I'm also impressed with Dan's ability to stay trim despite his love of beer. Some people have all the luck. I have seen him sitting here many times, slightly balding and gray but in great physical shape, putting my bursting belly to shame. At least I still have a full head of hair.

I would describe Dan as a progressive evangelical and an anomaly. Although he attends a fairly conservative evangelical church, he is politically and socially liberal. Like progressive Christian author Anne Lamott, he has a hard time loving George W. Bush. He's one of the few who welcomes my crazy ideas. Gina does, too, but she's a bit more skeptical of some of my conclusions.

Tonight, it was different. Dan and I were meeting our wives for dinner. It was 7:00. Before I entered the bar area, I had put in my name for a table for four. Since it could be as long as a thirty-minute wait, and the ladies weren't meeting us until then, I knew Dan and I had plenty of time for a brew.

Sometimes Dan and I come with a friend named Steve. Steve is a theologically conservative early-forty-something evangelical with a moderate streak. Out of this motley crew (my wife Lori and I, Gina and Dan, and Steve), it is usually Gina, Dan, and I who like to ask the tough questions about the Christian faith that we've noticed most believers are hesitant to address. Questions like, why did God command the Israelites to destroy whole towns, sometimes including women and children? Why do some of the actions of the God of the Old Testament seem at odds with Jesus' clear teaching on love? Why do evangelicals tend to be militaristic despite Jesus' pacifist teachings? Why would a God of love create an eternal hell? Why doesn't the church readily support environmental causes?

I wondered if we'd end up talking about my book—my spiritual journey into and out of conservative Christianity. Dan had recently read a draft of the manuscript. Since he actually liked it, it must have been way beyond what Anne Lamott calls the "Shitty First Draft"[4] stage. I glanced around. No sign of Dan. A family was called for their table. I noticed a teenage boy among them. *I was about that age when my journey began,* I thought. I took my first gulp of beer. That's when that unforgettable trip to Dallas, Texas, deeply embedded in my brain, began to play back. For now, I forgot about Dan.

The Jesus Revolution, 1972

I was fifteen years old and desperate to be noticed. My preference was to be noticed by Leslie McMahan—the well-endowed hot blonde in biology class. My mom and youth leaders in my Baptist church wanted me to be noticed by God—or more accurately for me to notice God and "accept" Jesus. I had serious misgivings about this. But I had to acknowledge tapping into a Higher Power was desirable.

Maybe not as much as getting on Leslie McMahan's radar screen, but desirable nonetheless.

On June 12, 1972, I stood in a church parking lot in suburban Massachusetts. It was a year after *Time* magazine's cover story on what it coined "The Jesus Revolution." War demonstrations on college campuses and in Washington, D.C. had dominated the previous five years. In Vietnam, the South Vietnamese Air Force, in coordination with American military, had just dropped a napalm bomb on a small village. A photograph of children running away in the aftermath became the 1972 Photo of the Year. My high school friends and I were reveling in songs by Deep Purple, the Doobie Brothers, and Don McLean, who wrote "American Pie."

I was about to embark with my Baptist youth group to attend Explo '72 (Explo being short for explosion) in Dallas. It wasn't my idea to go. It was Mom's. And the youth group leader's at church. I think it was a conspiracy.

I had to admit, Mom had had a genuine born-again experience. A few years prior, after floundering in liberal New England churches, she rediscovered Jesus among a group of Charismatic believers who had somehow infiltrated some Baptists. That was a miracle in itself. New joy and purpose filled her life. In her zeal to see me experience something similar, she encouraged me to attend Explo. Encouraged may be too weak a word. Cajoled is probably more accurate. I reluctantly agreed. Mom meant well.

"Your life will never be the same," said the youth leader at the Baptist church.

Other than being geared toward youth, Explo was similar to Jesus Festivals that would occur in later years on acres of farmland, like Woodstocks without drugs. In fact, some people called Explo the "Christian Woodstock" because of the last day's huge, eight-hour Jesus rock concert that drew 200,000 people. Coincidentally, the Watergate burglary in Washington, D.C., occurred during the concert. The weeklong event, organized by Campus Crusade for Christ, included Bible teaching, evangelism training, and outdoor music throughout the city of Dallas, including the Cotton Bowl.

Over 75,000 high school and college students attended. The vision was to equip these youth for world evangelism. My goal was a tad less dramatic: to survive the week without turning into a straight-laced Jesus freak.

I occasionally attended youth group to please Mom and Dad and make life at home a bit more bearable. I'd attend when I wanted a favor, like permission to stay over a friend's house or borrow Dad's brand new Toyota Corona.

Part of the message at youth group was appealing: the part that claimed that God loves all and wants to forge a close relationship with each of us. For me, who yearned to be accepted by my peers, the thought of being connected with a loving, accepting Higher Power was comforting. Maybe this was a way to feel like I belonged, to be at peace with myself and overcome my inner doubts and fears. Maybe even get enough confidence to have an in with Leslie McMahan or some other pretty girl.

Part of the message was disconcerting though: the part that said one needed to repent of one's life of sin and begin to follow Christ and obey His Word, the Bible. Not that I didn't have any sins to repent of or didn't need some positive change in my life. I most certainly did. But some of the things I was hearing that were considered "His Word to obey" were pretty narrow and restricting. Things like don't curse, smoke, drink, party, or feel up your girlfriend...at all. Beware of popular youth culture, secular music, school dances, and rock concerts. Start attending church and regularly share the gospel message—called witnessing—with your friends and perfect strangers. You know, become a Bible thumper. Hell, I'd probably have to swear off the swimsuit issue of *Sports Illustrated*, most certainly *Playboy* magazine, and possibly James Bond movies.

These types of thoughts flooded my mind for days until the day Dad dropped me off at that parking lot. Other youth group members and two parent chaperones stood talking while we waited to climb into church vans and drive to the airport to catch our flights to Dallas. With moderately long brown hair parted on the side, a T-shirt, flared jeans, and sandals, I stood alone, hands in my pockets. I didn't really connect with the other youth group members. One thought filled my mind. *I can't believe I'm going. Will I return a Bible thumper?* Suddenly, I noticed my friend Jim and another acquaintance named Ted had arrived. I sighed in relief. *All right! Some people I know to hang with.* Jim, Ted, and I didn't exactly fit the youth group mold.

"Hey, Jim!" I called. "I wasn't sure if you were coming."

"Yes, I guess our moms won out, huh?" he responded. Jim was my age. He and his parents attended the Baptist church. We were both pretty much in the same boat: we were expected to attend this event. Sounded like Jim got the cajoling treatment too.

"Hey, Ted, what are you doing here?" I asked, since I knew he didn't attend youth group and his parents didn't go to the church.

"Explo's going to have some huge Jesus rock concerts I wanna see."

That was a shock. I didn't know Ted very well, since he was a year older. I soon learned that Ted, with his torn, flared Levis, T-shirt, cross necklace, sunglasses, and shoulder-length hair parted down the middle and tucked behind his ears, was a self-described Jesus freak. It was his idea to go, not his parents. Later, I realized his parents were a lot like me. They were the ones who were apprehensive. I imagined them worrying his Jesus conversion meant he'd end up in a cult, maybe dropping out of school and joining a Children of God commune in California. He didn't attend a church but read Jesus Movement literature and had discovered Christian rock music, probably someone like Larry Norman who wrote the lyric, "Why should the devil have all the good music?"

"I discovered Jesus is cool, and He changed my life," Ted told Jim and me in a matter-of-fact tone. "But I don't have to go to church to follow Him."

Despite describing himself as being "into Jesus," I liked Ted. He wasn't in your face about it, nor straight-laced. He must have been an early independently-minded post-evangelical. He apparently found Jesus without the influence of an institutional church. The big sin he abandoned was smoking weed. Thankfully, he hadn't given up trying to pick up girls. Being particularly shy around girls, I learned a lot of tips from Ted about how to flirt. Ted soon learned that at Explo, flirting was acceptable. Picking up girls was not—particularly Southern born-again Christian girls.

A day later, on our first full day at Explo, I witnessed Ted making inroads with the ladies in the air-conditioned lobby of the college dormitory where our group was housed with other youth groups from all over the country.

"Something tells me you're not from New York. Where are you from?" he asked a girl. *Boy, they make them gorgeous down South,* I thought.

"Near Atlanta. Where are y'all from?

"We're from New England. I hope you don't hold it against us that we're Northerners," he said.

"Of course not. It's exciting that the Lord has brought people [together] from all over the country."

"Rebecca...nice name. I just love your accent. Tell me what Georgia is like," he continued.

Eventually, he led into a subtle request for a date. "Man, I love to hear you talk. How about if we meet after tonight's meeting, and I'll buy you an ice cream?"

Then he made the mistake of lighting up a Marlboro.

"How can you follow Jesus and still smoke? Don't you know your body is the temple of the Holy Spirit?" the girl said. Like some of the members of our youth group and the leaders, most of the people we met were seriously into the Bible. For most of them, spirituality and smoking didn't mix. For that matter, swearing, beer, drugs, and sex outside of marriage didn't either. When it came to beer, cigarettes, and an occasional slip-of-the-tongue, Jim, Ted, and I were renegades. Group meetings in hotels, special speakers in the Cotton Bowl, and Christian soft-rock music saturated the week in Dallas. In smaller group meetings, the big questions I heard over and over from zealous teens and vibrant youth leaders were "Are you saved?" or the more popular, "Have you accepted Jesus Christ as your personal Lord and Savior?"

"*I* have," they might add, "and He walks with me every day," as if they had him in their back pocket. If you made the mistake of answering "No," they would typically launch into a long blurb on the "four spiritual laws," and try to convert you right there on the spot. The goal was to get everyone saved.

The Four Spiritual Laws was a popular tract that outlined the problem with sinful mankind and the solution found in Jesus, which was, of course, to accept him as your personal Lord and Savior. Then he could be in your back pocket too. The laws went something like this:

(1) God has a wonderful plan for your life.

(2) You are in sin and separated from God.

(3) Jesus is the only provision for your sin.

(4) You must individually receive Jesus as Lord and Savior.

Without "receiving" or "accepting" Jesus, this wonderful plan would not kick into high gear or, for that matter, any gear. I had mixed feelings about this message. A wonderful plan for my life? I wonder if it includes hooking up with Leslie. Probably not. Okay, maybe a Christian version of Leslie. The plan sounded like God would be looking after me. Does that mean I'll overcome my low self-esteem and gain the assurance to meet life's challenges? That would be nice. Since God had the plan already, maybe I wouldn't have to think for myself. That takes the pressure off. But is that a good thing?

"After I accepted the Lord, He changed my life and filled my heart with love. He can do the same for you," they might say after explaining the tract. If they had "accepted the Lord," the questioner might ask them to share their "testimony," which is the story behind how they came to the Lord.

The questioning about a personal relationship with God made me uncomfortable. That's not where I was. Yet, Lord knows, I could use a personal touch from a Supreme Being if there was one to be had. And for the most part, it did appear these people sincerely cared about a person's spiritual condition. I had met others like them in the youth group. But something was wrong. I began to ask myself why I hadn't accepted the Lord. It seemed everyone else had. I was the oddball who had wandered into a private club. When people discovered I (or anyone else) wasn't a member, they immediately went into witnessing mode: "Mike, you'll never find peace in your life unless you repent and accept Christ," implored one in a private conversation.

"Will you be ready to meet the Lord when He returns?" asked another in a small group meeting.

"Make sure you're not left behind," said a third who was referring to something called the Rapture, a prophetic event about which I would soon learn.

When asked about being saved by one of the many refined and dollish girls with sparkling eyes and a strong Southern accent, the temptation to say "yes" even though I really hadn't "accepted Him" was irresistible. Although Ted was not your stereotypical believer, I believe he was honest. He *had* accepted Jesus, in his own independent way. He could say "yes" all day long and proceed to lay on the charm. Trouble was, I hadn't, and if I said "no," to the big question, I might have to endure another earnest description of *The Four Spiritual Laws* and the peer pressure to join the "club" that accompanied it.

Blue-eyed with long blonde hair, a vivacious girl whom I met in our small group meeting approached me once. I was glad she wasn't shy but wondered if she or one of her friends would ask me the big question.

"Nice to meet you, Mike. Where are y'all from?" she said with her Southern drawl, even though it was only me standing there.

"Our group is from Massachusetts," I answered. "And where are you from?"

"We're from South Carolina." After some more chitchat, the question came: "How about *you* Mike, have you accepted the Lord?" Her blue eyes locked on mine, waiting for a response.

"Well, umm... yeah, I have," I said, hoping she wouldn't notice my insincerity or ask me to share my "testimony."

"Praise the Lord!" she said.

Her genuine excitement caught me off guard. But I had just discovered a way to get off the hook from another round of witnessing and another explanation of *The Four Spiritual Laws*.

The other popular subject at the conference was the pre-tribulation version of the Rapture, a belief in the imminent return of Jesus to take believers back to heaven and leave unbelievers to suffer through a seven-year period of tribulation during which the Antichrist, mentioned in the New Testament book of I John, is revealed. The believers would be "raptured," taken bodily up to glory, or maybe beamed up like on *Star Trek* with Jesus in the heavenly transporter room, so whatever place they occupied at the time would become unoccupied. Planes and cars would be left unattended, causing mass catastrophe and confusion. It was popularized by the new national bestseller by Hal Lindsey called *The Late Great Planet Earth*. Lindsey predicted that we were living in the generation that would see Christ's return at the end of history and therefore the Rapture. The book was at the peak of popularity in the summer of 1972, and I remember seeing people carrying copies of it along with their Bibles.

At Explo, earnest evangelist types couldn't resist using this concept of the imminent return of Jesus or the Rapture in their witnessing to people to try to get them to "accept" the Lord. "God's Word says when Christ returns, everyone who hasn't accepted Him will be left behind to endure the worst period of suffering the world has seen since the beginning of time," I overheard someone say one day.

Other people believed in the post-tribulation version where there is no beaming up to heaven. Christ would return *after* the tribulation period, not before, to exercise judgment on unbelievers and receive believers at the end of history. At times I heard these folks say something like, "The Bible predicted our contemporary events, which means we are probably living in the last days when Christ will return." Either way, when witnessing, talk of the Rapture or the return of Christ would add a little incentive for the witnesees to more seriously consider giving their lives to Christ and to be ready for the end, although the "pre-tribulation" notion was definitely more dramatic and apparently the end-times theology of choice at Explo.

Admittedly, I was starting to buy some of this, although the beaming up to heaven part was hard to swallow. Some people appeared so sure and confident and undoubtedly genuinely cared that people get saved. They also talked as if the Rapture could happen anytime, possibly right after breakfast.

Part of me wanted that assurance. Not about the Rapture, but about knowing Love. I felt a powerful draw—a pull to finally know the answers to life's daunting questions. To feel like I belonged to a caring community. To experience a personal God. To gain His approval. But I also was skeptical about the religious expectations. Could they be reconciled?

One memorable early evening at the festival before one of the large rallies, where the general public would also attend, Billy Graham would speak and Christian bands would perform, Jim, Ted, and I went wandering into the downtown Dallas neighborhood around the stadium. It was stiflingly hot and humid and the air was still. We were sweaty, thirsty, and bored. Somehow Ted, being the oldest, managed to get someone to buy us a six-pack of Colt 45 malt liquor.

"Shit! How did you get that?" Jim said, when Ted reappeared after exploring the neighborhood.

"Ingenuity, my boy. A black guy with an Afro and beads had something to do with it," Ted replied.

Ted had sworn off smoking pot, but figured there was nothing sinful about drinking a couple of beers. Jim and I knew this wasn't exactly what the youth group taught, but couldn't argue with his logic—besides, the beers were really cold—so we sat down somewhere in a rundown secluded neighborhood in Dallas and consumed the whole six pack of 16 ounce cans between us. Soon we were filled with the "spirit."

Ted then noticed some kids playing in a vacant lot a block away and decided he wanted to go "witness" about Jesus to them. So off we went, with me extremely uncomfortable at the prospect of telling others about Jesus, whom I had not "accepted."

Ted managed to spout out some kind of line such as, "Hey, kids, did you know Jesus loves you and wants to change your life?"

Jim piped in a few words, and I stayed on the back burner observing my first experience with witnessing for Jesus when I wasn't the witnessee. After a few minutes we heard a van stop a couple blocks away and a man who was obviously involved with Explo yelled out, "You guys need some Bibles to give to those kids?"

Ted was flabbergasted. "How did you know we were here?" he asked the man. Jim was amazed. I didn't know what to think.

"I think the Lord must have led us here," the man said. We distributed Bibles to each kid, said a few more things to encourage them to read the New Testament stories about Jesus, and then headed back toward the stadium. There was an eerie feeling in the air as if something out of this world had just happened. Either that or the Colt 45s had kicked in. Ted was talking a mile a minute proclaiming it was a miracle, as we headed back toward the stadium—by then people were beginning to enter for the evening's event. He kept stopping people on the way and spouting how the Lord had just miraculously provided Bibles for kids we had witnessed to in a nearby slum. Personally, I had my doubts this was a miracle.

Energized by what happened, Ted hurriedly entered the stadium with his long hair flying in the wind, while Jim and I followed like devotees tailing a prophet; he proceeded onto the field straight to the front of the stage on the 10-yard line. We wound up sitting on the grass in the front row. Ted and Jim kept exuberantly sharing our recent experience with people sitting in the general vicinity. I was the shy one and just sat there with my beer buzz and listened to the conversations.

I couldn't help but make the following observation: the level of excitement about our "miracle" was in direct proportion to the amount of Colt 45s we consumed. Ted drank three cans and was ecstatic, as if he had just witnessed Jesus raising the dead. Jim had two and was excited as a fisherman who saw Jesus walking on water. Wimpy me had only drunk one; I was the reluctant disciple, the doubting Thomas. Later on, a male youth leader in our room, when hearing how we had "felt the presence of God," made a similar comparison.

Jim and Ted appeared to confuse their beer buzz with a Holy Spirit high. Did that make drinking beer wrong? Preachers of the day didn't just warn against the dangers of alcohol and drug abuse. They generally said *any* use of alcohol and drugs was worldly—even for those who weren't underage. I wondered. To me, apart from getting shitfaced, beer didn't seem so bad. Or maybe tying one on once in a blue moon was acceptable. Did things always have to be so black and white?

Several bands performed before Billy Graham spoke that evening, including André Crouch and the Disciples, Love Song, and Johnny Cash. Love Song was a popular rock band affiliated with the denomination Calvary Chapel. Its members all had beards and long hair—in a curly afro-style or tied in ponytails. The leader, Chuck Girard, later became a famous contemporary Christian rock musician. Their music was sweet and their voices earnest, singing lyrics about the reality of God and the power of Jesus to deliver folks from whatever ailed them—addictions or fears.

Although I was enthralled and impressed with Billy Graham's preaching, I honestly don't remember the main message he gave. It must have been that can of Colt 45. But based on hearing him in later years, I'm sure it had something to do with God's love, being born again, and living for God. He probably read the story of Jesus and Nicodemus from the book of John, which is when Jesus made his famous statement, "You must be born again to see the Kingdom of God." Billy was a very likable preacher.

I remember the end of his sermon, when he gave the obligatory altar call, explained the gospel message (similar to the *The Four*

Spiritual Laws) and, as a call to action, challenged those who were unsaved to "give their hearts to Christ" so they could have their sins forgiven, be reconciled to God, and live a new and exciting Spirit-filled life, but not without some persecution. As an Evangelist, this was Billy's main event, his urgent appeal. Like most revivalists, he implored those who hadn't to publicly "trust Christ" before it's too late, meaning before the Rapture or before they die an untimely death or before they get so caught up in the world that their hearts become hard. If not, the Bible says you must face eternity separated from God. Although he wasn't an in-your-face, hell-fire-and-brimstone preacher, the message was loud and clear. Your eternal destiny hung in the balance that very night. It was an invitation with dire consequences if you didn't accept it.

After his call to the crowds and as a public sign of their decision to follow Jesus, he asked people to come down to the front of the stage where "counselors" would be there to pray for and encourage the new converts. "All over this stadium, people are giving their lives to Christ. You can come too. Don't worry, the buses will wait for you," he said in his trademark drawl as lines of people who responded to his appeal moved out of their seats and walked down to the field level and up the aisles to the front.

I distinctly remember that by then I had progressed to a pseudo-acceptance of Jesus; a superficial decision that at least made me feel I wasn't an outsider. I had grown tired of people imploring me to invite Christ into my heart when I had so many misgivings. So I pretended to be one of them. I used this as an excuse to *not* respond to Billy's altar call, reasoning that I had already "accepted Christ." If I were honest with myself, I would have admitted I just wasn't ready, but the psychological and emotional pressure to conform and convert was overwhelming. Whether I was being addressed individually or as part of a larger audience in front of an evangelist, there was little space given to take more time to consider the claims, address intellectual objections, or have the freedom to just say "no, thank you," without feeling like I was the devil incarnate who had the unmitigated gall to reject an irresistible offer of eternal life from the Creator of the universe. No, this was revivalism.

Billy and other speakers never said, "It's okay to doubt the Gospel message. God doesn't want you to 'accept' Christ tonight if you're skeptical." That would be too reckless. After all, someone might get in an accident and die on the way home and have to face eternity without Christ. And maybe God would call the preacher to account. No, the speakers expertly set the stage for the "unsaved" to make a decision to follow Jesus during this meeting. What would be called manipulation in another context was called "the Holy Spirit tugging on your heart" at a revival meeting. Undoubtedly this approach explained why in later years the Billy Graham Association admitted a high percent of crusade converts were not members of a church a year after their "decision." They probably felt the same pressure to convert that I did.

Despite all this, in the midst of the enthusiastic crowds, I was impressed with the heartfelt Jesus-rock music and the thousands of young people praising God with honest expressions of joy on their faces. It was infectious. I was also impressed with the tight-bell-bottom-blue-jeans-clad, beautiful young woman sitting next to me. She and her lucky, longhaired, bearded boyfriend were the quint-essential Jesus people flower children in bell-bottoms with Bibles rather than bongs, sporting Jesus buttons in lieu of passing joints.

At one point, ominous dark clouds rolled in over the stadium blocking the sunlight; it started to rain lightly. Whoever was speaking encouraged everyone to "praise God anyway." A roar of shouts and voices rose up heavenward and after a few minutes, a glorious sunshine broke through some parting clouds with bright yellow rays highlighting the throngs of worshipers. The crowd paused in wonder and then broke into thunderous applause, raising hands in thanksgiving to the Lord, who apparently spared us from a threatening thunderstorm and torrential downpour.

Was this a supernatural occurrence caused by a transcendent Higher Power? Or was it simply a natural coincidence? To me, it seemed miraculous, unlike the incident when that man brought us Bibles to distribute to kids. The timing of the sunshine breaking in was spot on. If it was God, did this mean He approved of the religious dogma being espoused? At the time I assumed it did. I was grateful to see such a sign but confused about some of my doubts.

The next morning, at breakfast, we saw on the front cover of the *Dallas Morning News* a full-page-wide photo of a scene at ground level in the stadium. There they were, that pretty woman and her boyfriend standing in the front row of the huge crowd at the Cotton Bowl, arms lifted up, bodies captured in sway to the music with thousands of people surrounding them. Many had their hands raised with one finger pointing heavenward—the "Jesus-is-the-one-way-to-God" sign of the movement.

"Hey, we were right next to them!" we all shouted.

I believed you could just see my elbow off to the side of the photo. Or maybe it was Jim's. Regardless, my friends and I were now on the grid of the Jesus Movement. That same day, we three "Jesus people" played hooky from the day's training and hitchhiked to Fort Worth, found a hole-in-the-wall bar and tattoo parlor, and got crosses tattooed on our upper arms. At least Ted and Jim did. Always the hesitant one, I chickened out. I wasn't ready to take up my cross, even if it was only a superficial mark. Despite our age, the bartender served us Lone Stars on tap and told us to put salt in it to make it taste better. This wasn't your Northeastern, sophisticated cocktail lounge. This was the heart of Texas.

Unfortunately, since our flight home was early, we missed the last day's big "Christian Woodstock" concert, where other performers, like Larry Norman—the father of Christian rock music—joined those we had already heard. This final rally was captured on the cover of *Life* magazine the next week with the caption "The Great Jesus Rally in Dallas."

At home, I was a bit embarrassed admitting I attended Explo. It was a completely surreal experience. Nevertheless, despite the fact that I was turned off to much of what I heard there—the pushy witnessing exchanges and the notion of God abandoning unbelievers to face seven years of tribulation—I was impressed with my glimpse of a real and powerful God, who actually could show up. At the time, I wasn't motivated enough to "accept the Lord." I still wondered about some of the baggage and doctrines these Jesus people pushed along with the spiritual experience. Within seven years, something happened to me that changed my hesitancy. It was only a matter of time before I "accepted" Jesus.

REFLECTIONS AT THE MICROBREWERY

"There you are," Dan said, interrupting my recollections of Explo. "I'm surprised you found some seats."

"I got lucky."

Dan looked at his watch. "Good, we still have time to kill. I'll grab a brew too."

After Dan ordered a Fat Woody (a Scotch Ale), we got into a typical conversation. This night, as I had thought, he wanted to talk about my book. He didn't hesitate to dive in. "Man, from the start, you touched on so many things that resonate with me. We've talked about a lot of this stuff before, but now I see it with more depth. For example, your adventures in Dallas—I never went through the Jesus Movement like that."

Brett, the friendly bartender, plopped down Dan's tall mug of beer. Dan continued. "It was fascinating reading about your experiences with your two friends. I'm curious. What do you think was real and what was phony at this Expo?"

"Explo, not Expo," I corrected him. "Well, I believe God was there at Explo. Yet there were some strange things that didn't jive. I mean, it was weird. Like the pushy witnessing exchanges. I don't think God was cheering those on."

"I can see how that would make you feel antsy," Dan said. "I've encountered those earnest evangelist types myself."

"Yeah, it really was uncomfortable. It was like at every corner you'd meet someone who felt obligated to get you saved, including the speakers who made you feel foolish if you didn't make a commitment to Christ. Another thing was *The Four Spiritual Laws* tract. Knowing the Bible better than I did in the 70s, I see that not everything in it was derived from Scripture. For instance, that phrase 'accept Him as your personal Lord and Savior,' is not even in the Bible."

"Right, I always wondered about that," Dan acknowledged. "I never saw where that came from. Another thing. I've always been fascinated that Jesus never evangelized like modern evangelists do."

"That's a great point, Dan. He didn't try to get crowds to 'accept' him as Messiah. He only told select people to follow him."

"You also mentioned they pushed the Rapture doctrine a lot; you know, the same stuff in today's *Left Behind* series by what's his name."

"You mean Tim LaHaye," I offered.

"That's him. That whole thing seems to contradict Jesus' teaching on love."

We both marveled how people could believe God threatens non-Christians, regardless of how good or bad they are, with seven years of harrowing trials and pestilence unless they convert to Christ—even though Christ was the one who told people to be like God and love their enemies. I was also thinking of another angle. The imminent nature of the Rapture encourages an individualistic view of salvation.

"Fear of the Rapture—the end of the world and all that—distracts people from what really matters," I added. As I spoke, the memory of dire warnings from end-times books rang in my ears: a looming worldwide tribulation is coming soon, under the diabolical control of the Antichrist. "People become protective. They end up worrying about saving themselves and their friends and family from future judgment rather than making the world a better place."

"Yes!" Dan agreed. "And people lose hope that things can get better. They just think things are supposed to get worse. In reading your manuscript, I appreciated your explanation on how people get these bizarre interpretations to begin with."

"Yeah, people insert pet theologies into the Bible."

"Why is that?" Dan wondered. "It must be a real blind spot for people to read into Scripture what's not there."

"When people take things literally or out of context and don't try to understand whole narrative, the historical background, the original language—things like that—it's actually not hard to do," I said. "I've fallen into that trap myself."

Dan and I continued to talk as we sipped our microbrews. We would agree that these issues we were addressing—manipulative evangelistic techniques, Bible abuse, and unwarranted end-times beliefs—reinforce the problems with religion—organized and created by humans to control others—as distinct from spiritual inspiration, the belief that there is a Higher Power, a First Cause, a God or gods if you will, with a stake in or a stamp on our existence. Jesus had a problem with religion, not spiritual inspiration. When he confronted the Pharisees, he exposed the fallacy of religion and the way it stifled people's freedom and the free flow of God's grace.

Right then, my cell phone vibrated in my pocket. Lori was calling to let me know how things were going. We already knew that she and Gina would arrive separately.

"Lori might be a tad late," I let Dan know. "Oh, something else interesting happened at Explo," I continued. "During the last concert, Kris Kristofferson performed" (the soft-rock musician well known in the 70s).

"Oh, yeah, Kristofferson," Dan said. "He became a famous actor. I didn't know he was part of the Jesus Movement."

"Well, it's unclear how much he was. According to reports by members of Love Song, the event promoters held him up as a new convert to Christ. You know, they basically paraded him as a trophy at the concert. The crowds were surprised and excited that he apparently was a Christian. Thing is, he wasn't the right variety."

"Not meeting their expectations, huh?" responded Dan. "I've

heard of other musicians who have suffered that fate too, like B. J. Thomas. Performers have some kind of Christian experience, and suddenly they're expected to use their celebrity status to reach the lost or spout some religious agenda. After his conversion, Christians booed B. J. Thomas at concerts because he still played his secular songs. Can you imagine that?"

"I know. I heard that too," I said. "It's the idea that converts are obligated to fit a certain mold and buy into an evangelistic mentality. You know, getting someone saved like Kristofferson is, as some people would say, 'an incredible opportunity to reach young people for the Lord.'"

"Right. Whether the 'saved' celebrity wants to, or feels called to, or not," Dan added.

"So at this last concert, Kristofferson and his band were heard swearing and seen smoking cigarettes in their backstage room," I continued. "As a result, other devout performers freaked out. They apparently doubted the authenticity of Kristofferson's faith, kind of like Ted's wannabe girlfriend I wrote about did when he lit up a Marlboro."

"That's too bad," Dan said. "These celebrities are human. If they experience Jesus, why do we think they should immediately clean up their act and fit some stereotype?"

"Exactly. Not to mention that the expectation to quit smoking and swearing is just a man-made behavior code. I mean, the use of profanity and the practice of smoking cigarettes are superficial indicators with no direct correlation to a person's heart condition. So what if he smokes and swears?"

Our conversation continued for a while before we changed the subject. Something dawned on me as I recollected things; it was at Explo I first saw how organized religion insisted on gauging one's spirituality in terms of how well one conformed to a narrow view of behavior, speech, and thought codes. I saw signs of it back then, but I didn't understand its ramifications until years later.

Reminiscing with Dan triggered thoughts of many other

experiences through the years. As Dan and I checked out the Celtics-Lakers basketball game on one of the wall's flat screens, more memories flooded my mind. I didn't realize it, but this evening would prove to be more than a time out with friends. My reflections on my journey and the others' responses would become a mirror in which to see who I had become and reveal what the present-day implications would be for a more reasoned faith. Dan was a sympathetic listener. Not everyone would be. It was going to be a long night.

Watching the Boston Celtics got me thinking about the next step in my search in the mid-to-late 1970s. It was then that I discovered something about God outside organized religion that blew me away. It opened up a whole new path to experience the Divine that didn't exactly mesh with what I saw at Explo. As Dan got caught up in the game, I couldn't help recalling the details.

CONFESSION 2
COMING OF SPIRITUAL AGE

"I wanted to meet God, but they sold me religion."

– Bono

New England, 1974-1979

I came home from Explo uncomfortable with attitudes in the Jesus Movement that reinforced certain behavioral and doctrinal codes. Nevertheless, I was impressed with the spirituality I experienced and hankered for more. A God of love did appear to be real. I exulted in the joy, camaraderie, sense of purpose, and concern for others that these believers exhibited. It made me feel safe, accepted, and loved. It touched an inner void that yearned to be filled. Looking back, part of that longing was spiritual hunger for meaning. But part of it was a psychological need to be accepted and approved. I wasn't confident in my own sense of self. Was I missing out on a relationship with God?

Leaders at our local Baptist church said I was and that I needed to give my life to Jesus. Throughout the next several years, I went on with my life, eager to receive recognition and find some inner peace. There were only two ways to do that, so I thought. Either pursue popularity and satisfaction within the youth culture, or find God. So far the Leslie McMahans and other youthful endeavors of my life— sex, drugs, and rock-and-roll, in other words—weren't delivering the peace I craved. Maybe I should try God. I only knew one way to find God, and that was the evangelical way. Yet over the next few years I would get glimpses of a Supreme Being outside of the box.

In the mid 70s the unrest of the previous ten years had largely subsided when the Vietnam War deescalated and finally ended in 1975. In its place were other global concerns. Typical news stories were about apartheid in South Africa, the controversy over the escalating construction of nuclear power plants, the potential danger of accidents, and the improper disposal of radioactive waste. The no-nukes movement was just getting underway, and earlier that year 1,400 protestors were arrested at Seabrook Nuclear Power Plant in New Hampshire. Jimmy Carter was our new president, and songs from Fleetwood Mac's Grammy-winning album, *Rumours*, dominated the airwaves of radio and turntables of college dorms.

In those days, when hitchhiking, born-again Christians would pick me up and tell me about the love of God and how they had accepted Jesus. I usually could tell if they were evangelical Christians before I even got in the car. There was a bumper sticker that said something like "Honk if you love Jesus," or "Jesus Saves." These believers also told me God loved me and had a wonderful plan for my life. They must have read *The Four Spiritual Laws*. They were more serious about Jesus than my friend Ted and were willing to give up the "ways of the world." Although not as prevalent as in places like the South and California, the Jesus Movement had made an impact on notoriously liberal New England. Still, my misgivings about believing this stuff remained.

For our youth generation, the big sins to repent of weren't a lack of action and concern for social justice, but the hedonistic lifestyle associated with the drug culture and sexual revolution. In the world of my friends and me, drug use was perennial. Sex was, too, but mostly in our adolescent and young adult minds.

I really didn't make a good druggie. I looked the part with my long hair, leather cord necklace, wide leather belt, bell-bottoms, square-toed biker boots, and corduroy jacket with a pack of Camels sticking out of the top pocket. My taste in music fit the role, with my affection for British rockers and the progressive rock music of Jethro Tull and Yes. I just didn't play the part well. Compared to many of my friends, who included devoted Deadheads, I was tame.

I smoked pot for a number of years. Eventually I became paranoid after several experiences I had with hash oil and marijuana varieties we used to get with crazy names like Cheeba Cheeba or Panama Red. One night I drove some underage acquaintances to the liquor store, and to repay the favor they passed me some "really good stuff."

"Mind if we light up a joint?" one of them asked.

"Be my guest," I said.

"In return for buying us beer, have some new Columbian we just bought," he added. "It's outrageous." He said that last word really slow with a sly smile on his face.

The familiar aromatic smell filled the car, and I heard inhaling sounds as my two passengers took long hits and deep breaths and then passed the number to me. I followed suit with a strong toke, and we continued sharing the thin cigarette as I drove. Within five minutes I found myself in another world. Suddenly every thought I had took me on some crazy tangent of introspection that lasted an inordinate amount of time. Then, I'd come back to reality and realize I'd only walked from my car to the door of the liquor store. I kept trying to figure out why it took over an hour—as it seemed—to drive five miles, buy a case of beer, and return home. It drove me batty. I got so high that night, when I went to my girlfriend Kathy's house, I cancelled our plans, and we just hung out at her house while I recovered from marijuana la-la land.

The paranoia that developed from experiences like this made me hesitant to experiment with other drugs. While some of my friends snorted coke, dropped acid, and did speed, I eventually became the conservative, occasional light toker who drank a lot of beer and said no to other substances. When a friend became disoriented after smoking weed laced with angel dust and tried to get out of my car while I was driving forty miles an hour on the streets of Cape Cod, I decided I had made the right choice to quit smoking pot. This wasn't supposed to happen, by the way. To make their testimony more dramatic, evangelicals are supposed to quit smoking marijuana *after* they come to Jesus, not *before*.

My girlfriend, Kathy, was a breath of fresh air in my life. We met in high school and became inseparable for almost two years. We enjoyed each other immensely. We partied, laughed, loved, and enjoyed an active sex life. I may have failed life's Drug Culture 101, but at least in this relationship, I got moved to the head of the class in Introduction to the Sexual Revolution. Homework was fun. But there was a down side. To my shame, I treated Kathy badly when I broke up with her and lived to deeply regret it. She took it hard. The free physical-love message of the sexual revolution was missing an important component: personal responsibility and respect and love toward others.

One weekend during this period, something happened that helped chip away some of my doubts about The Jesus Movement. I was a senior in high school. Mom invited three Christian musicians who were visiting our church to stay over at our house. When she told me, I envisioned some choirboys or fat ladies with a "ministry of music." I was shocked to see three twenty-something guys walk in with long hair and beards. One of them looked like Ian Anderson of Jethro Tull and another like Kenny Loggins. They were born-again Christians but of a variety more like one of Explo's hip bands than Billy Graham.

"What rock groups do you listen to, Mike?" one of them asked me at dinner.

I was shocked. Mom's friends are interested in the music I like? I enthusiastically shared the groups I was into. Their genuine interest in me later led to a tour of my room, where I proudly showed off my personal collection of self-recorded reel-to-reel tapes of rock music from The Allman Brothers to Led Zeppelin.

"Would you be interested in checking out our albums?" one of them asked. At least two of them had their own albums with them, and each gave me a copy. The one that looked like Kenny Loggins had a photo of himself on the front cover with a flannel shirt, acoustic guitar, and a glowing smile that made him look like he had just been rescued from a yearlong ordeal on a deserted island. He looked glad to be home. The name of the album was *What a Day*. Later, I listened to the albums, and although they were pretty tame acoustic stuff, they had great guitar rifts and quite a few memorable melodies.

As I talked to these musicians, all I knew of Christian rock was a vague memory of groups named Love Song and Andre Crouch, who performed at Explo. Little did I know that I was in the presence of some who would be considered founders of the contemporary Christian music industry in America. The Kenny Loggins look-alike was named Phil Keaggy. Unbeknownst to me, he was touring off and on with Love Song. He would go on to write over 50 solo albums. One of the others was Paul Clark, an avant-garde artist who would later produce 17 solo albums.

"How did you come to accept the Lord?" Mom had asked our guests at dinner.

"There was a lot of social upheaval when I was in college," someone said, possibly Paul Clark. "I was trying to find meaning in my life, but all the things I tried left me empty—grass, speed, LSD, Transcendental Meditation. When I read about Jesus, something touched me, and I prayed to follow him. Soon after I began feeling loved, forgiven, and at deep peace."

Keaggy probably had a similar story. Years later I learned more about his life. In 1968 he founded a secular rock band called Glass Harp. Glass Harp's first album was recorded at Jimi Hendrix's Studios in New York and was produced by Lewis Merenstein, who also had produced Van Morrison's *Moondance* album. For a brief period, the band performed live and opened for groups like Yes and Traffic. Keaggy's conversion was also associated with a life crisis. He converted shortly after his believing mother died in a car accident on Valentine's Day 1970.

Years later, Keaggy would become disillusioned with the contemporary Christian music business. Christian label executives told him his songs were not marketable enough and tried to influence his sense of creativity. Apparently he got screwed in contracts and "lost years and years of [his] publishing."[5] He once warned students in a music clinic not to sign with Christian labels and confessed he regretted making a clean break with the mainstream rock industry. Today, he commends bands like U2 and singer Bono for speaking to the issue of poverty as progressive believers and remaining in the mainstream.

My weekend with born-again rock artists fascinated me. A few years later, there was one other experience that drew me to take Jesus seriously. I watched acclaimed Italian film director Franco Zeffirelli's *Jesus of Nazareth* on television. Famous for his Academy Award nomination of *Romeo and Juliet,* Zeffirelli directed this star-studded drama. It had a profound impact on me. Its portrayal of Jesus was spellbinding. Played by Robert Powell, Jesus exhibited a magnetic personality, uncanny wisdom, and genuine concern to relieve human suffering. He stood up to the niggling legalism of the Pharisees. I wanted to follow a Jesus like that. Ironically, Zeffirelli was openly gay, and his film never received widespread support from evangelicals like several other poorly produced Christian films on Jesus.

As time wore on, my position on becoming a Christian slowly moved. I was more receptive to the idea, but still had my doubts. Besides, I was having too much fun in college. At least at first. What I lacked in drug-culture chic I made up for in alcohol consumption. Cheap beer and occasional shots of hard liquor eventually became my standard controlled substances of choice. At the ripe old age of twenty-one, thanks to 18-year-old drinking laws (and my poor choices), I was burned out on bars and clubs, depressed, and in danger of becoming an alcoholic. It could have led to the slow burn variety of alcoholism that Stephen King described. He gradually succumbed to it by refusing to put boundaries in place to practice moderation. One Thursday night he went into his garage to toss some empties and found the large recycle container almost full of 16-ounce cans of Miller Lite. Trouble was, three nights earlier the thing was empty. And this wasn't even the weekend.[6] I appeared to be headed in the same direction.

HITCHHIKING TO GRACELAND

One day on the way home from the college I attended in Rhode Island, I found myself standing on a freeway ramp entering I-90 east, holding a cardboard sign that read "Boston." It had been over an hour since my last ride, and car after car drove past in the increasing darkness and cold as if I didn't exist. I inhaled my Camel filter one last time and threw it down on the pavement, angrily stamping it out with my boot.

This line about God's love is bullshit, I said to myself. *Where is this loving God when I need him?*

In the mid to late 70s, I hitchhiked all over the Northeast. Sometimes rides came quickly; sometimes it was an endurance test. This particular afternoon in November 1977 was of the latter variety. As I stood there on this crisp autumn day, I began to reflect on my journey over the years: spotty memories of Explo, the Baptist youth group, my initiation into high school, smoking pot afternoons at Julian's house, exulting in rock music—both the exuberance of groups like Tull and Zeppelin and the soul searching of Dylan, Cat Stevens, and the Moody Blues. Moreover were ruminations of my affection for Kathy, adventures with hometown friends, and drunken nights at parties, friendly Jesus-freak musicians, and my illusive quest for self-acceptance.

As car after car drove by that late fall afternoon, I got desperate and decided to test out this notion of a loving God who cared about the affairs of our lives. Out came the mocking about God's love. Then came a most irreverent demand.

Okay, God, if you love me, like these people say, why don't you get me a fuckin' ride for chrissake? If you love me, goddamit, get someone to pick me up and drive me at least to the next exit!

I was shocked by my boldness. That's the confession. I've been known to use profanity in prayer.

I continued to stand and watch the parade of cars head toward the tollbooth at exit 20 of the Massachusetts turnpike. Then a few minutes later—I kid you not—a nice four-door sedan pulled over. I seem to remember an Audi. I hopped in next to a very attractive, bright-eyed woman in her mid-twenties with long brown hair, with a beautiful Irish Setter in the back seat.

Amazing! Maybe Mom is right, I immediately thought. *God does answer prayer and apparently threw in a hot woman as a bonus.*

Honestly, as I climbed in, I was thinking this was a coincidence, not Providence. The woman told me she was a teacher in eastern Connecticut commuting to her home.

"How far are you going?" I asked her.

"Wellesley. How about you?" she responded.

I was flabbergasted. "Really? That's where I'm going!"

"Well, it looks like it's your lucky day," she said. She was kind enough to go out of her way and drop me off at my front door.

Later on, I reflected on what happened. Was that a God thing? A divine intervention?

No way, I thought. *It was a coincidence. If it was God, he would have had a born-again Christian or a charismatic nun pick me up, not some foxy lady.*

Then there was my prayer. All I asked for was a ride to the next exit, and I got a ride to my front door. That had never happened in all my years of hitchhiking.

Hmm, I mused. *Did God laugh at my request? "Only the next exit? I can do better than that!"* I couldn't deny the synchronicity of the situation. Maybe there was something to this God and Jesus rigmarole after all.

Looking back at this memory years later, I became enamored with the thought that it wonderfully illustrated what became my favorite theological concept: the grace of the Eternal knows no favoritism nor insists on right doctrines or codes of conduct before accepting and loving His children. A God of love responds to cussing prayers.

BORN AGAIN PARADOX

What is it that propels someone to take the step of conversion to a new religious belief system? The lion's share of conversions associated with The Jesus Movement, which was gradually spreading across the United States in the 1970s, were the result of a life crisis or deep inner need. My mother, for instance, went through a midlife stage of questioning the materialistic philosophy of the "God is dead" movement of the 1960s. Frightened by the possibility that godless materialism was true and therefore life was meaningless, she sought a real experience with God and found it in rediscovering Jesus among charismatic Christians. I was hearing of dramatic conversions from excited youth and young adults at places like Explo '72 and Mom's church. Amidst the social unrest of the era, disgruntled youth got burned out on the promise of free love and drugs and turned to God.

"I tried to fill the void and pain in my life with marijuana and then later cocaine, but it didn't work," a person might say. "When I experienced the love of Jesus, my inner pain was healed, and I no longer craved drugs."

Others' conversion involved political intrigue. Chuck Colson, President Nixon's special counsel, converted to Christ amidst the investigation of the Watergate cover up. After pleading guilty to obstruction of justice, he apparently "accepted" Christ in prison. Later he became a leading evangelical and founder of a prison ministry.

I wasn't a drug addict or criminal, but I did have a drinking problem at this time in my life and felt a void inside. I wondered whether I needed to take this notion of becoming a born-again believer more seriously, despite my misgivings.

In the Spring of 1979, I attended the University of Massachusetts in Amherst, nicknamed "Zoo Mass" for its reputation for Animal-House-like parties. It was my junior year, and I was living off campus with friends. It was in this setting when things came to a head.

"So, what do you want to do?" my girlfriend Amy asked. Her

sparkling eyes and pretty face, framed by long red hair, betrayed a longing inside. "Sounds like you don't think our relationship is going anywhere."

She was right about that. We had been dating for four months. Despite her adorable smile and accepting personality, we hadn't connected on a rudimentary level. And I wasn't good at breaking up.

"I guess I'd rather just be friends," I responded. She began to weep. I was crying *inside*. It was my third girlfriend since Kathy, and again, it wasn't working out. The truth was that I still missed Kathy, partly because I couldn't find anyone who replaced those wonderful feelings we shared. I knew Amy would be okay. She knew this day was coming. As much as she tried, she could never break through my melancholy disposition and lighten my soul. And I couldn't make her soar.

I was at that awkward moment of a young adult life when we try to find meaning. To complicate things, years of heavy drinking had taken their toll—the empties were piling up in the kitchen at a faster and faster rate, and my party weekends were getting longer. I was battling a moderate depression. Floundering in school with no sense of direction, I lacked a sense of purpose and excitement about my future career. Girlfriends were supposed to solve these problems, I naively believed. When they didn't, I'd slide deeper into a funk. The breakup with Amy was no exception.

Rather than thinking of these issues as personal choices for which I could take responsibility if I put my mind to it, I kept thinking my problems were a result of my not doing what Christians told me I should do—accept Jesus and give my life to God. The echoes of Explo and other evangelical encounters rang in my ears. I was seeing things in black and white. Either have a born-again experience and get a new life in God the evangelical way or remain lost and purposeless.

This tension grew stronger. I felt trapped. I needed to wake up spiritually to experience personal meaning and hope, but I wasn't willing to accept the narrow rules that I thought were required. One night a few months after Amy and I broke up, I prayed what I later called a dangerous prayer: *I'm not willing to change and become a born-again Christian, God. It seems too strict. But if that is the only way to get some peace, I'm willing to be made willing.* A week or so later I had a nervous breakdown. I'm not even sure what it was all about, but everything came crashing down, and I lost my ability to think clearly and cope.

Remembering my earnest prayer from the week before and desperate to gain some peace, in the next few days I began to seek God for help. One evening, overwhelmed with fears and anxieties, I voiced a sincere prayer to Jesus. Suddenly I sensed a compassionate Higher Power was present in my room. The Power completely understood my plight and encouraged me without a trace of condemnation or expectation of religious performance. It wasn't the Jesus I had imagined through the lens of religious books or other peoples' testimonies. It was a believable Jesus, anointed to heal humankind—in this case me—and connect me with my Source. The experience itself was otherworldly, devoid of religious overtones. Jesus was consoling me, stroking my hair with his hand, burning away my anxiety by His loving presence. I was a soul now strengthened by a Divine touch.

The experience left me at peace. Although it didn't show me what to do next, I assumed it meant I was born again and needed to go public. I would also need to join a whole-Bible-believing church. This is what evangelists had taught. Someone in the Baptist church back home connected me with a guy named Jake—a born-again Christian attending UMass Amherst who would later become a good friend. Jake helped me find equilibrium and introduced me to evangelical campus ministries.

Within a few months, I had changed dramatically. Part of it was a spiritual transformation, not unlike what Paul Clark described at dinner about his conversion. But part of it was my conformity to the image of the evangelical mindset. True believers get delivered, not only from drugs, but cigarettes, drinking, swearing, secular music, and whatever behavior the church decides. Alleviating the agony of drug addiction or the pain of personal unrest wasn't enough. Enjoying things like alcohol in responsible moderation wasn't acceptable. I began a wonderful connection with Divine Power but also entered the world of black and white. Like my fellow born-again believers I began to meet, I now considered myself a "real Christian" who wasn't merely going through the motions due to my cultural upbringing.

That summer I went with friends from the same Baptist church that sent us to Explo to another Jesus Festival at a place called Agape Farm in central Pennsylvania. One night, a former Hell's Angel spoke and made a dramatic challenge for people to forsake the things in their lives that represent the world: cigarettes, alcohol, drugs, rock music, pornography, extramarital sex, and anything that smacked of Satanism. He told people to toss their cigarettes, substances, albums, magazines, books—whatever represented their worldly addictions—into a massive bonfire. I remember running back to my tent, grabbing my carton of Camel filters, and tossing them into the fire as I swore them off, along with alcohol and secular rock music.

Welcomed like a returning prodigal into evangelical churches and a college ministry called InterVarsity Christian Fellowship, I was suddenly a celebrity. Dramatic conversions like mine reinforce the evangelical worldview and make people feel good. The things of the world don't work, and Jesus, or at least their version of Jesus, is the answer to all personal problems. Today I wonder how much of my "new joy" and improved self-esteem was because of this instant acceptance and recognition in the Christian community.

I discovered Christian rock music had come of age and began reveling in the music of people like my old acquaintance Phil Keaggy and talented musicians like Randy Stonehill and Keith Green, the latter known for his unwavering calls for his listeners to repent and more wholly follow Christ. To my utter amazement, only a few months after my conversion, Bob Dylan became a born-again believer through a ministry in Southern California called the Vineyard. I exulted in his passionate songs about believing in and following Jesus. I relished his first two Christian albums *Slow Train Coming* and *Saved*. I took Dylan's conversion as a sign that I made the right decision to follow Christ. The Jesus Movement was entering a new era and beginning to influence popular culture. Not only did I feel like I had found the truth, but also the way to express it—through the evangelical church movement.

GINA JOINS US AT THE PUB

Dan sat at the bar engrossed in the basketball game on the screen overhead. I eventually broke from my reminiscing and began watching too. The Lakers had the ball. Kobe Bryant suddenly leapt toward the basket, grabbed a pass from Lamar Odom, and slammed the ball into the net.

"Damn! I hate that guy," I shouted, slamming my fist on the counter. My Celtics were trailing 22-16, but it was only the first quarter. Right then I heard Gina's voice from behind.

"I should have known you two would be here and not in the lobby," she said.

"There you are," said Dan. "We're still waiting to be paged for our table."

Gina greeted me. When she asked about Lori, I told her she'd be late.

"Would you like a drink while we wait?" Dan asked her.

"No, I guess I'll wait 'til we get in the restaurant."

Gina was right at home at Silver City. Right before Dan offered her his seat, she stood next to us in the standing-room-only aisle adjacent to the bar, with short brown hair, a trim physique, and her trademark infectious smile. Not as inquisitive as Dan, nevertheless Gina was much more open than most evangelicals I knew. She and Dan had entered evangelicalism later in life through the influence of their daughter, who became a believer while involved in a Presbyterian Church youth camp.

"So what have you guys been talking about?" Gina asked.

Dan explained about reading my book and our discussion.

"Oh, yes!" Gina declared. "Dan told me he read a draft of your manuscript. Sounds intriguing."

Dan gave her a short version of the Explo and Jesus Movement story. He began to explain how I came to Christ, but stopped. "Well, you tell it, it's *your* story."

I gave a brief overview of my circumstances right before my nervous breakdown, how I felt the presence of Jesus in my room, and my initial involvement in the Baptist church.

"What's interesting to me," Dan said when I finished, "is how you saw God working through events in your life, but you also recognized the religious trappings."

"True enough, but I really didn't recognize all that until a few years later. I quickly got caught up in the culture of the church."

"I can see how that can happen," Dan said.

"You know, sometimes I wonder. Like, how much of my transformation was spiritual and how much was more like peer pressure? I mean, my experience sensing Jesus was amazing. And later, during times of prayer and reading the Gospels, I felt what only could be God's love. But still, I quickly became driven to follow a behavior code that was a bit obsessive."

I shared how I began to fit a mold. I couldn't see things in gray. The only way to find God was through giving allegiance to an organized religious movement—evangelicalism. I didn't consider there could be another way to find peace beyond that. It was good for me to quit smoking, but I wonder if I did it more to conform than to improve my health. Rather than learn to drink in moderation (as I finally did later), I stopped drinking altogether for twelve years. I got rid of my secular rock albums to swear off the world rather than learn how to be discerning. How much did I change from an inner transformation and how much from a desire to create an image and meet the church's expectations? I even bought into the one-party politics of conservative religion for a time.

"I know exactly what you mean," Dan raised his voice when I mentioned politics. "I feel that way when I encounter people at church who act like there's only one party to vote for. You know, to be Christian means you must vote Republican. That drives me crazy."

"For me, I wonder," I said. "If I had converted later in life, would the pendulum toward conservative faith not have swung so far?"

"Maybe so. Young people tend to go to extremes," Gina piped in. "And the road to adulthood is rife with drama."

"That reminds me," I continued. "It seems like most born-again conversions are associated with a life crisis. And I learned recently that most people convert when they are children or in their formative years."

"Hmm, that's fascinating." Gina said. "Has there ever been any research on that?"

"Actually, yes, I read about it somewhere. A research group did a poll. Something like, out of all the people who convert to conservative Christianity, I think it was 77 percent, do so before their 22nd birthday,[7] or something like that."

"Really?" Dan said. "That's interesting. You mean the older people get, the less likely they are to convert?"

"Sure," Gina declared. "That makes sense. People become set in their ways. And the youth-to-adult stage is often traumatic."

"And it's why some mission groups focus their evangelism efforts on children and youth during their more impressionable years," I added.

"I never thought about that before," Dan said.

"I guess that means we're the exception, rather than the rule," Gina observed.

"That also might be why we sometimes feel like a fish out of water," Dan added. "We didn't grow up in an evangelical church."

"Anyway, given the groupthink imposition I felt at Explo, I wonder if you could explain some conversions as the result of psychological pressure. Perhaps even a subtle form of brainwashing rather than a real encounter with God."

"Okay, now you're getting controversial," Gina exclaimed. "You sound like you're discrediting born-again experiences."

"I'm not saying most conversions are like that, but perhaps some. Let me give you an example. Are you guys familiar with L'Abri Fellowship?"

"Yeah, it's in your book," Dan said. "You studied there once."

"Yes, in the eighties." I looked at Gina. "It's an evangelical retreat center in Switzerland founded by Francis and Edith Schaeffer. Anyway, their son Frank—looking back over the years—wonders if some of the students were converted by his parents' magnetic personalities rather than God. I mean, some converts reported how hard it was to maintain their faith after leaving his parents' powerful circle."

We got into an interesting discussion on this. Dan agreed that perhaps there was a better way to look at salvation in lieu of certain sociological facts. Gina wasn't so sure. Dan and I were asking questions: If born-again conversion is the only way for people to make peace with God, what of the adults who statistically only have a 23 percent chance of converting? How much of a chance do people have of converting when they're 40, 50, or 60? Evangelism becomes a race for the cure. Reach them when they're young before it might be too late. Salvation becomes a magical formula. Reach them when they are impressionable and vulnerable through an evangelistic method to get them instantly saved. Salvation as a life journey or through means outside the proscribed method is not possible. You are either "saved" or "lost," and there are no loopholes.

"But, Mike," Gina responded. "You have to admit, it's natural for people to seek answers during times of personal development or crisis, and I'm sure many people find God at those times. After all, Jesus says he searches for the lost to rescue them."

"I have no problem with that. But a church that sees salvation as a destination—you know, to believe, act, and think in a narrowly defined way—rather than salvation as a journey, always judges outsiders as lost. And targets them to get saved. The easiest people to 'save' are the young and weak, who are often battling life's demons. Maybe there are other ways for people to be saved—besides having a

traditional conversion. You know, maybe it's not so much the destination, but whether one is headed in the right direction."

"Right," said Dan. "We get nervous if a Christian smokes or
swears or doesn't believe in the Trinity or something. Or we write off
liberals and unbelievers as deceived. Isn't becoming a more decent,
loving person more important?"

"I suppose," Gina answered. "But isn't that just like saying being a
nice person is all that counts? What good is becoming a Christian?"

At that point, Dan, who was tired of standing next to us in the
crowded bar, noticed two couples sitting at a nearby pub table had
stood up to leave. He hit my arm and pointed. Like vultures circling
dying prey, we prepared to descend on the open seats. After we were
seated, I jumped in to respond to Gina. "What good is it to become a
believer? Well, it frees your soul if you really experience God's grace.
But maybe God also works through people who aren't Christians,
Gina. I think believing in Christ is best, but maybe Christ—the
expression of God's love—works in the lives of unbelievers whether
they acknowledge it or not. I mean, as you said, Dan, it's love that is
most important, not a Christian membership card."

Dan and I had bounced these ideas around before. I had discovered from my studies that these notions actually weren't foreign to
the Bible. I could tell that the wheels in Gina's head were turning.
I still wanted to add something about my conversion story and see
what their reaction was, so I went back to that. I explained how I
could clearly see both the good and the phony elements of my
conversion. I needed to know a benevolent Creator loved me and I
wasn't just the result of random, materialistic acts in an impersonal
universe—a lucky being in a cosmic craps game. God is personal and
His or Her nature and the universe really are an expression of love.
(In the last year or so I had started referring to God in the feminine
sometimes). Because I experienced that love and its twin, forgiveness,
I was free to be myself and love others. This part of my experience was
genuine, I told them.

Both Dan and Gina acknowledged my point and said they

experienced something similar. But Gina interjected. "Not to get off topic, but why did you just refer to God as 'His or Her?' Doesn't the Bible reveal God as our Father?"

"Well, yes," I responded. "But in Proverbs, it also refers to God's wisdom as feminine. I don't think we're confined to think of God as a He, since the Divine has masculine and feminine qualities. God is spirit, not a male figure. In another instance Jesus says he wants to gather lost people like a mother hen protects her chicks. Although the gospels speak of God as Father, I have no problem using both male and female pronouns. I guess that's why I liked how God was revealed in the book *The Shack*."[8]

Gina accepted my explanation and told me to continue. She and Dan were familiar with *The Shack*. I was pleasantly surprised. From past experience most Christians I knew were uncomfortable with female pronouns for God.

"Where was I?" I asked.

"Something about what was genuine in your experience," Dan said.

"Oh, yeah."

I told Dan he was onto something when he said being a loving person is what counts. The paranoia of the church and the Jesus Movement about beliefs and behaviors that in and of themselves have nothing to do with the condition of a human heart—whether one smoked, drank, listened to secular music, attended church, or believed the whole Bible was true. This attitude influenced me greatly. Throughout most of my Christian life, I chose to live in a conservative evangelical enclave where there were few, if any, shades of gray and where only through conformity is genuine acceptance ensured.

"I think I know what you mean," Gina responded. "Sometimes I feel that way in our church."

"You know," said Dan, "what you're saying reminds me of when Jesus told some guy who didn't follow him that he wasn't far from the Kingdom of God. I think He told him that because the guy understood that love is the greatest commandment. Love is more important than religious dogma."

"That's true." Gina had to agree.

I glanced at my cell phone. It was almost 7:30. "Lori should be here by now." Dan and I noticed the game was into the second quarter. The teams were neck and neck. We all took a break from our discussion. Dan and I gulped our brews. Suddenly, the large pager I had put on the table lit up. It was time to move into the restaurant.

Our discussion got me thinking about what it was like to be a new believer 30 years ago. In the early 1980s, I had a profound spiritual experience and had been touched by Jesus' teachings. I felt whole and loved inside. But I was also being formed into the image of a particular organized religion: evangelicalism, a religion with a behavior code defined by a carefully measured box. We evangelicals were not to cuss, smoke (cigarettes, cigars, or marijuana), drink, go to questionable movies, listen to secular rock music, publish music on a worldly label, put erotic scenes and swear words in our books, or engage in premarital sex. We were to "accept" or "give our heart" to Jesus, faithfully attend a local whole-Bible-believing church, submit to its leaders, go to home group meetings, have a daily "quiet time" of prayer and reading the Bible, pray at meals, look forward to the second coming of Christ, believe our faith is the only way to God, and promote world evangelism. That being said, we were generally really nice people.

In the 80s, this had become my new image. I was now serious about following Jesus and eager to please God. The church was teaching me that Christ was calling his "body" to reach the world. In the next step of my journey, I answered that call but soon was confronted with a theological question I wasn't prepared for. As we got up and walked to the restaurant, these memories occupied my thoughts.

CONFESSION 3
AN INCLUSIVE THEOLOGY

"Mahatma Gandhi... has taught me more of the spirit of Christ than perhaps any other man in East or West."[9]

– E. Stanley Jones

The Horn of Africa, 1982-84

OFF TO SAVE THE WORLD

Stifling hot air blasted my face as I stood on the bed of a four-wheel-drive pick-up truck racing over a sandy track on the edge of an arid refugee encampment. I watched with curiosity as a group of small children in tattered clothes ran after the truck excitedly shouting, "Gaalo! Gaalo!" which I later learned meant *infidel* in their native language. All of us white European-stock passengers were considered pagans by these African Muslims, even if we claimed allegiance to a Christian God.

I've finally arrived! That thought brought a feeling of elation, but I wasn't prepared for the paradigm shift in my mind that lay ahead, not to mention the physical change that would occur in my digestive tract.

It was a mere three years since my conversion when I found myself a "holistic missionary" in this country that in a hundred lifetimes I never dreamed I would live in. Those familiar with it often describe this remote part of Africa by saying, "It may not be the end of the world, but you can see it from there!"

"We desperately need aid workers in Somalia," Dave, a recruiter, had told me seven months earlier, to which I naively replied, "Where the hell is that?" In late 1981, Somalia was an obscure nation. I actually had the f-word in mind, but as a twenty-four-year-old new believer, I was learning to clean up my language.

What led me to pursue such a mission? It started shortly after coming under the teaching of an evangelical church. After hearing sermons and studying the Bible through an evangelical lens, I became committed to the mandate to share the gospel (good news) of Jesus Christ with the "lost." My motivation was simple. I had felt a loving touch from a living God. I wanted others to experience the same. Conversations with some of my friends from high school and college were my first attempts at sharing the gospel. In fact, to my dismay, a college friend began to call me a Bible thumper.

Being in a mission-minded church, I soon learned that although sharing the gospel with my American neighbors was God's will, it was far too small a vision. Whereas Americans had ample opportunities to convert in our "Christian nation," the "lost" living in Muslim, Hindu, Buddhist, and secular countries didn't. Obeying Jesus' Great Commission[10]—to make disciples of all nations—outside our borders was a far worthier goal. The unbelievers of the world were "unreached" peoples or tribes in places where evangelical-style[11] churches were not well established or were nonexistent—places like Somalia.

At the same time, I also developed a heart to obey the commands of Christ I saw in the Bible to serve the poor of the world[12] and "love your neighbor as yourself" through charitable work. Some called this the Great Commandment.[13] It was really putting love in action and is sometimes associated with social justice. I learned that many evangelical churches in the 1980s didn't put much of a focus on love in action. They saw evangelism as the major outreach of the church. Fundamentalist churches sometimes accused people of pursuing a "social gospel" if love in action was emphasized at the expense of evangelism. For some churches, if they did make love in action a mandate, it was often a means to an end—to fulfill the Great Commission (evangelism). In other words, the core purpose of doing good deeds was so people would see Jesus in us and consider converting as a result. To me, this bordered on manipulation. It wasn't genuine love. It wasn't doing good deeds simply because it was right.

I became attracted to evangelicals who wanted to focus equally on both—without a manipulative agenda. This was sometimes called holistic mission. For me, after reading literature from Christian aid organizations like World Vision, I felt an irresistible urge to serve overseas in a developing nation and balance these two calls. I applied to another evangelical aid agency and soon after was on the phone with Dave.

Dave filled me in on the pressing needs in Somalia. Reportedly, 1.2 million refugees, mostly ethnic Somalis from eastern Ethiopia, had crossed the border two years earlier to flee the war raging in their native country. Thankfully, the widespread hunger and starvation stage of this tragically familiar refugee crisis was largely over. Aid agencies were now starting to pursue development projects to enable refugees to become self-reliant.

"We need you to join our team and help transition [refugees] from relief to development," Dave said. "You would help downsize feeding centers and develop new self-help projects."

"Is your organization finding opportunities to share the gospel with Muslims?" I asked.

"Yes, our work is opening doors for evangelism."

I wanted to share the love of God practically through community development work and spiritually through sharing the good news of Jesus that I had experienced first hand, starting after my nervous breakdown in college. This assignment seemed like the perfect fit. I answered the call. I initially signed up for a twelve-month assignment that ultimately turned into twenty-four.

Seven days before I climbed onto that green Toyota 4x4 with the UNHCR[14] logo emblazoned on the door, I had landed in Mogadishu. It was May 1982—eleven years before a US Blackhawk helicopter was shot down by Somali rebels and well before the devastating civil conflict to come.

Mogadishu was a bustling, rustic city full of whitewashed buildings, buzzing scooters, honking Fiats, lumbering diesel trucks, and inattentive drivers. I thought the streets of Boston and New York were crazy. Mogadishu motorists were downright dangerous. And this was the decade before the *technicals*—improvised fighting vehicles full of young men with automatic weapons that were common in the 1990s when civil unrest escalated. Local custom allowed for drivers—while driving—to converse with friends who were walking nearby on the sidewalk. Socializing was more important than watching the road!

One local joke among expatriates was that the word "Fiat" didn't represent the Italian-made automobile but was an acronym for a common phrase spoken among its owners: Fix It Again, Tony. In reality, Somali mechanics tended to be named Mohammed. Actually, it seemed almost every male in the entire country was named Mohammed; if not their first name, then their middle or last name, which represented the names of their father and paternal grandfather respectively. I even met someone named Mohammed Mohammed Mohammed.

The refugee camp where I rode on the truck was called Bo'O (Bo-Oh) and had the same bustle of the city, but with mud-covered stick huts called *akals* which replaced the whitewashed buildings. Little did I know that 1960s folk singer Joan Baez's mother, also named Joan, was a relief worker in Bo'O a year earlier. She would later write a book about her experiences called *One Bowl of Porridge*.

The sprawling camp seen from a nearby hill appeared as if thousands of these domed *akals* were splattered over a thorn-bush desert like little scoops of chocolate ice cream. In the bush, a million goats and the ubiquitous camels replaced the scooters, Fiats, and trucks of

Mogadishu. A proud people mistaken for being stern, the Somalis are in fact very hospitable with a keen sense of humor. Today, when I hear of the tribal infighting, widespread violence, piracy, and civil war between Somali nationalists and Islamic extremists that has been going on for years, my heart grieves, and I wonder how things could have changed so dramatically. It was at Bo'O I met my fun-loving and gregarious young interpreter named Ghedi, whose real name was—you guessed it—Mohammed.

Talk about culture shock. White, middle-class, and filthy rich by African standards, not only did I have to adjust to East African culture, 110 degree-plus temperatures, and frequent jaunts to the latrine, but also to Islam, the 99.8 percent majority religion of Somalia and of most of the refugees.

I remember my first steamy night in Mogadishu. At around five in the morning I was awakened by an eerie sounding voice in the night. *Allaaah akbaaar* (Arabic for "God is great") blasted from a crackling loudspeaker from the nearby mosque. The first few times I heard the Muslim call to prayer, it left a spooky impression—strange and counter-cultural—that remained with me for days.

Then there was the socially obligatory spicy Somali tea. Painfully sweet, it never failed to give me a whopping headache. I saw Somali men in their traditional colorful tube skirts walking hand in hand down the street. No, they weren't gay. It's socially acceptable for male friends to hold hands. Some months later, a male Somali friend of mine would take my heterosexual hand as we strolled down the street. That also left a spooky impression that remained with me for days.

The evangelical agency I joined was conservative theologically but progressive in some ways; they promoted a balance of the biblical mandates described above. Hence, their focus was on helping the poor through community development projects that used technology appropriate to the local culture and economy. This was a concept developed by secular author E. F. Schumacher in his popular book *Small is Beautiful*. Still, the agency literature stated, "the bottom line is sharing the good news of Jesus Christ." My colleague Jay and I completed training together in rural development and cross-cultural ministry along with others heading for other countries. We then joined a team of six already in Somalia.

Jay was an independently minded evangelical who was used to living cross-culturally, having spent part of his childhood in Pakistan when his parents worked there. He played a profound spiritual role in my life. He introduced me to an important, deep theological publication. No, not Augustine or Calvin's treatises, but *The Wittenberg Door*—the satirical and controversial *Mad Magazine* of Christendom. Today, its exposés of outrageous televangelists have become a source of the "God Stuff" material on *The Daily Show*. For me, it became a lesson on how to lighten up.

Most Somali women were strikingly beautiful. Even when wearing a head covering, women with high cheekbones, long facial features, enticing eyes, infectious smiles, and alluring curves were an ever-present draw to a young, unmarried man. Come to think of it, they were a draw to any man who was breathing.

Social and religious mores insist women never wear pants or shorts, but rather long and brightly patterned dresses that cover up legs down to the ankle but allow the exposure of much of a woman's breasts—no big deal to a culture that accepts public breast-feeding. A nice surprise was that my job required that I hang out with these remarkably attractive women.

I became manager of a wood conservation project that helped curtail the huge problem of deforestation. The only cooking fuel affordable to poor refugees was firewood and charcoal. In traditional cultures there is a well-defined division of labor, and women are the customary transporters of firewood. Without cars for transportation, the women would walk up to eight to ten hours roundtrip to collect enough wood to last five or six days. In refugee camps with 40,000 to 50,000 people, deforestation was occurring rapidly. It was my job to spearhead a project that introduced environmental solutions to deforestation and practical assistance for women. We helped refugees plant trees and I managed the training of women on how to make, use, and sell fuel-efficient cook stoves made of mud or fired clay. I wondered how to word that on a future résumé.

When I tested the stoves for fuel efficiency, the women offered me the food and drink they had cooked while leaning over floor-based stoves. I consumed massive quantities of sweet tea, fried goat liver, and eyefuls of partially covered women's breasts in a variety of shapes and sizes. I wasn't trying to gawk; as an American and a young man, I really couldn't help but notice that most Somali women went braless and wore very loose clothing. The Muslim Brotherhood movement, which later came to Somalia, would have prevented these women from dressing this way. But these women were from a moderate Islamic tradition that accommodated African culture.

Eventually, like Jay and a few others, I went native to a degree. I occasionally wore the traditional men's tube skirt called a *maoiis* (similar to the *dhoti* in India). Once, while inside someone's *akal*, I tried the mild narcotic that Somalis are known to consume for its amphetamine-like qualities—a leafy plant that is chewed known as *qat*. But my drug days were over, and besides it was too much work, so a mouthful was all I chewed. People would munch it in large quantities for hours and hours to gain the desired effect.

Cushitic ethnic groups like the Somalis don't think of the core of the human soul as being the heart. To them it's the liver. I confess, one of the women stove workers I trained, Selima, became more like a girlfriend than a subordinate staff member, although we never had a physical relationship. Selima wrote me letters. She signed them, "With all my liver."

Selima, from a similar Muslim tribe in Ethiopia called the Oromo, represented the best of all I loved about the people of the Horn of Africa. Like Ghedi, Ahmed, Hiis, Halimo, and many others, she had a captivating sense of humor, kind heart, and keen sense of justice, developed out of her recent forced journey. Her ravishing smile and unique personality soon won me over. I was slowly falling in love. For an evangelical man, falling in love with a Muslim woman was out of the question.

It wasn't long before I was faced with a theological problem I was unprepared for. I was taught that Jesus was the only way to God and heaven,[15] the "one mediator between God and men."[16] Since I could feel His love in my heart—or should I say my liver—Jesus must be the way to God, I reasoned. Furthermore, my evangelical teaching interpreted certain verses in the Bible and Jesus' words to mean that unless people accept Christ as their Lord and Savior, they would not go to heaven when they died. They would be separated from God and punished in an everlasting state called hell. Although this made me uncomfortable, who was I to question the Bible? But I also believed that God loved everyone in the world and desired all to go to heaven, for the Bible also said that somewhere.[17]

My mandate was to share the gospel with those who did not know Christ in hopes that they too would be saved. In fact, our small team adopted a method of sharing Christ, tailored for Africa called "teashop evangelism," as in teashops it was culturally natural for conversations about God to occur. This wasn't an in-your-face-four-spiritual-laws approach at all. We merely talked about Allah with Muslims and casually explained what we believed. For those of us on the team like me who had an evangelistic passion, it sometimes led to sharing the good news of Jesus—that through Christ, people are reconciled to God. When the conversation was with a particularly dedicated Muslim, we would actually evangelize each other.

Although God apparently wanted all to be saved, the Bible apparently said that would not happen. One well-known scholar put it this way. "If we take Scripture seriously, we must admit that the vast majority of persons in the world are condemned and will be forever lost."[18]

This scholar had thought through the implications of this belief system, but I hadn't until I experienced the religious realities of Somalia. It was at a rustic teashop one day when its ramifications hit me like a ton of mud bricks.

"So you Christians believe *Isa* [Arabic for Jesus] is the Son of God and the way to heaven?" asked Abdulahi. The dark "shah" I just sipped from a small glass was overwhelmingly sweet. But drinking Somali tea no longer gave me a headache. Now the spicy treat with cardamom, cinnamon, and cloves, was a daily addiction.

"Yes, but it's not that God had a physical son," I said. *"Isa* is like God in a human form."

"We Muslims know that Mohammed is God's last and only prophet for today," Abdulahi said. "Believing in Jesus like you do is blasphemous to us. God is one and can't have a son, period."

This is harder than I thought, I often mused in these teashop conversations. *Muslims are like us. They believe they already know the truth.*

A handful of young Muslim men we met were disillusioned with the strict rules of Islam and were attracted to the grace message of the New Testament (for instance, one is saved by God's grace, not by purifying oneself through washings, five daily prayers in set positions, ritual fasting during the month of Ramadan, and the Hajj pilgrimage). These included Ghedi, who was very open-minded, read the New Testament, and said he wanted to follow Isa. Yet most Muslims we shared with were not coming to Christ—including my Salima. Islam was an entrenched part of their culture. It wasn't merely taught in their mosques on Fridays but was drilled into young children in mandatory Koran schools and family interactions.

Abdulahi's strong faith made me think. He believed in the God of Abraham and was a decent human being. *How can evangelical teachers be so confident that only those who "accept" Christ will go to Heaven?* I thought. The logical conclusion of this doctrine was that the overwhelming majority of Somalis and Oromos were...well, toast, and if you were a literalist, burnt toast. That meant, unless she broke with cultural heritage, came to Christ, and became a virtual outcast, my girlfriend Salima was doomed too! As were dozens of other Muslim friends and acquaintances I had grown to love with a deep affection I believed was divinely inspired. The majority of Muslims I knew would remain Muslims, and those who died before them had died Muslims. Unless someone did some fast and furious widespread Bible thumping, around 99.7 percent of those alive would end up in hell for eternity! My heart broke when this reality struck me. This was incongruent with what I was experiencing.

I said to myself, *The Bible also says "God is love,"*[19] and *God is not willing that any should perish.*[20] How could an all-powerful, loving God allow the vast majority of these people to be lost? If that were true, I would have joined another believer struggling over this same issue during church who said, "I can recall one Sunday morning when I had to stop singing, for I was no longer sure whether I believed that God deserved worship."[21]

It was then that I rejected the traditional evangelical doctrine of salvation—my first major break with conservative theology. I didn't know how to explain the Bible verses that the doctrine was based on. I surmised there must be some other information I wasn't aware of. I also rejected it based on reason and other Scriptures I had read that reinforced God's love and mercy extended to all.

In time, I developed a theology of salvation that incorporated the compassionate character of God as demonstrated through Jesus and people's belief in God based on creation. I came to believe that God would judge people of other religions differently, according to what they did in light of what they knew, and many would be saved even if they didn't become Christians. Yet I still believed that some people—the wicked who reject God—would go to an everlasting hell, not a torture chamber as many presumed, but nevertheless a place of painful separation from God out of their own choice. The writings of C.S. Lewis had helped shape my view on this. He had written somewhere that, "the doors of hell are locked on the inside."[22] It wouldn't be until over twenty years later that I would confront head-on the traditional doctrine of eternal punishment in hell and discover some alternative conclusions that actually have basis in Scripture and church history.

This new belief of mine that I had developed while in Africa was a form of inclusivity—the notion that salvation can exist beyond Christendom. As I learned more, I realized that the evangelical church predominantly taught an exclusionary view of salvation; that it can only exist for those with faith in Christ. I also learned first-hand the church often silences those who disagreed.

THE MISSIONARY SYNDROME

Progressive evangelical sociologist Tony Campolo, now a professor emeritus at moderate evangelical Eastern University (where I later received my master's degree in 1997), tells the story of when he was on a television show with Jerry Falwell. Falwell had asked him a question he wasn't expecting.

"He asked whether or not people who did not know Jesus as personal Savior could go to Heaven. He demanded an immediate yes or no," Campolo reported.[23] After hesitating, Campolo referred to the passage in Romans 2:14-15 and answered taking a similar position that I embraced after my experience in Somalia, that God judges people, including those who have never heard the message, on the basis of the light and truth about God made available to them.

But for fundamentalists like Falwell, and I dare say most evangelicals, this is not the theologically correct answer, and it created quite a firestorm. Campolo was called on the carpet by the supporters of some of his mission's endeavors for this terrible sin. Many of them stopped supporting his organization because of his "heretical" answer.

This belief that only born-again Christians can be saved is one of the elements of what I call the "missionary syndrome." Fundamentalist and evangelical missionaries, for the most part, are motivated to go overseas to evangelize (The Great Commission) because millions face a "Christ-less eternity," whether they also balance that with love in action (The Great Commandment) or not.

Although I was just as zealous to evangelize, putting Christ's love into action was my main motivation for missions, as I studied and implemented both community development and micro-enterprise programs wherever I served. I believe God gave me a deep desire to empower the poor, and I met many evangelicals like Jay and my teammates in Somalia who had that same passion.

However, we often felt like we were in a minority because it was typical for love-in-action programs (physical ministry) to get short shrift, as if they were a distant cousin to evangelism (spiritual ministry). Some evangelical agencies, such as Food for the Hungry, World Vision, and World Concern, focus primarily on physical ministry, while still acknowledging the importance of evangelism. Yet as it was then, even today, the images of millions of lost souls in a sea of ethnic groups unreached by the gospel message looms large in the mind of the conservative missionary and is the core motivation for today's 250,000 missionaries in 4,000 evangelical mission agencies from 200 countries.[24] It also is the major motivation for churches trying to reach secular society. Supposedly, the eternal destinies of millions of people are at stake.

Since I ultimately served as a rural-development missionary to Muslims for seven years (after Somalia, I would serve in Malawi for five years), I experienced this syndrome or burden and relate to how one missionary put it. "We have attended many Muslim funerals. We grieve every time we see another Muslim friend buried, having passed into eternity without salvation in Christ."[25]

Statements like this can be a subtle form of hellfire-and-brimstone preaching without saying the word hell. If they have arrived in eternity without salvation, where are they? The implication is the traditional interpretation of the afterlife. They are in eternal punishment in hell. Being uncomfortable with the concept of hell, some evangelical preachers, teachers, and missionaries tend to partially conceal their true position on salvation by purposely being unclear through ambiguous language. Rather than saying flatly regarding the lost in the world, "millions are going to hell," as some fundamentalists might, they will say something like, "millions face a Christ-less eternity." If recruiting for missions, they might add "unless we obey Christ's command and go to them with the gospel."

With such talk, the evangelical missionary begins to feel a heavy burden and responsibility to go off and save the world, share the gospel, or monetarily support those who do, or else millions of Muslims, Hindus, Buddhists, Animists, Catholics, and liberal Christians would have no chance of salvation. The weight of the world rests on the shoulders of evangelical missionaries, whether Western or nationals, who are on a global rescue mission because Jesus has given the Great Commission.

Although today I feel these exclusionary beliefs are seriously misplaced, I still admire the zealous dedication behind them. The majority of the missionaries I knew and worked with were sincere in their love and concern for the people they went to. We labored hard to learn the language, understand the culture, live amidst unsanitary conditions, and risk disease to share about a life-changing experience—one that I still believe can set people free to receive the love of God. Today my question is, is it the only legitimate experience? The commitment to traditional missionary work may be admirable, but it can also alienate the very people it seeks to reach by insisting that conversion to another organized religious tradition, namely Christianity, is necessary to be "saved" from their sins and avoid the wrath of God and the threat of eternal torment. Moreover, submission to some form of an organized Christian church is necessary or Divine displeasure remains.[26] Is this really the heart of God?

DON'T TEACH THAT IN AFRICA

Immediately after returning from Somalia in 1984, I enrolled in a small, unaccredited cross-cultural mission school called William Carey International University (WCIU) in Pasadena, California. I also took several classes at Fuller Seminary School of World Mission. My two years in the Horn of Africa got me hooked on the idea of doing long-term holistic missionary work among Muslims, which would include church planting. I had little formal training in Islam, cross-cultural ministry, or international relief and development, and sorely needed to take graduate courses in these subjects.

This was the period of time when I met my wife Lori. This beautiful woman with a heart of gold walked into my life on the campus of WCIU. When I learned she had lived in Liberia for a year at the age of 17 and was studying missions and preparing to return to Africa to work in a Muslim culture, I pretty much dropped everything to pursue her. She wasn't impressed, at least at first. Within seven months of starting to date we were married.

Lori and I began searching for an African tribe to target in our future mission work and we eventually settled on an ethno linguistic group called the Yao of Malawi (or Chiyao), who were considered "unreached" with the gospel. It wasn't until 1990 that we left, having partnered with another couple and arranged financial and spiritual support by two evangelical churches. I was up for ordination as a Pastor by *our* church, the same American Baptist congregation in Massachusetts that sent my youth group to Explo. In this localized ordination, the leaders of the church could simply vote on ordaining someone to ministry under their local oversight, rather than a national ordination. At the ordination meeting and vote, a group of six men[27] asked me questions about my faith to ensure they were ordaining someone with doctrines that matched the church. After reading the church statement of faith, they asked me if I could wholeheartedly agree to it.

There was something in there about "salvation is in Christ alone," and I shared with them my concern of rigidly applying that to all people, such as Muslims. I was forthright in telling them the belief I had adopted shortly after arriving in Somalia eight years earlier— that God saves *some* people outside the church who demonstrate faith and love as best they can given the knowledge they have.

I held my breath and braced for a shocked reaction. Would they turn me down for ordination because of my unorthodox belief? To their credit, the ordination committee didn't reject me. I know some evangelical churches and most fundamentalists would have, the same way they reacted to Tony Campolo. But my ordination committee came up with a compromise. The pastor said they could tolerate that belief only on the condition that I don't openly teach it.

Thank God I don't live in the Middle Ages. I probably would have been declared a heretic, burned at the stake, or beheaded. Nevertheless, they told me to be silent. Despite the fact that they accepted my ordination, they did it with a condition, because my inclusionary belief pushed the envelope of evangelical theology. I agreed to their condition, thinking I had no alternatives. I allowed someone to limit my expression of my core religious values. Actually, I censored myself to keep peace and avoid conflict. Although my sending church sent two pastors to visit our work three years later, they had little means to prevent me from teaching what I wanted. I had more to fear from our Team Leader, who would have spurned such teaching (and who was sent by another, more conservative, evangelical church).

Since my focus at that ordination meeting was on getting accepted, I failed to think through the implications of the committee's decision. I quickly forgot it and refrained from questioning the traditional view, i.e., that there are no exceptions to the need for conversion to Christ. I also avoided definitive statements about hell.

Years later I regretted my acquiescence. I would have loved to have a sending church's endorsement to teach our Muslim hearers that God's acceptance of them now or in the hereafter is not dependent on their converting to Christianity or some orthodox view of and commitment to Christ.

"If you choose to trust Christ or formally join our church,[28] great," I would have said. "But that's not the most important thing. The most important thing is to open your heart to receive God's love."

One can have an assurance of God's love while remaining Muslim.[29] God is concerned with the heart more than doctrines and is able and willing to save people without their formal adherence to a new religious belief system.

This is wholesale heresy and watering down the gospel to evangelicals, who insist that formal conversion to Christ is necessary for salvation. There can be no accommodation for the majority of Muslims who will never be ready to make a break with their religion—one that is highly ingrained in their culture and formally instilled in them since early childhood.

My experience shows, although much of Islam needs a measure of grace (that Jesus' teachings can bring), Western Christians can learn much from common Muslims, the majority of whom are moderates and haven't been indoctrinated by radical extremists. As an example, all the missionaries to Muslims I knew were duly impressed with their Muslim friends' fervent dedication to God. Most of them were more spiritual than Americans. The Muslims I knew in Somalia, Kenya, and Malawi, both Africans and East Asians, were also some of the most hospitable people one could ever meet. The *us vs. them* mentality of missionaries and evangelicals—*we're saved and they aren't*—doesn't serve building cultural bridges. The fact that some Muslims have the same mindset doesn't excuse Christians from setting an example of tolerance. Islam needs reform,[30] as do most religions, including Christianity. This doesn't mean a God of love rejects individuals within a particular religion, let alone automatically sends them to hell when they don't convert.

In the early- to mid-1980s I had broken with a major evangelical belief about the nature of salvation. I was trying to navigate my way within the church and had chosen to be largely silent about what I really believed. Yet, my inclusionary view did not entirely satisfy my reasoning mind. Apparently, some people would still go to an eternal hell. Yes, people ignorant of the gospel would be judged differently. If they did their best with the knowledge they had, they would be saved. But what of people who heard the gospel and rejected it? Or couldn't grasp the love of God and how it can transform their life? Or evil people resistant to God's authority? If they died unrepentant, would a loving God send them to hell with no hope for parole or pardon? Why don't people have opportunity to turn in the afterlife? Furthermore, what advantage is it to share the gospel with the "ignorant" masses, particularly Muslims, when the majority of them won't convert to Christ? Would God judge them more harshly because they had this knowledge and didn't act on it? Upon my return from Malawi in 1995, it would be another twelve years before I would find satisfactory answers to these questions.

DINNER AND BILLY GRAHAM

Dan, Gina, and I had just moved from the bar to the dining room. Right as a hostess was seating us at a table, Lori showed up.

"Sorry, I'm late. The lines are long at Penney's." Lori had done some Christmas shopping at the mall, which was only a hundred yards from Silver City. Twenty-five years after we met in California, she didn't look much older—vibrant, pretty, perpetually young, and golden blonde. My very own Goldie Hawn.

I greeted Lori and told her we had been conversing at the bar.

"You missed a great discussion," Dan said. "We were talking about the nature of conversion."

Everyone was hungry. We immediately started looking at the menus while the ladies chatted and Dan and I noticed the seasonal microbrews available. We ordered, talked about our kids, and ate dinner. Dan and I couldn't help but keep one eye on the basketball game. The second quarter was winding down, and the trailing Celtics were closing the gap.

Dan had my book on his mind. After dinner he brought it up again, and we eventually picked up where we left off. He brought up my experience in Somalia and the concept of inclusive faith. I'm not sure how it happened, but eventually we started talking about Billy Graham.

"I like Billy Graham because he's honest." I said. "He's humble enough to admit when he's wrong and in need of changing his view."

"Really?" Gina said. "What did he change his view on?"

"Well, let's see," I looked up trying to recollect. "The nature of the Bible and salvation are two things. Yeah, despite his conservative credentials, he became a moderate evangelical voice. He was one of the few calling for nuclear disarmament—that's another one. Ultimately, he refused to be absolutist on abortion, taking the Bible literally, and on the nature of salvation—things like that."

"Unlike his son, Franklin," Dan offered. "I think he can be extreme."

"Yes, I agree. Franklin is a hardliner compared to Billy," I said.

"What did he change about salvation?" Gina asked.

I began to explain about the first time I heard Billy Graham give an unorthodox view of salvation in the mid-1980s, ten or fifteen years after I saw him at Explo. I told them he was answering the same types of questions I raised during my experience in Somalia: What is the destiny of sincere adherents of other religions like Islam? What happens to those who have never heard the gospel? What about those tribes who have been cut off from missionaries?

"Those are good questions," Dan said. "How did he answer them?"

"Graham taught that God judges those people according to what they do in light of what they know," I said. "If they have had no opportunity to genuinely understand the gospel message, God will judge them differently. This was comforting to me. It meshed with the inclusionist belief I had developed."

I didn't mention it but I recalled how I rarely heard such views from the pulpit all these years. Although I did remember once hearing a professor at Fuller Seminary saying something similar and conclude, "We may be surprised whom we will see in heaven."

Lori interjected. "Isn't there a magazine article on Billy Graham in your office?"

"Oh, yeah," I said. She was referring to a 2006 *Newsweek* interview

I had copied. I shared with everyone as best as I could remember his quotes. Ones like, "I'm not a [Bible] literalist in the sense that every single jot and tittle is from the Lord. This is a little difference in my thinking through the years."[31] When an interviewer asked him whether heaven would be closed to good people from other religions or belief systems besides Christianity, he said, "Those are decisions only the Lord will make. It would be foolish for me to speculate who will be there and who won't... I believe the love of God is absolute. He gave His Son for the whole world, and I think he loves everybody regardless of what label they have."

"That's fascinating," Dan said, after hearing my paraphrases. "I didn't realize he was like that. The possibility of good people from other religions going to heaven is not a typical statement we hear in church."

"Yeah, but he didn't say everyone will go to heaven, right?" Gina asked.

"No, he didn't," Lori said, as she had read the article. "So, he didn't say God routinely saves people from other religions," Gina continued. "He said he couldn't speculate who will be there."

"Good point," Lori said. "The Scriptures still teach the need for people to believe in Jesus and that Jesus is the only way to God."

I knew if we got into this much deeper, there would be some sharp disagreements. My wife is an extremely kind person—always going the extra mile to help others and putting me to shame. We just don't see eye to eye on this issue. I knew Gina was skeptical of my views as well. Once when I had brought up the possibility of *universal reconciliation*—the notion that *all* of humankind would ultimately be reconciled to God—at a Bible study and suggested there were biblical grounds for it, Gina scoffed. She said it sounded like the New Age teaching she had dabbled in years ago. Another man had done one more. He sounded a warning that the whole idea was dangerous.

No, I didn't want controversial topics to ruin our nice dinner. *I'll have to wait to talk to Dan about this at another time,* I thought. I had given Dan a book on the subject called *The Inescapable Love of God,* and I knew he was aware of Rob Bell's new book, *Love Wins*. I was looking forward to hearing his thoughts. And of course, he had read my manuscript.

"Well, I was relieved when I read Graham's interview," I said, trying to keep the conversation in a less dangerous area. I explained how it confirmed the position I had for years ever since my experience in Somalia. That it's reasonable God will save *some* people outside of Christianity. I gave Gina a brief explanation of how I came to that view—Lori and Dan had already heard this story.

"That makes sense to me," Gina said. "That *some* people outside the church—but not all—will be saved."

At least she's open to that, I thought. As I shared, more recollections filled my mind. I remembered the missionary syndrome. After Somalia, I wondered why any type of inclusive theology—similar to what Graham said—was rarely, if ever, expounded in churches I attended. Nor was it explained as part of my missions training, with the exception of hearing something cursory at Fuller Seminary. I concluded pastors and teachers were afraid to go there. It might be construed as denying Jesus' teaching in the New Testament when he said, "I am the way and the truth and the life. No one comes to the Father except through me,"[32] the verse that Lori referred to. Or when the writer of Hebrews said, "Just as man is destined to die once, and after that to face judgment..."[33] Jesus was the "only way to God," and after you die it is too late to "repent" and receive the atonement for sin if you hadn't already accepted Christ. People's sins would still be upon them, and they would be separated from a holy God for eternity. This was Salvation 101 taught in evangelical churches.

But there was a whole ton of interpretive questions people refused to ask that were demanded by the context, what the original audience perceived, what other Scriptures taught, and what was the character of God. Again, I didn't want to bring this up now. But I couldn't help but think about people who were asking these questions. Like Tony Campolo, who addressed the salvation issue in his book, *Speaking My Mind*. Although he didn't endorse it, he introduced Christian universalism as at least worthy of consideration. When I attended Eastern University in 1995-97, where he taught, I wish I had known he was also grappling with these notions. These types of questions are not broadcast openly among evangelicals because people are afraid—afraid of spiritual rejection, and in the case of pastors, missionaries, and college professors, afraid of losing their jobs and livelihoods. No, I would talk to Dan later about this and the new conclusions I had come to.

Our topic of discussion died. Dan began viewing the game again. As the ladies fantasized about eating the delectable desserts on the menu, I recalled where I was in my spiritual journey in 1984. After living two years in a Muslim country, I had to address something more foundational than how to interpret the Bible. I needed to decide on the fundamental nature of the Bible. Is all of it inspired by God? Is it infallible, as my fellow evangelicals claimed? In my next adventure, I got my answers. Left to my own thoughts, I recalled that fateful trip to Switzerland.

CONFESSION 4

INVESTIGATING INERRANCY

"The Bible says not a word about its supposed infallibility."

– *L. William Countryman*

Switzerland, 1984

A stunning view of the Alps awaited me as I walked outside the L'Abri study center on a gorgeous spring day. My natural tendency was to stop and stare and breathe in the awe-inspiring beauty. Not today. I was preoccupied with an important decision I had just made, one that pushed me to the outer edge of evangelical orthodoxy, if not off a steep cliff and tumbling toward apostasy. Could I reconcile my new conviction with my evangelical faith? I wasn't sure. How did I get in this predicament? Walking up the stone path to the main chalet, I was keenly aware of the dilemma that brought me to this moment.

After completing my two-year assignment in Somalia with an evangelical peace-corps-like aid agency, I traveled to Switzerland and an innovative spiritual mission called *L'Abri*, French for "the shelter," founded by American evangelical guru Francis Schaeffer— at the time my favorite theologian—and his wife Edith, a popular evangelical author and speaker in her own right. Compared to the arid landscape of Somalia, the grounds of L'Abri were a virtual paradise, nestled among the snow-capped peaks, a short train ride from

Geneva. I was a man on a new mission, this time to dissect the doctrine of biblical inerrancy.

Five years earlier, as a fresh "born-again" believer, my new evangelical friends and mentors told me I was a babe in Christ. I needed to grow spiritually. Besides getting involved in the fellowship of the church, one important way to do that was to read, study, and memorize verses in the Bible. I needed to get into the Word, so I could get to know Jesus more, hear God's voice, and obey.

One of the first things I noticed was how much my fellow believers revered the Bible. It was God's Word—the holy book with authority to guide one's life. Statements of faith often referenced it as "the only authoritative rule of faith and practice." I heard it quoted in Sunday sermons; I studied it in Bible study groups and adult Sunday school lessons. "Let's get into the Word," a devout believer would say. "Your word is a lamp to my feet,"[34] as the Psalmist declared.

All teachings apparently had to be proved by the Bible, as was evidenced by the widespread practice of "proof texting," that is saying or writing some statement authoritatively and referencing the Bible verse it came from. Over the years, I learned how proof texting was one of the most common ways to abuse the Bible, since so many times the verse or verses were plucked inappropriately out of their literary and cultural milieu.

To a "real Christian," the Bible was more than a human book. It was the inspired Word of God; it spoke individually to people; it was a guide for daily living. We were to look to the Bible to develop a grid for decision-making. We were to seek answers to spiritual and moral issues specifically mentioned in the Bible. For issues not directly addressed, we were to use its principles as a guide. I began to read and study the Bible this way for the first time in my life.

On one of my first times cracking open the New Testament, I experienced an amazing phenomenon. Despite some of his teachings being difficult to accept, the Jesus of the Scriptures was the wisest, most radical and loving personality I had ever encountered. I was experiencing what Albert Einstein did when he read the accounts of

Jesus. "I am enthralled by the luminous figure of the Nazarene...No
one can read the Gospels without feeling the actual presence of Jesus.
His personality pulsates in every word. No myth is filled with such
life."[35] Although he was a deist at most—one who believes in a God
who doesn't regularly intervene in creation—Einstein apparently
believed in the historical existence of Jesus and encountered his presence and powerful personality. For me, Jesus leapt from the pages
of Scripture as I read the gospels seriously for the first time. Now I
knew why people revered the Bible. It had a radical and encouraging
message that enthralls the reader. I also saw a similar element when I
read the Old Testament prophets with their denunciation of the rich
and powerful and defense of the poor and oppressed.

On the other hand, not everything in the Bible was clear-cut,
consistent, or obviously inspirational. The Bible had intrinsic problems. When God told the Israelites to kill the inhabitants of whole
towns, which sometimes included women and children,[36] I squirmed
and internally rejected this morally repugnant god who contradicted
Jesus' message of love. When it appeared to teach that the world and
all living things were created in six 24-hour days,[37] I wondered how
that meshed with scientific evidence that earth is four billion years
old. When God ordered harsh punishments, even the death penalty,
for cursing one's parents, adultery, certain heterosexual liaisons, men
having sex with men, and working on the Sabbath,[38] I cringed. *Shit!*
I screamed inside (yes, it warranted *that* word). *Why is God so merci-
less? Jesus was just the opposite!*

The trouble was, the New Testament had its own dilemmas.
Jesus' teaching on God's care and love was encouraging, but what he
taught on divorce[39] seemed narrow and unrealistic. There was only
one justification for divorce (sexual immorality). Even physical abuse
apparently wasn't a good reason. His take on a person who is angry
with his brother was problematic. If one calls his brother a fool, he
is "in danger of the fire of hell,"[40] he flatly declared. How could Jesus
be so loving in one instance and so stern in the next? It was as if I
just met this wonderful friend and suddenly he stabbed me in the

back. Then there was his statement that anyone who blasphemes against the Holy Spirit would not be forgiven, in this age or the age to come.[41] This seemed to contradict his other teaching on forgiveness that we should forgive people who sin against us seventy times seven times.[42] The Apostle Paul had his own issues. When he taught that women cannot teach men and should be silent in the church,[43] I shuddered. These were some of the hard passages of the Bible and part of the reason that there was such a thing as "the Bible wars."

The Bible wars were fought around three major issues. First, there was the question of the nature of authority of the Bible. Is it always authoritative for modern society, or are there places where it is culturally or historically conditioned? For example, conservative evangelicals and fundamentalists take the Apostle Paul's words about women literally and teach that women can't be pastors or even leaders in a Bible Study. Moderate evangelical churches teach that Paul's teaching that limited women in ministry is not relevant for our modern culture, although they won't go so far as to permit a woman to be a pastor of a church. *So why do liberal churches have no problem ordaining women?* I wondered.

The second issue was an extrinsic problem, the question about how to properly interpret the Bible, which is rarely straightforward. Over the years a host of denominations developed their own way to interpret certain passages. Even though all churches taught that Jesus would return, there were churches that taught the pre-judgment Rapture I learned about in Texas and churches that taught against it. There were churches (Charismatic or Pentecostal) that taught that "spiritual gifts," such as prophecy and tongues, were normative throughout church history and other churches (Dispensationalists) that taught they weren't. There were churches that appeared very strict about how they interpreted the Bible—they tended to take things literally—and churches that tried to be more nuanced with the text.

The third major issue was considered by some to be the litmus test for a genuine Christian church. It was the doctrine of biblical inerrancy or infallibility, typically found in a church or organization's statement of faith. In some evangelicals' eyes, if a church or individual did not believe in this doctrine, they might as well have sold their soul to the devil. At the very least, anyone who rejected this doctrine was viewed as succumbing to the religious liberal agenda of the Protestant mainline churches.

Liberal. Now there's a loaded term and label commonly used among us. Liberals were those nasty folks outside acceptable evangelical doctrines and practices. They were the enemy, even more so than atheists because they claimed to be believers. We "knew" they really weren't. The root cause of their heresy was how they treated the Bible. The major front of the Bible Wars was between conservative and liberal Christians over the nature of authority of the Bible, its interpretation, and the doctrine of inerrancy. (Ironically, over the years I learned that despite vehement arguments on both sides, both conservatives and liberals are guilty of misreading and mishandling the Bible.[44])

Years later I learned a fascinating tidbit about the semantics of the terms *inerrant* and *infallible*. Most evangelicals used these two terms synonymously. Inerrancy is the belief that the Bible, in its original form (I will explain the implications of this below), is absolutely without error and free from contradiction in all its teachings. This includes its pronouncements touching theology, history, creation, and science. Nevertheless, some evangelicals made a distinction between *inerrancy* and *infallibility*, although your average believer wasn't unaware of this. In 1972, Fuller Theological Seminary revised its statement of faith and removed the word *inerrant* replacing it with the term *infallible*. It said the Bible is "the only *infallible* rule of faith and practice." According to other statements it made, the school's new definition reinforced the trustworthiness of the Bible in matters of theology, but left open room for it to have misstatements about historical and scientific details. This development angered many evangelicals. Since then Fuller has developed a reputation for being, you guessed it, too "liberal." Fuller's more nuanced

view was not the norm. When I reflected on it, it seemed disingenu-
ous. According to any dictionary, the two terms essentially mean the
same thing.[45] It was as if Fuller just couldn't bring itself to say the
Bible *wasn't* inerrant.

Why do people believe in inerrancy? The reason, I learned, was
based on a fear of undermining biblical authority. In other words, if
we conceded that the Bible wasn't always accurate, let's say historically or scientifically, how could we trust its theology? By admitting
there are *any* mistakes in the Bible, the door would open for the presence of errors in matters such as the historicity of Jesus, his teachings,
the crucifixion, the resurrection, and biblical morals. The authoritative house of cards of the Word of God would come tumbling down.

In my evangelical circles, the Bible was always handled as if it
were inerrant. No one ever stood up and said, "There are some contra-
dictory accounts in the New Testament," or "This verse is probably
not accurate, since it contradicts other more probable accounts," or
"Matthew got it wrong here." If there was ever an acknowledgement
of inconsistencies, they were always explained as "apparent inconsistencies," with some sort of explanation that claimed to harmonize
the accounts.

As a new believer, I had many questions about this doctrine
that plagued me, and I consequently needed to come to terms with
it. By 1984, my thinking followed this rationale: I was struck by
the otherworldly power of Jesus' teachings but also cognizant that
there were discrepancies in the Scriptures, i.e., contradictions in the
gospel narratives pertaining to historical details, different takes on
certain teachings, and varying depictions of God's character. How
could the Scriptures really be error-free? Could inerrancy really be
defended? And why did the Bible never claim itself infallible? There
was one verse in the New Testament that stated God inspired the
"Scriptures."[46] But that was actually referring to the Old Testament.
And it didn't say they were error-free. Besides, why can't the Bible be
inspired and still contain some mistakes? What difference would it

really make? These were biblical thorns in my flesh and were what led me to L'Abri.

ADDRESSING INERRANCY IN THE ALPS

Why choose L'Abri for this mission? Mostly because of its founder, Francis Schaeffer, who with his intellectualism and love for culture and the arts, was a fresh breeze in the often-stale atmosphere of modern evangelicalism. Starting in the 1960s, after outgrowing some of his fundamentalist roots, he developed a reputation for defending orthodox Christianity with rational arguments. Schaeffer was a fascinating combination of theological conservative and cultural progressive, who supported environmentalism,[47] studied popular culture, and was known for insights into the 60s generation and folk and rock music, which he deemed acceptable. In his son Frank's memoir, Frank remembers attending a Jefferson Airplane concert with his father in San Francisco, respectfully passing up offers to smoke joints, but enjoying the music and purchasing albums. No self-respecting American fundamentalist would be caught dead doing that!

L'Abri attracted an eclectic variety of people, including visitors Timothy Leary, the Harvard professor famous for experimenting with LSD; Billy Graham's daughter; President Gerald Ford's son; and Os Guinness, who later became a moderate evangelical leader and author from Britain. Mick Jagger and Keith Richards called on several occasions from their nearby chalet to say they would visit but never showed. Bob Dylan scheduled a visit. Once, when Frank Schaeffer met Jimmy Page of Led Zeppelin in 1969, Page had a copy of his father Francis' book, *Escape from Reason*, in his back pocket. Page told Frank that Eric Clapton gave it to him.[48]

One project for which Schaeffer became famous was his 1974 book and documentary on his view on the rise and decline of Western thought and culture, *How Then Shall We Live?*. In it, he criticized the shallow materialism and bourgeois attitude of middle- and upper-class America. The youth rebellion of the sixties was correct in its assessment of our culture, he had said. The hippie solution (drop out of society, abuse drugs, and pursue free love) was wrong, but they were right about the core problem. This point was largely unnoticed in the evangelical world, which continued to romanticize the good old days and middle-class values of the 50s and early 60s.

To Francis Schaeffer, long hair and rock music, with its often-revealing lyrics about the human condition, was fine. Even smoking a little pot was at least on par with the older generation's practice of having cocktails over dinner. This open-mindedness influenced his own trademark personal look. By the 1970s, he sported almost-shoulder-length hair, a goatee, and a Nehru jacket. On speaking tours he donned knickers and 18th century buckle shoes. He was a cultured, intellectual, theologically conservative hippie!

As an aside, there is a strange irony to this. Francis may have outgrown his strict fundamentalism of the 1950s, but he was still a tried-and-true Calvinist, who defended the Bible from attacks by liberal theologians and developed a traditional argument for the doctrine of inerrancy.[49] When Francis and his son Frank began working with the Christian Right to promote their books and documentaries on culture and human rights (i.e., abortion, infanticide, and euthanasia), Francis secretly detested the prevailing attitudes of conservative Christian America.

"That man is really disgusting," he once remarked about Jerry Falwell, after hearing a comment Falwell had made at a private meeting that disparaged homosexuals. In Schaeffer's mind, the Jerry Falwells, Pat Robertsons, and James Dobsons were their co-belligerents at best in the fight against abortion, not their allies. Today this incongruity hasn't escaped me: Despite this uneasy relationship, Schaeffer's defense of biblical inerrancy helped fuel the Christian Right's misuse of Scripture and their literalist, narrow mindset. A mindset that disgusted Francis Schaeffer!

Regardless, if there were anyone who could help me come to terms with the inerrancy question, it was Francis Schaeffer. Unfortunately, Francis wasn't at L'Abri during the week I stayed in May 1984. He had moved back to the States to be treated for lymphoma at the Mayo Clinic. In fact, the whole Schaeffer family was absent. Just my luck. I was too young to enjoy the 60s, and now this. But my misfortune at not meeting this esteemed evangelical theologian was nothing compared to what he and his family were going through. In fact, Francis passed away that very week. It was a somber few days at L'Abri.

Moreover, by 1984 the hippie-type spiritual seekers were gone from L'Abri, including the young women in bell-bottoms and short skirts that Frank Schaeffer pursued as a teenager. Believe me, I wouldn't have minded meeting them. I was a horny follower of Jesus trying to live a pure life. Despite the fact that everywhere I went in the Christian world I secretly hoped God would arrange for me to meet my future wife, I was supposed to be at L'Abri for spiritual answers. The Schaeffers had trained their people well; I found some very intelligent and considerate leaders at L'Abri, ones who helped me to address my gnawing questions.

L'Abri was set up like a guesthouse where visitors worked every morning on the grounds or in the kitchen for part of their room and board. During lunch and dinner, leaders entertained questions from visitors—and I mean any question was fair game—about Christian theology, the Bible, world religions, popular culture, sex—anything. A lively discussion would ensue. Since goateed Francis wasn't there to wax eloquent and intellectual over each inquiry, young seminarian-type prodigies led the discussions. Each afternoon, students could pursue their own research in the cozy study center adjacent to the main chalet, called Farel House, full of books and lectures on cassette tapes. On some evenings there was a lecture and Q & A on a particular topic. The healthy attitude of open-mindedness, acceptance, and a remarkable intellectualism I found there was something I seldom saw in my narrow traditional evangelical experience.

My first full day, after a morning of cleaning up in the kitchen and working in the garden on the footsteps of mountainous majesty, I began my quest. Over the next few days, I studied several books and teaching cassettes on the issue, including some by Francis himself. Later I bounced my findings back to the L'Abri workers during evening discussions.

The first thing I learned was a fascinating detail I hadn't known. Scholars who support inerrancy believe only the original manuscripts of the Bible are inerrant. And the originals have never been found! Our modern Bible is derived from extant copies of now long-lost originals. But everyone I knew—my evangelical friends and pastors—all acted as if they had an infallible Bible in their hands. They never entertained the possibility that something written in a modern Bible could be inaccurate due to copyist errors (not to mention translation errors, which I will address later), even if one believes in the doctrine of inerrancy! Even for an inerrantist, it would be perfectly appropriate to believe we have a fallible Bible in our hands, because we don't have the original copies. I concluded most evangelicals must believe that God preserved the integrity of the Bible through the copying process. But this wasn't the true inerrantist position! Inerrantist scholars knew surviving copies have too many variant readings to support this view.[50]

I had to process this point. Did it make sense that God would direct the communication of the exact history and doctrines of the faith in the original writings but not preserve them in the copies we have today? If we don't have an inerrant copy of the Bible in our hands, then what was the purpose in having an original inerrant Bible? According to the doctrine, the error-free character of the Bible was lost because the evidence did not support the notion that the original Bible was preserved. Since we can't retrieve the inerrant originals, we can't verify the doctrine of inerrancy. It must be accepted on faith. Even more so because the Bible doesn't claim to be inerrant. *Maybe there never were purely inerrant originals.* I filed that thought.

Despite these facts, the teaching tapes at L'Abri included attempts to harmonize inconsistencies in the Bible as a way of defending inerrancy (rather than argue our copies were tainted).⁵¹ The assumption was that however our modern Bible was derived, apparent problems were not genuine mistakes. I distinctly recall one recorded lecture (not by Schaeffer) on the problems with the order of events between Jesus' crucifixion and the resurrection described in the four gospels. *Aha!* I thought. *This will get to the core issues.* Those familiar with doing a critical analysis of the gospels—the books of Matthew, Mark, Luke, and John—will know that some events described in one book are contradicted in another book. For example, the book of Matthew says *two* women went to the tomb, Mary Magdalene and another Mary. The book of Mark says *three* women went to the tomb, adding Salome to the two Marys. Luke says *more than three* women went: the two Marys, Joanna, and still others. Finally, John lists only *one* went to the tomb, Mary Magdalene.

In addition, Matthew and Mark say there was *one angel* at the tomb, while Luke and John says there were *two angels*. Matthew and Luke say the women went back and told the disciples about the resurrection. John says only Mary told the disciples, while Mark says the women didn't tell the disciples because they were afraid. Luke states that Peter went to the tomb in response to the women's report, and John says Peter and John went to the tomb. John says that Mary went to the tomb twice, once alone without seeing angels, and later on with Peter and John when thereafter she saw two angels. The other writers say she only goes to the tomb once. There were a number of other details as well that revealed contradictions. As the teacher on the cassette described these scenarios, my head began to spin.

Most people don't compare these four books, so they don't realize there are discrepancies at all. The teacher began going through these accounts and making an attempt to reconcile them. In my mind, the original chroniclers had gotten the details wrong. But rather than chalk up the differences to human error or poor memories, the lecturer offered a scenario that might harmonize the contradictions and thus make each account accurate and therefore inerrant.

Some of it made sense. Perhaps in reality there was a group of women who went to the tomb, but each writer focused on the women or woman he deemed important. But most of it made no sense at all. Overall the attempt to reconcile these four sources through constructing elaborate scenarios made me dizzier than the actual discrepancies. In my mind, the lecturer was forcing the texts into an inerrant belief system rather than allowing the texts to speak for themselves. It appeared he desperately wanted the doctrine of inerrancy to be true! His efforts to harmonize inconsistencies violated what I later came to know as *Occam's razor*—a principle that recommends that one should select the hypothesis that makes the fewest assumptions, often the simplest explanation. The lecturer's convoluted rationalizations were based on too many presuppositions. It seemed obvious and simpler to acknowledge that the gospel writers got some of the details wrong. I concluded that the Bible at least had some minor errors. A few years later I gained an additional insight. If the Bible were entirely free from historical errors, it would actually harm the cause for historicity, not help it. Historians and legal experts will tell you that when eyewitness accounts are identical, that is evidence that there was collaboration. In other words, minor discrepancies in the accounts of the gospels could be evidence that the writers are not guilty of collusion. People see things from variant perspectives and recall things differently, including getting factual details wrong. It's not evidence that their testimony is a fraud, but rather that eyewitnesses often have memory fallibility.[52] If it can be shown that the core, major points of the testimony are the same, even with incidental details being different, then this is evidence the overarching testimony is true.

This is what happens in this example of the accounts about the morning of the resurrection. The accounts are remarkably similar on important matters—a woman or women went to the tomb, an angel or angels were present and spoke the same general message, and at least one woman, Mary Magdalene, and probably more saw the risen Jesus. Three out of four accounts said they reported it to the disciples. On the other hand, the lecturer on the cassette, like all inerrantists, could not acknowledge the possibility of an eyewitness's faulty memory or an historian inadvertently (or purposely) misrepresenting details. They *must* reconcile all contradictions.

I didn't buy it. All the arguments I heard or read didn't add up in my mind. I still trusted the Bible to be substantially correct, even though it had minor mistakes. I didn't see it as a collection of mythologies. But neither did I see it as an infallible, one-hundred-percent-accurate document down to each minor detail. I could still believe the resurrection was true even if I believed the accounts of the events following the resurrection had errors. The church was insisting the Western value of textual precision be imposed on the Bible. But "an experienced historian knows that a source may be mistaken in many matters of detail and still correct in others or in the general run of its narrative."[53] I just couldn't believe every statement of the Bible was entirely without error. God still allowed fallible humans to relate the stories and fallible copyists to preserve them.

I agreed with what one theologian concluded when faced with inaccuracies in this story of the empty tomb. "Granted that there are a dozen or more problems of detail in the four versions of the incident, does that deprive each individual narrative of its power?"[54]

As I walked up the path from the study center to the main L'Abri chalet that bright afternoon, I was relieved I had found answers. In some ways, my faith in the gospel message was strengthened. But I also was distressed. What I concluded would be interpreted as misguided at best and heretical at worst by the overwhelming majority of my evangelical friends and acquaintances. In fact, at L'Abri, it was an issue of theological purity for workers. Unbeknownst to me, Francis Schaeffer had L'Abri staff sign a loyalty oath to the inerrancy of Scripture. Francis' son-in-law, John, being more open-minded about the nature of inspiration, refused to sign it and was banned from teaching any longer.[55] Even though I wasn't aware of this, I knew this kind of thing frequently happens in churches and seminaries. To me, this discredited any intellectual power the movement claimed.

I was left with a choice. Since I could not in good conscience accept the doctrine of inerrancy, or the muddled alternative doctrine of infallibility, I could either reject them and risk alienation from the evangelical community or tolerate them without accepting them outright. I chose the latter. You see, I was still addicted to other people's approval. I knew sharing openly what I believed would bring only censure and pressure to conform. At this stage in my life, my psychological need for acceptance was stronger than my desire for open intellectual honesty.

Yet inside, I always wondered. Why didn't we evangelicals allow people to believe the Bible is sometimes wrong and still accept them as believers in good standing, let alone leaders or teachers? Why was it paramount to insist everyone accept the whole Bible as one hundred percent true? Why did we make certain peripheral beliefs like biblical inerrancy or infallibility non-negotiable?

I ended up avoiding churches and organizations that had a strong adherence to this doctrine, although that was easier said than done. When faced with situations where I heard that doctrine taught, I would rationalize that the Bible was only partially inerrant, not altogether so. It was still trustworthy generally, if not so in specific details. I saw mistakes where others saw *apparent* inconsistencies. For the most part, these mistakes were minor. Although they contradicted the doctrine of inerrancy and made me think twice about the nature of biblical authority, I saw no evidence they contradicted central Christian dogma. In the ensuing years, however, my view of the Bible would shift again—as I learned more about how to uncover its original meaning and interpret it in our modern context.

REFLECTIONS ON BIBLICAL CONTRADICTIONS

They say politics and religion make for bad dinner conversation, but that didn't stop Dan from plunging into the inerrancy debate. The ladies decided to forego dessert and order after-dinner drinks.

Gina got a Heifewizen and Lori ordered a coffee with Baileys. Dan and I were overdue for another round and both asked for one of the seasonals—a spicy Pumpkin Ale.

"All right, Mike," Dan started, after our server brought our drinks. "I need to ask you about the inerrancy of the Bible." Dan looked at Gina and Lori. "It's in one of the chapters of his book," he told them. "Besides the resurrection story, what are some examples of contradictions in the Bible?"

"Man, this Pumpkin Ale is good!" I declared, in an attempt to hint that inerrancy might be too controversial a topic to broach. I was worried how Lori and Gina would react. "Oh, I'm sorry, Dan, what did you say?"

"He asked for examples of inconsistencies in the Bible," Gina said. "I wanna know too. May I taste that?"

"Sure, go ahead." I pushed my tall glass toward Gina. She at least seemed interested in the topic.

"Yum. That *is* good!" Gina pushed the glass back my direction. "I'll have to have one sometime. So, what about the contradictions?"

"Okay, where do I begin?" I tried to recollect some of the many discrepancies I had encountered. I had seen lists of up to 142.[56] "Okay, for one—I think it's in Matthew—Jesus said John the Baptist was Elijah, as prophesied in the Old Testament, while in the book of John, John the Baptist denies he is Elijah. Oh, and Matthew says the disciples got two donkeys and Jesus sat on both of them when He entered Jerusalem; the other writers say there was only one. Let's see...what else? Oh, Matthew, Mark, and Luke recorded the last supper was the feast of the Passover. John said it was the night *before* the Passover."

"Yeah, but I'm sure there's an explanation for those," Lori piped in. "It doesn't mean there's a mistake. Like maybe John the Baptist didn't realize he fulfilled that prophecy."

"I wouldn't dispute that some are only apparent contradictions— as you said, there might be a way of harmonizing them. But there are so many more where such explanations are a stretch, or where an error fits the evidence better."

I shared what I had learned from historian Garry Wills. He explained how Matthew was tying Jesus' entry into Jerusalem with a passage in the Old Testament that used Hebrew parallelism. In Zechariah, it says "...your king comes to you, gentle and riding on a donkey, on a colt, the foal of a donkey." Matthew claimed Jesus told his disciples to bring him a donkey *and* a colt. Then later said Jesus rode *them*. But in parallelism, the same thing is said more than once with varying words to make an impression, not to denote two different concepts. Zechariah was only talking about one young donkey, and Matthew misinterpreted it as two, a donkey and its foal. Matthew got it wrong.

Wills also said Matthew, Mark, and Luke were in error when they said the last supper was the feast of the Passover. John is the only one who got it right; it was the night before the Passover, which is why the Sanhedrin were able to arrest him and put him on trial. Otherwise, if it were the very night of Passover, it would have been against the Jewish law to hold a trial.

"Wait a minute," Lori objected, when I had finished. "You're just going by what that one guy said. Other Bible historians have alternative explanations."

"I'm sure some do," I responded. "But maybe they presuppose the Bible is without error—and therefore come up with a rationalization for a problem—rather than start from a neutral position and let the chips fall where they may."

"That makes sense," Dan said.

"I don't understand," Gina offered. "If what you are saying is correct, then our church is not teaching the truth. They frequently say the Bible is the infallible Word of God. God doesn't make mistakes."

"But God works through fallible human beings, Gina," said Dan.

"You two are blowing my mind," Gina said.

"I think you need to read some *evangelical* scholars," Lori suggested. "There's another way to look at this that supports the truth of the Bible."

"Yeah, but why does it have to be black or white?" Dan asked. "It seems to me that these stories could be essentially true with some details wrong. After all, these differences he's citing are minor. Maybe God inspired fallible authors."

"I agree," I said. "I don't think the Bible has to be spot-on to reflect spiritual authority."

"So, Mike," Gina said. "Why does the church insist the Bible is inerrant? There must be something to it."

"Actually, the doctrine of inerrancy is relatively new," I responded. "As a formal doctrine it developed in the 19th century—out of a fundamentalist reaction to modernist theories about the Bible—you know, as a means to protect it from 'liberal' attacks. Many churches hang on to it out of fear. If the Bible isn't inerrant, then people would have to rethink their faith, and that's frightening."

"You're getting these ideas from certain scholars," Lori interjected again. "Gina, there are plenty of biblical scholars that would disagree with what he's saying. They support the total reliability of the Bible."

Dan asked Lori what scholars she was referring to. She had read some while taking Bible classes in college years ago. "J. I. Packer for one," she said. "Probably John Piper. In fact, there were something like 200 leaders who signed some statement on biblical inerrancy back in the late 70s."

"She's right," I said. "It was called the Chicago Statement. Francis Schaeffer and R.C. Sproul were among the signers."

"So how does this statement differ from what Mike is saying?" Gina asked Lori.

"It's been years since I studied this," Lori said. "But they say the Bible is reliable in theology, science, and history. And that it must be interpreted properly according to the type of genre—you know, history read like a history, poetry like poetry, metaphors like metaphors. Things like that."

"That makes sense," Gina said.

"Also, it says only the original manuscripts are considered inerrant," Lori continued. "So it's possible copies we have today have very minor slips at most—numbers, misspelled words—but overall what we have is amazingly preserved."

"That's true," I said. "About only the originals being considered inerrant."

"Yeah, but isn't it true we don't have the originals?" Dan asked.

"Yes, our best copies are still hundreds of years removed from the original autographs," I said. "So, logically, we really don't have a mistake-free Bible. The confusing thing is the church downplays the originals being infallible, and over-emphasizes the belief that the Bible has been preserved. Consequently they never entertain the possibility we have a fallible Bible today—that in transcribing the originals, mistakes were probably made, beyond misspellings. As I said, that follows logically if only the originals were error-free. Or if the originals were never infallible to begin with, for that matter. But the Chicago statement still insists discrepancies are only apparent. You should read it. To me, it has fuzzy logic. And there are plenty of other scholars who don't subscribe to it." "Another thing to put on your reading list, Dan," Gina said, turning and smiling at him.

"I think my reading list is long enough, thank you," Dan said. "But, no, it's good to look at this more critically. It seems the church just tells us to accept stuff like inerrancy at face value without explaining the evidence for and against."

"I agree," I told Dan. I then explained why few of us ever approach the Bible with pure objectivity. We approach it with our pre-existing beliefs and biases in mind—one way or the other. As I talked, I tried to recall what one Episcopal priest said who rejects the belief in the inerrant Scriptures but still believes they carry authority. I did my best to explain a summary of his quote. "This guy made a great point in his book. Most of us come to the Bible in the context of its use in the church or Christian books, so we have preconceived ideas and expectations. But most of these ideas are unexamined. We just accept them as true."

"Makes sense," Dan agreed.

"So if someone comes along and claims the Bible is not infallible, it threatens us because it contradicts our expectations. But these expectations may or may not be good ones in the first place."[57]

"Well, I think it's a real problem when we come to doubt Scripture," Lori said. "It makes reading the Bible subjective, like you can just toss aside what you don't like."

"It doesn't have to be that way, though," I offered. "Look, someone had to decide what goes into the Bible and whether it was reliable history. We take it on faith they made the right decisions. Also, someone had to copy the originals down through the years. We take it on faith they transcribed it accurately. Why do people in the past get to decide what's inspired or true in Scripture, and we just have to accept it? Why can't we look at the best biblical scholarship, use a little common sense, and make our own decision about whether every word of the Bible is true?"

"I think those are fair questions," said Dan. "And if the evidence points to some of these mistakes you brought up, that doesn't mean the whole thing is bogus. I mean, if Matthew got it wrong about the donkey the disciples fetched and Jesus rode, why does that threaten the obviously inspirational stuff he wrote that Jesus said?"

"Because if he got it wrong on a small thing, how can we trust him for the big stuff?" Lori said, repositioning herself in her seat. "No, I think it's fine to emphasize that God protected it. From what I've read, compared to other historical manuscripts, the Bible is remarkably preserved."

"Well, preserved up to a point," I responded. "The reason you can trust the big stuff is because an historical-critical approach to the Bible may show its faults, but it also reveals how it contains verifiable history and a theme, you know, of a just and compassionate value system under a loving Creator. Even despite problematic passages."

I took a deep breath before I continued. "Look, I understand how this can be scary; I was freaked out too when I first encountered the evidence for this. But actually, I've come out a stronger believer, I think. In fact, I learned that if all biblical stories matched exactly, that would be proof of tampering, or editing, or a conspiracy to create a myth. Historians know this—that eyewitnesses or researchers or whoever wrote the history sometimes get it wrong, because that's the nature of human memory and fact-finding. Precision is illusive. Besides, you know, Dan's right. Most of these differences we are talking about are immaterial—and I've only mentioned a few. There really are a lot.[58] Isn't the gist of what is said more important than the details?"

"That makes sense, Mike," said Gina. "But Lori's concern—about making the act of reading the Bible too subjective—seems valid too. I'll have to think about this."

It seemed we had exhausted this topic. I leaned back and checked out the game without registering the time or the score. Although I didn't bring it up to the group, I was all too aware how my new understanding of the Bible led me to move on and address other concerns. Inerrancy was just the tip of the iceberg. One of these other issues was my discovery about the traditional view of the church— how it clashes with a reasoned look at the New Testament. That was a particularly rocky path of my journey. And I remembered the details all too well.

CONFESSION 5
SAVE THE ALES
(FROM THE CHURCH)

"I'm not often so comfortable in church. It feels pious and so unlike the Christ I read about in the Scriptures."

-- *Bono*

"Loving God while you are selling Him is close to impossible."

– *Frank Schaeffer*

After a few years' involvement in several evangelical churches after my conversion, something happened. I began to notice how much the church squelched personal liberty. In an effort to ensure members were properly discipled in Christ, church leaders would stifle one's freedom to enjoy (not abuse) certain pleasures and one's choice of personal conduct. Whether intentionally or unintentionally, we evangelicals, I discovered, tended to be freedom busters. Drinking ale in the local pub is but one example. I realized the ales needed saving. Not from greedy profiteers, but from fundamentalist mindsets. These "ales" aren't confined to alcoholic drinks, but are a metaphor for personal and spiritual liberty. Another example is being free to choose how to practice one's faith outside the strictures of the church. If, as a believer, you doubt this, take the sage advice that "...you ought to live your life with such freedom and joy that uptight Christians will doubt your salvation."[59]

To me, the two major causes of this squelching of liberty—the free flow of ales so to speak—are one, literalist approaches to the Bible (which I will elaborate on in a forthcoming chapter) and two, that age-old relic that began in the Constantine era, the institutional church. With some rare exceptions, what we call "church'" has become the perpetuator of organized religion, a legalistic system that controls. This wasn't what I bargained for.

Initially, like other newly born-again evangelicals, I was told about the importance of the church—the body of believers in Jesus— and how I need to commit to a local expression of one. At the time, I had no reason to think otherwise. But years later, I found evidence that our contemporary concept of "church" is seriously misunderstood. I discovered our modern model of church, whether Protestant or Catholic, is foreign to the New Testament. Professional salaried clergy, a clergy-laity distinction, meetings in buildings, church budgets, hierarchal leadership, and legalistic requirements were not present in early Christianity, and most were borrowed from pagan culture after the Roman Emperor Constantine made Christianity the state religion.[60] Since they are so entrenched in contemporary tradition, they are read into passages in the Bible, not derived from them. What we envision as "church" today, in the first century was more accurately an organic gathering of people touched by God's love. It was not a formal institution. Jesus did not found a new religion, an institutional church,[61] or expect his followers to set up a Christian version of the synagogue.[62]

How can this be? How can the modern concept of church be unbiblical? And how is the church limiting the freedom of believers? It took me twenty-five years to discover the answers to these questions. This isn't a deliberate deception by pastors, and it doesn't mean there's nothing good in modern churches. Most of the pastors I know are honest and dedicated. Undoubtedly some churches are healthy places to grow spiritually. But many aren't. I found most I encountered to be legalistic, authoritative, and spiritually abusive the more closely they followed modern false notions of church. These notions derive from highly ingrained traditions that are not easily recognized or abandoned. Because of that, to the degree that churches inhibit liberty and exercise control over their members (and I daresay, in my experience, practically *all* church institutions do to some extent), they are detrimental to one's spiritual and emotional health. This phenomenon slowly dawned on me over my first decade as a believer.

Massachusetts and California, 1980-1989

CHURCHIANITY

I never considered myself a fundamentalist Christian. In my mind, fundamentalists had those outrageous narrow rules: don't play cards, smoke, drink, dance, date, or listen to rock music. My friends and I were products of the counterculture Jesus people who relished rock-and-roll as a legitimate expression of heartfelt worship, wore bell-bottom jeans and T-shirts to church, and challenged the status quo. This wasn't all true, however. There was a deception going on in my mind. In reality, I had my own narrow rules.

"I hear you're going to see Bill Gothard," Anne, my friend from College Church in Northampton, Massachusetts, said. It was 1980, and this popular fundamentalist teacher who sold out arenas across the country with his Basic Youth Conflict seminars was coming to nearby Springfield.

"Yeah, some people recommended I go, since he's a good Bible teacher," I answered.

"Well, he may have *some* good Bible teaching, but you need to beware of some of his *other* views," she warned. "He claims that *all* rock music has an inherently evil beat. He thinks even Christian rock is of the devil."

"Are you kidding?" I responded. "That's crazy! Where did he get that idea?"

"Something about an African witchdoctor hearing Christian rock and claiming it was conjuring spirits. He also takes the Scriptures on submission to the nth degree, saying men over women is part of God's ordained authority structure. My advice is to think hard about what he's teaching, take what you see as good, and reject the rest," she concluded.

"Okay, I'll keep that in mind."

As a new believer, I was still in the naïve stage and was shocked that my fellow evangelicals were often not in agreement on what the Bible taught. I learned that many of us were moderates; we believed the orthodox doctrines of the faith, but were suspicious of the stricter beliefs and limiting practices. And we loved Christian rock music. (Mind you, we weren't as moderate as we thought. With a few minor exceptions, we condemned secular rock music.)

Bill Gothard proved to be as Anne said. It was one of my first encounters with fundamentalism. Years later it came as a shock to me that despite this concept of myself as a moderate, I really did go through a long and arduous fundamentalist stage. Not the super-restrictive version, but the moralist, legalistic variety. Fundamentalism-lite, in other words. Some of this started when I became enamored with a popular Christian musician.

"Hey, Jake!" the brother of my best friend declared. "Mike would love Keith Green. Put on his first album." I was unaware of contemporary Christian music at the time, and Jake, whom I had met shortly after my conversion at UMass Amherst, and his brother Don were giving me a crash course. They were duly impressed when I told them I had met Phil Keaggy and Paul Clark personally.

"Check this out, Mike," Jake said as he queued up the first song on his turntable. "This guy will blow you away."

Green was a soft rock musician from California who wrote compelling melodies with challenging lyrics. He blossomed musically at a young age—at 12 he had signed a five-year contract with

Decca Records—but secular fame never materialized. After dabbling in drugs and mysticism for years, he came to Christ in 1975 shortly after a bad mescaline trip. The song "You Put This Love in My Heart" leapt from Jake's speakers and touched a chord inside me. After years of floundering in low self-esteem and depression, the hopeful message of that catchy song was real for me. A year earlier I had come to feel that Divine Love in *my* heart.

"What do you think of this next one?" Jake asked as he lowered the needle onto another disc entitled "No Compromise," which included Green's popular song, "Asleep in the Light." Its lyrics included a scathing rebuke to the evangelical church for ignoring the needy. It was consistent with Keith and his wife Melody's life; they were known for taking outcast and homeless people into their home.

"Wow! Great tunes and lyrics. This guy cuts to the chase."

I was hooked. Green infused his fiery personality not only into his music, but also into his writings on Christian discipleship. I bought his albums and began obsessively reading the magazine he and his wife published called *The Last Days Newsletter*. I loved the way he challenged conventionalism and promoted total commitment to Jesus, including helping the poor.

On the other hand, much of what he said grated on me. I later concluded he was unconsciously promoting a performance-oriented approach to God. If you really loved God, you'd swear off television, labor tirelessly against abortion (which his wife did), and then move to Africa to save the heathens (which I did); that kind of stuff. Reading Green left you with the impression that whatever you were doing to serve God, it was never enough. You could always and should always do more.

This isn't always bad advice. Some people, like me, need a kick in the butt. In fact, I attribute some of my motivation to serving in Africa to Green. But performance-oriented religion has a way of draining you. I began to feel that I could never measure up to the picture of dedication and devotion being painted. I could never seem to do enough daily prayer, reading the Word, sharing the gospel, controlling my thoughts, and being a zealous nut for Jesus. Despite the fact that Green later toned down his message with some much-needed grace, I bought into other similar revivalist teachings and slowly began looking at my relationship with God differently.

It was then that I started thinking I needed to be in a more radical Christian community or church. No more compromising, business-as-usual Christianity, but faith that truly lived out what Jesus and the New Testament taught. The revivalist material I was reading made me yearn for a deeper spiritual experience. These thoughts occurred shortly after returning from Africa in 1984 when I joined a conservative charismatic church in Pasadena, California, called Abundant Life Community Church (ALCC). It was part of a church movement called People of Destiny International (PDI)—today called Sovereign Grace Ministries (SGM)—founded by Larry Tomczak and C.J. Mahaney. ALCC claimed to be a "New Testament church."

It was at this time, when I was studying missions at WCIU and Fuller Seminary's School of World Mission in preparation to return to Africa that I met my wife Lori, who was at WCIU. ALCC was a church plant, meaning people were sent out from an established large church to start a new congregation. The leaders desired to see people transformed by the love of God. When I joined there were only about 40 people. Almost a year later, after Lori and I were engaged, I was delighted that she joined me at ALCC after one year of attending Jack Hayford's Church On The Way in Los Angeles. Now attending church together, we watched ALCC grow to hundreds. I started playing the piano in the church band. We were a zealous younger crowd who sincerely believed we would be a catalyst for revival.[63]

Despite our well-meaning passion to help others find peace with God, it took me a couple of years to finally figure out this church was one of those we-alone-and-the-ones-who-agree-with-us-are-the-only-ones-who-are-doing-it-right churches. PDI/SGM claimed they were planting their churches after the first-century model. That was appealing to me, since I wanted authentic Christianity, not a milquetoast version. But the line between dedication and dogmatism is sometimes very thin. It was here that I learned about the phenomenon I later came to call *churchianity*—the practice of making belief in Jesus largely focused on the habits and demands of the institutional church, rather than on the love of God, which leads to the abandonment of freedom and the subtle instillation of legalistic religion.

ALCC had two personalities. One was the personality of the church from which it came, the PDI/SGM home church in Washington, D.C. This was a conservative, charismatic, Calvinistic church movement focused on middle-class Americans. They believed in what they called "apostolic authority," the notion that since there were "apostles" in the Bible, there should be modern apostles who oversee groups of churches. PDI/SGM "apostles" would occasionally come to visit our church. They also put a lot of emphasis on the local pastors' having the role of watching over the flock in terms of ensuring that their life conformed to sound doctrine and right behavior.

The other personality was of the Korean-background senior pastor, Che Ahn. He hadn't graduated from seminary yet (he was attending Fuller Seminary when I joined), but claimed he had received a prophetic word that he would be involved in "a great harvest of souls." His focus was on seeking revival and practicing "power evangelism," a term coined by John Wimber, the founder of the Vineyard denomination. That meant trying to reach the lost for Jesus through praying for supernatural signs, such as physical healing or having God orchestrate something in one's life. Che was well intentioned, but was the most driven pastor I had ever met.

The outcome of these two church personalities was a congregation with specific things for members to believe and lots of stuff to do. For instance, there were early-morning and all-night prayer meetings, long worship sessions with contemporary Christian music, people giving "prophetic words," speaking in tongues, home group meetings, occasional street witnessing, healing services, and drug addicts wandering in to check the scene out, falling under the conviction of God, and converting right there on the spot.

Well, er... maybe not that last one. That was kind of one of the coveted goals. The drug addict with dreadlocks getting saved on the spot, that is, or perhaps a celebrity. I think the best we did was see someone with a serious drinking problem saved over the course of a couple weeks. I'm not making fun of that. It was a wonderful thing to behold. The man needed help and after earnest prayer and encouragement, we saw him stop abusing alcohol. In fact, we were pretty good at building a caring community. Another time a man shared his testimony with Madonna on the streets of L.A. when he helped her with her broken-down car. We all prayed for her at the church service. We would have been thrilled if it had turned out she was "saved" through one of our members. Still, there was something wrong with our highly disciplined lifestyle that I couldn't put my finger on.

After a couple of years Lori and I began leading a weekly home group. I started to believe that we really *were* doing it right and most other churches weren't. We seemed to be doing everything by the book. I was even making inroads influencing the leadership to do more to help the poor by starting a "mercy ministry." Since senior pastor Che was into *world evangelism*, he was keen on cross-cultural missions. The church attracted many people like Lori and me who were preparing for global mission work. Eventually we began a church-based program with the goal to send teams abroad to developing countries that had large populations of "unreached peoples." We mission-minded folks had introduced a more holistic approach to missions that included community development, helping the poor identify problems and devise projects that build long-term self-reliance. Yet, despite the image of the church being on the cutting edge of Christian ministry, I occasionally noticed a disconnect.

"So, Mike, you've been to Africa as a missionary?" Lou, one of the pastors, asked me.

"Yeah, it was with a Christian relief and development agency. We were more like development workers who sometimes would share our faith."

"Where were you and how long?"

"In Somalia, mostly, but I spent six weeks in Kenya too. My whole term was two years. I was part of a team that helped bring aid to largely Muslim refugees from Ethiopia."

"Amazing," he continued. "Muslims are hard to reach. Maybe God will use you to plant a PDI church in Muslim Africa."

"Well, I don't think a church like ours would be a good fit there," I suggested. "It would have to be contextualized to fit African Muslim culture."

I tried to explain how much of what we do in church is really American culture and not conducive to African culture, let alone an Islamic one. He didn't seem to get it. I shared potential problems. American "apostles" with no understanding of the foreign culture could never presume to know how to oversee an indigenous church. American missionaries, even if they learned the local language and culture, shouldn't control a second-culture church, or else it would create an unhealthy dependency. I noticed he was more interested in evangelism than community development. He downplayed its importance as a vehicle to demonstrate concern for physical needs and social justice in and of itself.

The PDI church model is inflexible. It really wouldn't work in Africa, I thought. *Besides, without a vision for contextualizing the message and helping the poor out of love—not a means to an end—it wouldn't be authentic.* An inflexible church model meant a lack of freedom.

"Jesus commands us to preach the Gospel and make disciples of all nations," pastor Che declared one Sunday morning, referring to The Great Commission. "God gave me a vision that I was to come to Los Angeles and see a great harvest. I believe it will start in the greater L.A. area, and eventually this church will become a center from which missionary teams will be sent out to reach the nations."

This was a typical sermon and prelude to an evangelistic campaign we would often do. The church's interpretation of evangelism was twofold: one, invite friends to church to experience God and hear an evangelistic message, and two, hit the streets. I remember going out to Pasadena City College a few times and Hollywood Boulevard once to "witness" to people—that is to share our faith with the hope of leading someone to the Lord.

With my experience in Africa and my training in cross-cultural ministry, I should have known better than to buy into this method. I knew how much it turned me off in places like Explo in Dallas. In mission training, I was taught that we needed to "earn the right to be heard" before evangelizing. But I allowed the church to affect my thinking through subtle pressure to conform to their philosophy of ministry. I wasn't thinking for myself, or encouraged to do so. Another sign that personal freedom was being squelched.

I enjoyed talking to people and getting into an honest conversation about God and my faith, but street witnessing wasn't my style or one that followed American norms. Superficial, often one-sided conversations with strangers and handing out simplistic tracts that you would have to apologize for when talking to intellectual types wasn't my idea of touching people's lives. Besides, it was just really weird walking up to perfect strangers and asking them, "Do you believe in Jesus?" Well, maybe that wasn't the first line. But something similar was introduced as early in the conversation as possible.

Years later in 1996, I heard a professor at Eastern University sum up the reason this method of evangelism is perceived as obnoxious. "The gospel might be the most important message you can share with someone, but it's not the most urgent," he stated. "In every culture, people don't share important matters the first few times they meet. That would be premature and appear contrived." No wonder they called us Bible thumpers. In later years I realized even if one did "earn the right to be heard," our witnessing is usually an agenda, not a sincere concern. Our goal went beyond people coming to faith. We wanted to influence them to join our church. Then we would have authentic church growth, not merely transfer growth, where people just switch from one boring, dead church to some hip, happening church. This was another disconnect. The goal of new converts joining our church bothered me. I thought the goal shouldn't be conversion to our church or denomination but for people to come to know and enjoy the love of God. Who cares what church they go to? Why not help another church grow?

But in this particular evangelical subculture, people didn't think like this. Converts should come to our church so we can teach them to accept *our* brand of spiritual growth. If not, they might drop off of the face of the earth, end up in some less-than-pure church, or heaven forbid, a liberal church!

"Mike, you gotta hear this song by Steve Taylor," my friend Holly said. "It's so telling." Holly and I worked together for an organization on the campus of William Carey University. She attended a different church. One less conservative than mine, mind you.

Steve Taylor was a fiercely independent Christian musician who was often misunderstood. The song began loud. Holly turned and smiled at me, awaiting my reaction. Upbeat and funky, the rhythm was contagious. The catchy refrain, which was the title of the song, leapt from the speakers.[64] It summarized a new believer's desire:

I want to be a clone!

Each line referred to how this hypothetical convert played into what the church expects.

I want to be a clone!

He could never figure out how to serve God on his own.

I want to be a clone!

In fact, the church tells him he would fall away unless he did what they say.

I want to be a clone!

"Oh, my god." I said as the satirical words sank in. "That's happening to me at my church! I'm becoming a clone!"

"Well then, Mike, you better put a stop to it," Holly insisted.

It was true. Myself and those around me were becoming clones through social conditioning. It wasn't deliberate, but it was real and powerful nevertheless. Leaders of such churches manifest a style, usually patterned after the charismatic senior pastor or founder of the movement, that they inadvertently impart to members. It wasn't just how they dressed or looked but how they spoke—the Christianese—and the theology they espoused. In fact, PDI/SGM churches were a perfect breeding ground for producing clones, with their apostolic oversight, the pastoral training the organization provided (our pastor was one of the few pastors who additionally went to seminary), and the requirement that members accept their foundation teachings before they join.

We male clones were well groomed in casual dress with medium-length hair. We rarely wore jeans on a Sunday morning. We would alternately clap and raise our hands during worship, express adulation, and when open prayer time was announced, voice an articulate prayer with lots of code words like "anointing," "harvest," and "revival."

The women clones typically wore long, plain dresses, preferably with some lace but never too revealing. They also rarely wore jeans on a Sunday morning, let alone tight jeans. During music time or worship, they, too, would raise their hands. When praying, they expressed a more vocally subdued prayer, but equally fervent with those "biblical" code words.

Okay, maybe some of this is just human nature—people merely meeting their longing to be part of a community, as in level three of Maslow's hierarchy of needs: individuals wanting to feel like they belong through mimicking others' appearance and speech. Clone regulations weren't written rules in the back flap of the bulletin, nor were ushers checking for hairstyles and skirt lengths. All comers were welcome, regardless of how they looked. Yet the longer I attended, the more I noticed it was only the new people who were seen wearing attire outside the standard clone wardrobe or had the long hair or the sexy outfit or who were otherwise distinguishable from the long-standing members. The ones who stayed around and made a commitment to the church slowly began to look, act, and sound alike. When one of the "apostles" came to visit and preached a sermon, I noticed how much he sounded like one of the founders of the movement. When it dawned on me, it was kind of spooky.

Even more disconcerting was the way things were taught at ALCC. I started to notice that leaders and dedicated members would espouse their version of the truth as pretty much the only enlightened way. When it came to certain issues, rather than admit there may be more than one way to look at them, they would promote one version of it as *the* biblical way. A lot of it, of course, was good. We are to love God and love our neighbor. We should not judge, lest we be judged. Some things are straightforward. But the approach was to teach almost *every* biblical proposition with equal authority with little thought of the original culture, our modern context, or the need for nuance. As a result, it became black-and-white, neatly packaged morality derived from the Bible. But it really was selective reading of the Bible, interpreted through a doctrinal grid making almost every passage read (selectively) into a command from God. With my rejection of strict inerrancy, this way of teaching the Bible gnawed at me. I was beginning to see signs of what I later called Bible abuse.

For instance, the church taught that God wanted parents to spank their children, based on obscure verses in the Old Testament. They were careful to reinforce to do it in love and not anger, but if you didn't practice corporeal punishment, you felt like you were disobeying a direct command from God. They also taught that daily personal prayer, regular group prayer, and church and home group attendance are essential to the life of a mature believer—based on verses that only indirectly applied. If you weren't disciplined in these practices, you felt that you were a spiritual lightweight. Tithing was mandatory. Masturbation was a sin. Partying out of the question. Married women with children were not to work outside the home. When an "apostle" showed up, he taught members to submit to their pastors based on one questionable verse in the book of Hebrews.[65] There was no free flow of ales and spiritual freedom here.

As a result, the church developed a groupthink mentality. Questions were not encouraged unless they were very safe questions. Dissent was frowned upon. Conformity was expected, maybe not at first, but in the long run. The church had a specific model and style for members to follow. Attend church regularly, volunteer to serve, tithe your income, make a commitment to a weekly home group, promote the doctrines that the leaders taught, discipline your children the "biblical" way, and evangelize the lost. And, whatever you do, because we were a charismatic church, don't ever question someone's prophetic word[66] (unless of course it was heretical, in which case you'd better question it!).

"Evangelicals are enamored with power and control. That's why numbers and measures are so important to evangelicals, and why compliance is next to godliness."[67] There was little space for disagreement. The practice was calm acceptance of what was taught. Publicly confessing a difference of opinion was rocking the boat. Donald Miller describes this socialization phenomenon and its logical outcome:

> The real issue in the Christian community was that it was conditional. You were loved, but if you had questions, questions about whether the Bible was true or whether America was a good country or whether last week's sermon was good, you were not so loved. You were loved in word, but there was, without question, a social commodity that was being withheld from you until you shaped up. By toeing the party line, you earned social dollars; by being yourself, you did not. If you wanted to be valued, you became a clone.[68]

One night I had visitation duty—following up a new visitor to the church, hoping to influence him to return. He was a friend from my school and was brutally honest with me. "The reason I won't come back, Mike, is because your church has an attitude. You come across like you're the only church that does it right."

I was floored. But I knew he was correct. We may have been

sincere, but we were elitist. That was another clue I was in a funda-mentalist stage and had succumbed to *churchianity*. I didn't like it. I began to rethink why I was a part of ALCC. In reality, it wasn't just our church with the attitude, but the whole evangelical movement. We were supposedly the only ones believing and doing things right. We were squelching peoples' freedom to define "church," Christian community, and personal behavior the way they saw fit. We were making the Christian life a set of legalistic codes of conduct based on our interpretation of the Bible—without realizing we were highly susceptible to misinterpreting it.

Because of these concerns and other revelations about how the denomination's (PDI/SGM) authority structure clashed with our mission vision, Lori and I left ALCC in 1989. Actually, the clash was pretty serious. The "apostles" overseeing the local churches had told two families (who were on a church-planting mission in the Philippines), that they considered themselves in control of the Philippines ministry—despite the fact that these "apostles" had no experience in cross-cultural programs and were living halfway across the globe. This type of hierarchical structure was not what these two families agreed to. They left the mission, as did the director of the mission program in our church. They all felt they were misled and betrayed. The sense of betrayal ran so deep, some of these people stopped going to church altogether.

Malawi, Southern Africa, 1990-1995

LOVING AND LEAVING THE CHURCH

Lori's concerns weren't as serious as mine over this issue. Nevertheless, we agreed, since we felt called to return to Africa anyway, it was time to find a church that could fully support our vision. Ultimately, we returned to my home church in Massachusetts, the small evangelical Baptist church near Boston that sent me to

Explo. In 1990, we left for Malawi to begin work as development missionaries and church planters under that church's covering (but not control). One day in 1992, I was riding my mountain bike from our rural home in Namwera, in southern Malawi, to a neighboring village. A new revelation had been forming inside me.

"*Ali uli, baba?*" Our neighbor Mesi called out, meaning "How are you, sir?" or, literally, "How are you, Father?" She was walking on the muddy path carrying a ceramic jar on her head.

"*Indili chenene, mama, kwaliajetu?*" I replied in the local Chiyao language, telling her I was fine and returning the question. I had stopped riding my bike on the narrow way to greet her. All around us were green lush fields of maize. It was the height of the rainy season, a welcome period of abundance after an arid seven months of virtual drought.

Mesi responded that she was well and thanked me.

"*Sikomo, mama.*" I watched Mesi walk by, looking at her tough, muddied bare feet. Mesi, what a strong woman, I thought. She had raised three children, having lost two to childhood disease—probably malaria. I knew she walked as much as 10 miles a day doing chores like retrieving water from a shallow well or collecting firewood, and then carrying the heavy loads on her head back to her village.

By now I was accustomed to the grinding poverty that rural Malawians like Mesi and her family endured. Most were subsistence farmers with little discretionary income, no access to clean water, and sub-standard health care. One of the development projects we initiated was providing training and loans of seeds and implements to help forty families per year grow more vegetables during the dry season to improve nutrition and develop cash crops. But our efforts were only making a dent in their endemic struggles.

On this village pathway, I was struck again by how impractical our western model for church is for the poor in developing nations. Missionary best practices stated that Westerners should plant churches that would eventually become self-governing, self-support-ing, and self-replicating. This was based on the concept of church as an institution with a building, property, formal membership, and reliance on professional salaried pastors to lead the flock. *How can the poor be expected to sustain that model?* I had often thought to myself. "When we teach them to give generously to the church, aren't we making them more destitute?" I rhetorically asked Lori that night. "If they can't sustain this model and we insist on it, then the only alternative is for outsiders to subsidize it."

That's exactly what some people do. They end up subsidizing the indigenous church with Western money, e.g., paying the local pastor or funding the construction of a church building. To my dismay, our team was guilty of that. It has devastating consequences. Experience reveals the danger of trying to infuse poor churches or development projects with handouts that don't build self-reliance. The poor become dependent on the rich, and their dignity is stripped. Moreover, if a local pastor or religious worker has his salary paid by Westerners, church members and outsiders are suspicious of his motives, and he loses credibility.

More radical church planters advocate churches that require no professionally paid pastor or leaders and meet in homes. This was the only model that made sense to me for rural areas of Africa. It also seemed that it fit the practice of the early first-century church. After these thoughts crystallized in that village setting, I went back to the New Testament to confirm how the early church operated. It was true. There were no paid professionals. Even the apostle Paul was self-reliant, being a tentmaker by trade. There were no senior pastors, no hierarchy. In some churches, Paul appointed elders, but they were a plurality with no one person over the others. There were no buildings; the practice was to gather in homes. Hence, there was no overhead.

Pennsylvania and Washington State, 1995-2004

When we returned from Malawi to the States in 1995, I enrolled in the economic development graduate program at Eastern

University in St. Davids, Pennsylvania, and we began attending a Vineyard Church. Years of being in conservative churches like ALCC had influenced me to be wary of them. Lori and I had visited Vineyard churches in California and Massachusetts and had liked their freewheeling style, so we joined this one near Philadelphia. I began playing the keyboards in the worship band.

One doesn't actually "join" a Vineyard through formal membership. You just start attending regularly. This freedom appealed to me and seemed like a more biblical way of organizing a church. In fact, King of Prussia Vineyard was a breath of fresh air. They were not dogmatic about what they taught but still expounded deep respect for the Bible. They cultivated an environment of genuine acceptance, not conditioned on certain practices or adherence to doctrines. At the Vineyard, you felt like you could disagree with the pastor or the sermon or your home group leader, and it was all cool. When one of the associate pastors gave a message and confessed he liked the television show *Seinfeld*, I knew I had found a safe haven to be myself. Even George and Kramer were kosher. The church actually let people think for themselves. For the most part, freedom was encouraged.

On the other hand, Vineyard churches were still an institution. I had sat under the teachings of one of the founders, John Wimber, when I had taken classes at Fuller Seminary. Despite a more freestyle contemporary way of doing church, he still advocated that members make strong commitments to follow the vision of the local leaders and support the church financially through tithing. I heard him teach once that prospective leaders shouldn't be elected unless they tithed. At the Vineyard, church—and the accompanying rules that go with it—was still the pathway to spiritual maturity and pleasing God.

In 1997 I finished my degree, and we moved to the Seattle area. Since we would have preferred a Vineyard church and the area we lived in did not have one, we began church shopping. Over the next several years we attended three different evangelical churches. I ultimately saw major problems with each one.

When I tell my church-membership history, some people wonder why I kept going back to conservative evangelical churches. There were several reasons. First, despite misgivings with evangelical theology, most restless evangelicals like me feel a very strong impulse to remain "evangelical." Years of subtle and not-so-subtle teachings against "liberal" theology take their toll. There's a fear of leaving the evangelical fold, being exposed to unorthodoxy, and facing objections from friends and spiritual leaders. Although I preferred a "progressive" evangelical church, I had two strong convictions that today I consider misguided: One, I *had* to make a commitment to a local church (this is Evangelicalism 101) and two, it *had* to be sufficiently orthodox, in other words solidly evangelical.

Furthermore, there are not many "progressive" evangelical churches around, such as the Vineyard, to choose from, so for me, conservative churches were sometimes the only choice. Moreover, despite all this talk about manipulation and spiritual abuse, most churches are full of nice people with good intentions. I know this comes as a shock to my secular progressive friends, but that was my experience. I daresay, even Sarah Palin is well-meaning. When I noticed particular teachings in a church that bothered me, I would often tolerate them because I had forged friendships with people I liked, and I didn't want to lose them. Finally, it took time for me to notice the damage that narrow teachings can have on members and society. I was amazed how many times I would attend a church for months, even years, and then begin to notice negative consequences of certain teachings. I heard similar stories from others.

During those years in the late 1990s and early to mid 2000s, Lori and I attended three churches: a Calvary Chapel (a popular denomination born out of the Jesus Movement and founded by Chuck Smith), an independent evangelical church, and a large Pentacostal-lite Assembly of God. At Calvary Chapel, they believed the pre-tribulation Rapture doctrine. Despite my vehement objections to it, I decided to overlook it because they had a great rock-n-roll style worship band. Now there's a decision based on deep theological thinking.

After a few months at Calvary Chapel, a former member and leader in the community approached me. "I was one of the elders. Be cautious. It took time for me to see it, but they are cult-like. They are very controlling and tend to shame you if you don't buy into their doctrines." That sounded familiar. I told Lori that was a red flag for me, and she agreed we should leave.

We developed good friendships at the next congregation, an independent evangelical church in Silverdale, Washington. It wasn't long before I began to notice the Pastor's teaching was bordering on legalism. Sermons were predictable and included lots of admonitions to *do* things to get closer to God—give more, pray more, examine yourself for sins, etc. Once after going to hear Brennan Manning (an ex-Catholic who emphasizes the grace of God) speak at another church, the different approaches became obvious. Oh, well, I just won't buy into the legalism, I thought.

Eventually, I became a deacon. When I told them I drank a beer or two on occasion (after years of abstinence, I had started drinking beer again in moderation), they didn't know what to do. "We've never had a church leader who drank," the assistant pastor told me. "Don't drink in the presence of members who may be offended," he admonished. So much for theological discussions at the pub with this group.

At one of the elders and deacons meetings, they began pushing a book that encouraged spiritual preparation for revival. "Lack of genuine holiness is the predominant reason God withholds his mighty power and presence,"[69] the author wrote. His definition of holiness was astoundingly legalistic.[70] In my mind, this was pure performance-oriented Christianity. Do something more—repent of sin, fast, pray, evangelize, honor your church leaders, and have a revival meeting—and then, and only then, God will act. I ultimately left this church, despite my wife's objections. She loved her relationships in the church. I was allergic to legalism and yearned for freedom from ecclesiastical control.

Finally, at the Assembly of God that was at least void of

sensationalism, my tolerance was tested again. Despite the fact that pastors often gave two sides of an issue and encouraged people to think for themselves more than our previous church, it was their insistence on the teaching of tithing[71] that broke me.

Here we go again, I thought, during a sermon where the pastor was encouraging tithing to our church based on a passage in Malachi.[72] That passage is speaking to Israel about tithing their produce for the benefit of the poor and the Levites. How can he claim it pertains to our church?

I saw this as Bible abuse and manipulation. The Word of God tells us to tithe to our local church, so we should obey, the reasoning goes. But God tells modern believers no such thing. If you want to teach that giving 10 percent (or any percent) of one's income to an organization is an *option*, well fine. Make your case. Just don't tell people it's a matter of obedience to the Word of God or the mark of a mature believer. It's not.[73] To my wife's chagrin, I walked out the door of the evangelical church that day and haven't returned. Her focus is more on sharing her relationship with God in community. Mine is on living a faith true to my own sense of reason. But my wife is also gracious. We have since worked out our differences about church.

My reminiscing about my church history made me wonder. Lori and I didn't see eye to eye on this, but could I make clear my new feelings about church to Dan and Gina?

REFLECTIONS ON FREEDOM

Back at the restaurant, our post-dinner discussion on contradictions in the Bible had ended. Dan and I were checking out the game and nursing our Pumpkin Ales. The ladies announced that they wanted to do go to the mall and do more Christmas shopping.

"How long will you guys be here?" asked Gina.

"For awhile, I guess," Dan said. "At least til the end of the game."

The Celtics had bridged the gap. It was halftime, and commentators were expounding on the talents of Rajon Rondo.

"I may come back after I'm done," Gina told us.

Lori said she was tired and would probably go home after the mall. "It's been a long week."

Dan and I moved back to the bar. As usual, it was packed with a noisy crowd. Unlike my earlier entrance, there were no seats in sight. We had our work cut out for us. To position ourselves in the aisle just right, standing near a few occupied bar stools and small tables so we were ready to pounce on any empty seats when someone left. We stood there, glasses in hand, in close quarters, glancing around to see if there were signs of an opening.

"Hey, how's it going?" I asked a man squeezing by who looked familiar.

"Great, how about you?" he replied. "Hey, didn't you go to Covenant Fellowship?" He was referring to the church where I had been a deacon.

"Yeah, I remember you. I haven't gone there in years." I answered.

"Really? I finally left last year," he said.

"Interesting. Do you mind if I ask you why you left?"

"I got tired of jumping through hoops."

"I know exactly what you mean."

Jumping through hoops. As he walked away, I thought, *What a great way of putting it.* The encounter got Dan and me talking about the chapter in my book about *churchianity* and the lack of freedom in the church.

"So, Mike, I wanted to ask you. Why do you think the church puts up these hoops to begin with? Why do so many of us get caught up in a Christianity based on rules and expectations?"

At least I can see how Dan reacts to my new take on church, I thought. "Good question," I said. "I think the major reason is we misunderstand the core message of the New Testament because of two problems: misusing the Bible by reading it with a wooden literalism and looking at everything through the lens of the modern institutional church, which is really a man-made construct."

"Okay, then, I'd like to hear about those two problems," Dan said. "But first, what is the core message of the New Testament?"

"Well," I said, taking a moment to think. "It's good news, not bad news. Through Jesus, God has announced to humankind that His reign of love has arrived and we no longer have to submit to the Law of Moses in order to be at peace with God. Trust in Christ, who is available to all, and in his love message is what counts."

"I like that," Dan acknowledged. "The letter of the law is not the focus anymore, but rather the spirit of the law."

We then began to talk about how the religion of Jesus is a religion of the heart. Outward conformity to rules and laws, whether they are biblical, ecclesiastical, or political, does not guarantee the righteousness that Jesus espouses. Simply obeying law is limiting. Without love for God and people, obedience cannot engage the heart.

Dan made the point that a good heart does not necessitate following the letter of the law. He reminded me that Jesus ignored the purity code and Sabbath law to meet human needs and contradicted the Torah by declaring all foods clean (Mark 7:19).

"True enough," I said. "Jesus seemed to make exceptions to the law based on love. But he didn't seem to set aside the law entirely. As you said, he emphasized the spirit of the law more."

We then got into what the first cross-cultural emissary of the gospel, the Apostle Paul, taught. As we talked, I thought about Paul's teaching. He said a new path to righteousness, apart from law, was revealed in Jesus. The new way of right standing with God is no longer through obedience to laws. That is why Paul said, although all things are not beneficial, "everything is permissible for me,"[74] and "we are no longer under the supervision of the law."[75] I shared this with Dan. "You see, the way to righteousness is not by obeying the Jewish law or any other man-made law, but by believing the good news and living by a spirit of love. Without a set of rules that binds us to obey, practicing love becomes the fulfillment of the law. Love, not law, is the overriding guideline for behavior. According to Paul, this is the new way of salvation."

"Yeah, but why do so many of us not follow this?" Dan asked. "In our churches, we bring in a set of rules and make Christianity into a set of prescribed behaviors."

"It's pure *religion*, Dan," I said. "One reason is the widespread, mostly unintentional abuse of the Bible."

"Okay, give me some examples of this Bible abuse," Dan said.

"Well, Paul's teaching on the law, for instance. It can be found in the first eleven chapters of the book of Romans. Most people don't read all eleven chapters in one sitting so they take things out of context and twist what Paul says. When they read '...it is those who obey the law who will be declared righteous,'[76] and don't finish Paul's argument, they get the wrong impression, thinking we should still follow the law. They don't get to his conclusion in a later chapter that '...we have been released from the law, so we serve in the new way of the spirit, and not in the old way of the written code.'[77] Nor later when he says, 'Christ is the end of the law.'"[78]

"I see," said Dan. "Sometimes people don't get to the core meaning of a passage because they read things piecemeal."

"Yeah, that's it. Related to that is the literalistic way some people read the Bible as if every word, phrase, and verse is unquestionably God's Word. So larger ideas, concepts, and principals from other parts of Scripture get lost. You know, people get mired in one verse or phrase. Or people never consider that some passages of the Bible were not part of the original but added by copyists,[79] or that perhaps every passage isn't intended to be a directive from God. Finally, there's the problem with mistranslations we've talked about."

"Wait a minute, you said a lot there," Dan said. "I remember reading your manuscript about parts being added by copyists. I want to talk about that, but let's not get too far off the topic of the church. Now, mistranslations I understand. Like when Jesus said 'I haven't come to abolish the law but *fulfill* it.' I've read the word translated 'fulfill' is better understood as 'to complete its purpose.'[80] He came, not to perpetuate the law, but to finish it, so that it's no longer our master."

"Exactly!" I agreed. "That meaning makes more sense because it fits with what Paul teaches." I was excited that Dan and I were on the same page with this. He had told me once with his recent interest in digging deeper into his faith, and being somewhat of a compulsive personality, over the last year or so he had read everything he could get his hands on about the Bible's origin and composition.

"But let's get back to the church," Dan continued. "How does the institutional church contribute to misunderstanding the core message of the New Testament?"

Right then the two women we had initially sat next to at least an hour ago started to gather their things at the bar and appeared to be leaving.

"Let's be ready to grab those stools." I said. We inched our way toward them.

"Don't mind us," Dan said as the one with auburn hair turned toward us. "We're just hovering here waiting for a seat."

"Well, you're hovering in the right spot. We're leaving, and we kept the seats warm for you," she smiled as they stood up to leave. "Enjoy."

"Thanks." We settled into our new spot glad to get off our feet.

"Okay, where were we? Oh, the institutional church," I began. "Have you ever heard of Jacques Ellul?"

"Can't say that I have."

"He's a French theologian and prolific writer. Someone the evangelical church, unfortunately, has largely ignored. He makes the point that going back to the beginning, the institutional church abandoned the New Testament concept of freedom. You know, when Paul says, 'It is for freedom, that Christ has set you free,' in Galatians."

"Interesting," Dan said.

I had recently read Ellul's book *The Subversion of Christianity* and had some fresh memories of his points in mind. As best as

I could, I began explaining to Dan the history of the loss of freedom in the church. One of Ellul's notions was about the Roman church. "Ellul says it was impossible for church leaders of the fourth century to keep up with Jesus' movement of freedom. With thousands of new converts in the church, following proclamations like 'You are free by the Holy Spirit' and 'Everything is lawful' weren't practical. They couldn't bring themselves to tell new converts that they were completely free to choose their way of life and decide their own conduct. So they incorporated churches and put them under a head and when things grew, the authority structure became more complex." [81]

"So, that's how the idea of church hierarchy started," Dan offered.

"Yes, that's true. Now, Ellul isn't saying this freedom the church lost is license to do anything one wants. Christian freedom is constrained by love. It ends wherever the freedom of others begins."

"I see," Dan said. "People are free but still obligated to love their neighbors. But didn't the reformation correct this hierarchy and control problem?"

"Unfortunately, no. Ellul says that Luther resurrected freedom, but it was soon banished by the reformation churches. He says it's so hard for us humans to accept this concept of freedom, it's like, psychologically unbearable. Especially when people get into positions of power. Throughout the ages, with rare exceptions, believers have rejected Christian freedom." [82]

"That makes sense," Dan said. "The church would naturally find freedom intolerable because it would mean letting go of control over people's lives."

"Sure," I added. "If you are an institution with paid professionals, your whole outlook is self-preservation. I mean, teaching your members that they are truly free—free to *not* be members of the church, free *not* to give to the church, free to govern themselves under the law of love, and free from any other church-derived expectations—all undercuts your mission."

"You've had much more church experience," Dan said. "How much of a problem is this loss of freedom in evangelical churches?"

"A lot in my experience. With the church I attended in Pasadena in the 80s [ALCC, part of the PDI/SGM denomination], and even when I last visited in the mid-90s,[83] I saw how people were subtly manipulated to conform to a certain set of behaviors. You know, to become clones. If members weren't conforming—spanking their children, hyper involved in the church, joyfully accepting the teaching of the leaders—they suffered subtle discrimination.

"Just for grins, Dan, I recently did some research on the denomination to see what's happening today. Lo and behold, I found two websites made up of former members. One is *SGMSurvivors.com* and the other *SGMRefuge.com*. They are chock full of stories of how pastors and 'apostles' emotionally and spiritually abused members of the church. I was shocked it had become so bad."

"Really? What are some examples?"

"A new one since my involvement was the expectation to homeschool your children. What surprised me was what happened when people didn't toe the party line. The leadership corrected people, and if they didn't respond to correction, they were subtly ostracized, accused of having the sin of pride, or being unteachable. Sometimes people were even told to leave the church."

"Incredible," Dan said.

"Yeah, very controlling. Some engaged people reported needing permission to marry. Pastors told one woman not to marry her fiancé unless he agreed to become a member of the church. When they told the pastors they couldn't agree to that—that they would be attending another church (one that did not line up doctrinally with the denomination)—the pastors told the whole congregation not to associate with this couple for the protection of their souls! Can you believe that? The couple were treated like heretics and lost all their friends in that church. They were devastated."

"That's crazy!" Dan exclaimed.

"The ultimate example was what the newer 'apostolic' leaders did to one of the founders, Larry Tomczak. According to people I corresponded with on those websites they forced him to step down from leadership because he supposedly wasn't controlling his family—his son went through a rebellious stage."

"In other words, the son was normal," Dan added.

"Yeah. You should check out these websites to get a feel for what it's like. It's a huge case study on spiritual abuse."

"Okay, but not every church is controlling like that," Dan said. "That example is obviously a top-down structure. Many denominations have a more balanced model, you know, with elected elders that can just fire controlling pastors—so they are more accountable. Are you saying those churches are limiting freedom?"

"Well, it depends on whether they are legalistic in other ways."

I explained my conclusion that churches limit freedom by definition. Every church that has been institutionalized—with the exception of ones that truly don't practice *churchianity*—will at least insist that obedient believers be involved in and give to an institutional church, if not theirs.

"Think about it," I said. "Have you ever heard an evangelical pastor stand up and say, 'Involvement in this church or any local church is entirely optional. You are free to never set foot in a church again and, all other things being equal, you'll still be pleasing God?'"

"You're right about that." Dan answered. "Every church needs people to attend to survive. And the mega churches don't just want to survive; they want to build a religious empire."

I agreed. Although they wouldn't say it that way, Dan and I figured that was a fair assessment, given the focus on church growth, building expansion, and preachers that are treated like celebrities.

"But don't people need to be in relationships with other believers? Isn't that one purpose of the church?" Dan asked.

"Sure, but remember the original concept of *church* is simply believers who come together. The word translated *church* is the Greek, *ekklesia*, which simply means 'gathering.'[84] You don't need to be part of an institution to gather with like-minded people."

I had often told people that insisting that one be involved in our modern church to be a good Christian is like saying you can't be a good citizen unless you're a member in good standing of the Rotary Club. This reminded me of a book. "There's a fascinating book, *Pagan Christianity*,[85] about the history of our modern church and how its governance and practices are largely based on pagan practices."

"I've heard of it," Dan said.

"When I first saw it, I figured it was written by some New Age adherent trying to discredit the Bible altogether, but one of the co-authors is George Barna, the highly recognized evangelical pollster."

"Oh, that's right. I remember reading about that in your church chapter," Dan said. "What do the authors say is the right model?"

"I think the point is there is no correct mold. A modern church model can be a healthy community as long as it's optional and not a legalistic treadmill. *Pagan Christianity* promotes organic home gatherings that have no affiliation to an institution. But those could become legalistic if people insisted true believers must be a part of one. I think with some creativity, people could come up with all kinds of ways to be in group relationships. I even read about a 'church' that met in a pub. They called it *Holy Joe's*."[86]

"Now that sounds cool. Where do I sign up?"

"Perhaps you already have," I said. "Maybe when you and I and Lori and Gina get together here and talk about our faith, or just deliberately meet together as believers for that matter, it's like a New Testament gathering. After all, Jesus said 'wherever two or three are gathered in my name, there I am in the midst of them.'"[87]

"You may be right," said Dan. "I've always had other ideas for *church* too. Like it should go to the world outside rather than expecting the outside world to come to it. I've often had a vision of a gathering of believers who are so open and welcoming that atheists feel comfortable to attend a meeting. I mean, so you don't have the pressure to conform and believe a certain way."

"That's good. It reminds me of what they say about author Anne

Lamott. She's a Christian even an atheist would respect in the morning."

Dan laughed.

"Your vision is similar to mine, Dan. I envision progressive Christian meetings formed around common interests rather than doctrines. Imagine focusing on love in action. For instance, people could form groups around supporting micro lending in Africa or assisting resettled refugees or helping the homeless or practicing environmentalism. You know, creation care. Let's see, I had thought of several others. Oh, eradicating child slavery, fighting sex trafficking, or mentoring troubled youth, stuff like that. The possibilities are endless. Groups could give money and do service projects and community outreach that supports these causes."

"You know," Dan added, "that kind of grassroots effort, if it caught on, could do untold good. I mean, instead of pouring money into church institutions, more resources could go to making a practical difference in the world."

"You're right."

"I'm wondering, though, how could groups like these remain distinctively Christian?" Dan asked.

"How 'Christian' would they need to be?" I countered. "Can't people just be on a spiritual journey? Why can't the stamp of the group be *love*—the main thrust of Jesus' and Paul's teaching—you know, *love sums up the law and the prophets* and *love is the fulfillment of the law*, rather than particular doctrines or conversion? I think Christ would be present if that were the case."

"Hmm, that sounds pretty radical," Dan said. "Isn't the purpose of these gatherings—this organic church—to come together in the name of Jesus?"

"Absolutely. I'm not saying any group that does good deeds—helps the poor or fights injustice—is automatically Christian. I'm saying it's possible to form a group where core members are motivated by Jesus' teaching—primarily love—and still be non-sectarian."

"Do you mean it could be made up of both Christians and non-Christians?"

"Why not? Jesus welcomed all at gatherings, and although he challenged people, he didn't insist people be devoted disciples. You see, I think we are programmed to think of a church in a certain way—a group of people believing a set of doctrines under professional pastors in a Christian institution. I think if you focus on what really counts—loving one another and encouraging each other on our spiritual journeys—then Christ naturally shows up. I think the thing that makes groups 'Christian' is when the motivation is to follow Christ's one law of love."

"I actually like that idea!" Dan raised his voice. "It puts the focus on what Jesus taught us to do to love others, not on dogma or praying or worshiping a certain way. But again, it seems pretty radical. Isn't doctrine still important? I mean, you want to draw people to Christ, not some New Age gobbledygook or another religion, right?"

"Look, I haven't worked this out one hundred percent. I'm just trying to apply what I've learned about authentic 'churches' to our modern context in a way that's not legalistic. Let me give you a couple of examples."

I told him about the many aid organizations in Africa I had encountered that follow a similar model, like Habitat for Humanity. They retain their Christian identity while helping and employing people of other faiths and no faith. "People who join or work for them don't have to be Christians, Dan. They just agree to the Christ-based love values the organization holds. That model could be applied to organic gatherings. It naturally attracts Christians—well at least open-minded ones—but is inclusive of all. A gathering would only need to insist that those who join agree to one principle: loving others—love and respect for all of humanity—is what counts."

"I think you're onto something."

"Another example is from Jessica Maxwell's book, *Roll Around Heaven*. Her friend, Lory Misel, helps people 'wake up to God' by teaching the love of Christ. And stuff like how to overcome egotism and the reality of God's spirit available to all, whether one follows a religion or not. He says evangelicalism can be spiritually abusive."

"Interesting."

"He encourages seekers to form 'spirit families' that meet together regularly outside the strictures of an organized church."

"What does he mean by 'spirit families'?"

"His website says they're a forum for people to join with others to learn kindness, appreciation, forgiveness, and being of service to each other and the world—those kinds of things. Perhaps a good model would be an inclusive Christian version of a spirit family. And one whose members chose to focus on a particular common interest that changes the world for the good—some way of putting love in action."

"This is kind of bending my mind," Dan said. "It reminds me of what you wrote in your book about Anne Rice. She is still committed to Christ but has rejected Christianity. Maybe she's on to something. Maybe for too long we have confused Christianity with *churchianity*."

We continued to discuss how an inclusive organic "Christian" gathering might look. I latched on to what Dan said about wanting to have a group where atheists would feel welcome—at least ones who were open-minded enough to meet with people on a spiritual journey! I told Dan about former Muslim-turned-atheist Ayaan Hirsi Ali.

"Since Jesus considered anyone who helped 'the least of these' as serving him, even though they were unaware of it,[88] I consider Hirsi Ali to be a follower of Christ in disguise, and I don't mean to disrespect her choice of atheism, but to honor her. What she does to rescue oppressed Muslim women[89] is just what Jesus would commend. I heard her speak and know she is attracted to progressive forms of faith, even if she doesn't believe. Like Gandhi, she imbues the spirit of Jesus."

Right then, my cell phone vibrated. It was our friend Steve, who had tracked us down and asked if we minded him joining us.

"Looks like Steve will come later," I told Dan after ending the call.

"Good," Dan said. "The more the merrier. This could turn into a long night."

I had found an ally in Dan. We were thinking outside the box of evangelicalism, which is terribly threatening to people of conservative faith, who assume alternative models to church are unbiblical and dangerous because they don't put people under church authority. I wondered what Steve would have said about our musings. I know he would disagree with many of them, which reminded me how far I had come. It also triggered the memory of another experience; when I saw the evangelical church engaging in a culture war and using politics as a weapon. In the 1980s and 90s, abortion was at the forefront of that war, and I had the battle wounds to show it.

Dan excused himself to use the restroom. Sitting alone, my thoughts traveled to a scene on the streets of Los Angeles in 1989. Suddenly, it was like living that day all over again.

CONFESSION 6
ABORTING POLITICAL FAITH

"There is no lost golden age to which American Christians may return."

– *Mark Noll*

Los Angeles, March 25, 1989

In the intermittent morning rain, I sat cross-legged on a lawn observing the surrounding confusion with a cacophony of voices ringing in my ears. Hundreds of other protestors enveloped me. We sat pressed together on the property of Family Planning Associates. The massive crowd in the streets encircling us included spectators, counter-protestors, and a small army of LAPD officers, complete with their white riot-control helmets. Suddenly, one of our leaders stood up and raised a bullhorn to his mouth to address the crowd.

"An abortion does not eliminate a 'by-product' in the womb; it eliminates a being," he cried. "Obviously it is a human being. What other kind of being could it be?"

Throngs of counter-protestors, or "pro-aborts" as we called them, were mocking us. Strident and loud, they surrounded us, occasionally chanting "Read'em their rights, and take'em away!" A few held offensive signs portraying bloodied women's corpses killed from illegal abortions. Some, presumably employees of the clinic, had walked through our midst toward the front door we blocked, looking around

123

in awe at the sea of silent squatters. "If you're so concerned about life, why don't you stop wasting your time here and go out and help the poor?" a woman asked.

I became indignant. I felt like shouting back at her, "I took two years of my life to help the poor. I'm taking a break to help the weak and defenseless!" But I also knew what she referred to. Many in the pro-life movement seemed to care more about the unborn than those already born into poverty.

"You are preventing us from doing our job of helping women achieve their reproductive rights," shouted another. "That includes getting contraception."

Every taunt and challenge from them warranted a response. But there would be no response. All 800 of us were instructed to remain silent with the exception of designated marshals. Aside from a few whispers, the only time we opened our mouths during the four-hour plus standoff was to occasionally sing a worship song. We were well organized. We were Operation Rescue (OR).

Across the street was another group of pro-life activists that wasn't part of us. They held signs that read, "Abortion is murder" or "Thou shalt not kill," and had their own grisly placards with huge photographs of bloody aborted fetuses. They were disorganized, vociferously shouting accusatory statements toward the crowds of pro-choice supporters in the streets; the opposite of the quiet, passive-resistance approach we had learned a few days before at an OR preparatory meeting. I was shocked at their in-your-face approach. Since their numbers were small and they weren't blocking the clinic entrance, police ignored them.

It was nearing the time when the police would start taking us OR protestors away. At least the ones who had agreed to risk arrest. This is what we expected. Police had given us warning that unless we dispersed, we would be arrested. Things were unfolding exactly as planned. Our goal that day was to shut down the clinic so that no abortions would be performed and possibly persuade some women to change their minds about getting an abortion. That part was the job of other OR activists, called "sidewalk counselors," who were not risking arrest and were actively looking for women who might have an appointment that morning. Once the police began arrests, we were to passively resist by going limp and forcing the police to drag each person across the street to waiting buses, so it would take more time for them to clear the area. With hundreds of activists to clear away, that would ensure the clinic would never open. I was nervous. I had been conversing quietly for the last hour with fellow protestors, one being my friend Bart. We anticipated the arrests would begin soon.

Suddenly it happened. Police officers approached and started dragging each of us across the street. We watched quietly as they cuffed each one and led them into buses, separating the men and women. Some grimaced in pain as the plasticuffs—handcuffs of choice for large-scale protests—were tightened to their wrists. Hundreds of protestors in front of us were slowly being dragged away. It seemed like hours before they reached the area where Bart and I sat. I felt like I was in a dream or watching some documentary on television as the surreal event unfolded. With each person dragged, the police came closer to us. My skin began to crawl.

Finally, an officer roughly grabbed my ankles and dragged me across the street. I had to lift my head and fold my arms to avoid injury. The pavement grated my back through my light coat. Once across, he turned me over on my stomach and tightly bound my hands with the cuffs. Pain shot through the sides of my wrists as the plastic strips dug into my skin. Pulling me to my feet, they told me to get on a bus full of men. I sat close to Bart, who had already been taken in.

"My wrists are killing me," Bart said, as we sat leaning forward with our arms behind our backs.

"Mine too," I said. "He put them on really tight." I was also feeling a little faint.

In time, we got used to the discomfort and pain. As other men were loaded on the bus, we all began asking each other how we were, sharing our experiences, and speculating about our success. The experience was instilling within us a sense of camaraderie and pride in fighting for what we considered a worthy cause. After the bus rolled away, a man up front led us in several choruses of the old folk song, "Keep Your Eyes on the Prize," which was popular during the civil rights movement. My spirits were lifted. All the buses eventually arrived at a nearby gymnasium, where all 725 of us awaited further transport. It was there they took off the handcuffs, to my relief. After another hour or so of processing, we were finally taken to the L.A. County Jail. Bart and I stuck together and were isolated in a group of fifty or more and put in a very large cell that became our home for the next three days until we were finally released.

JOINING A MOVEMENT

I wasn't always pro-life. Before "accepting" Jesus I considered myself pro-choice. My conversion to the pro-life cause happened in 1980 after I read two influential books. The first was *Aborting America*, by Bernard Nathanson, a former co-founder of NARAL (known at the time as the National Association for the Repeal of Abortion Laws). Nathanson is a medical doctor who at one time was a strong pro-choice advocate working with Betty Friedan for the legalization of abortion laws. For years he presided over the largest abortion clinic in New York. Upon the development of ultrasound, however, he changed his views on abortion and became strongly pro-life.

In *Aborting America*, Nathanson called the human fetus "Alpha" and explained why it should be medically protected, despite his acknowledgement that a woman has a right to control her own body. His conclusion was "a humanistic philosophy, drawn from modern biological data, not from religious creeds."[909] At least after four to six weeks of pregnancy, when Alpha has an embryonic beating heart, a central nervous system, brain waves, and sexual identity, he suggested a woman's right to her own body may need to be circumvented by the rights of the unborn. I was struck by Nathanson's rational and irreligious approach.

The second book was *Whatever Happened to the Human Race?* by C. Everett Koop (who eventually became Surgeon General of the U.S. under Reagan) and Francis Schaeffer. The book and film by the same name was also the brainchild of Francis's son Frank. It was a well-argued case for the dignity and rights of the unborn without graphic images of dead fetuses and political overtones. I was deeply touched by Dr. Koop's passion, based on his career as a pediatric surgeon. He saved the lives of premature babies. It was obvious how those babies were comparable to those whose lives were terminated in late-term abortions. Sometimes the age of gestation was the same.

These were the types of arguments that appealed to me. They weren't from Scripture but from addressing abortion as a human rights issue. The biological facts coupled with the gruesome realities of the procedure—at least in the later stages of pregnancy—warranted respect and protection for Alpha. And it justified the promotion of the crisis pregnancy movement, which I began to support. We couldn't just be against abortion, we had to be for helping women and babies make an alternative choice and provide practical care for them. This was my mindset even as the single-issue political approach to abortion—a notion that made me and some of my friends very uncomfortable—had grown in popularity among evangelicals in the 1980s.

By 1989, Lori and I had been a member of the PDI/SGM church (ALCC) in Pasadena, California, for five years. We were making preparations for our move to Africa. Just a few months before we were to move, my pro-life convictions attracted me to an emerging anti-abortion trend. Young evangelical leaders I admired, like Melody Green and Larry Tomzcak, were endorsing it and its leader—a 30-year-old activist dedicated to fighting abortion with emotionally charged rhetoric and a new strategy: civil disobedience. One evening two weeks prior to that fateful day in Los Angeles, a contingent

from our church went to hear this famous abortion foe speak at the
Sierra Madre Nazarene Church, which at the time happened to be
the home church of James Dobson, the founder of the conservative
Christian organization, Focus on the Family. The activist's name was
Randall Terry.

"If you believe abortion is murder," Terry proclaimed, "then you
must act like it is murder." I sat there spellbound by this persuasive
leader from upstate New York who spoke about the new anti-abortion movement called Operation Rescue and the series of "rescues"
planned for the next few days in metro L.A., coined the "Holy Week
of rescues." A brilliant organizer, this young evangelical was heavily influenced by human-rights activist and Catholic, Joan Andrews,
who was what some called a consistent pro-life activist. Not only
was she fighting abortion, but also nuclear war and capital punishment—two issues that most evangelicals, and Randall Terry for that
matter, ignored. On abortion, Andrews was willing to go to prison
and in fact had spent 2½ years in a Florida jail for disrupting abortions. Terry's idea of risking arrest came from Andrews. I learned
later it also came from Francis Schaeffer, who wrote a book entitled
A Christian Manifesto, wherein he advocated civil disobedience to
protect the unborn.

Among evangelicals in the 1970s and 80s, abortion was *the* defin-
ing issue. In response to the landmark *Roe v. Wade* Supreme Court
decision in 1973 that effectively legalized abortion nationwide in any
stage of pregnancy (even the last twelve weeks, as long as a doctor
deemed it necessary to preserve the health of the woman), evangelicals were galvanized to stop abortion in obedience to perceived
biblical mandates. The evangelical literature and rhetoric of the day,
including that in my church, summed it up. American society was in
moral decline and in jeopardy of total collapse. We had lost our spiritual moorings and needed to return to our Christian roots. Through
STDs, AIDS, economic decline, and the threat of nuclear war, God
was releasing progressive judgment on the nation. With its tie to

sexual immorality, abortion—the slaughter of innocent life—was perceived as one of the major reasons for divine retribution.

Others included the predominance of pornography, homosexuality, and the elimination of prayer in public schools. According to the Religious Right, the solution to the moral crisis was to save America by bringing it back to its Christian origins through political activism. Some evangelicals also called for the restoration of the New Testament church as the "deliverer" that would redeem the nation through evangelism and further establish God's kingdom, readying people for the return of Christ.

PDI churches were among those who strongly promoted this vision with a sense of urgency. It was our duty to help save America, commit to a New Testament church, and fight immorality and abortion by electing righteous pro-life candidates and contributing to pro-life causes. By the late '80s, however, all these efforts had little or no impact on changing abortion law or rates. Despite eight years of Ronald Reagan, the Supreme Court had not turned back the clock on *Roe v. Wade*, and America was performing 1.6 million abortions per year.

In this context, Operation Rescue arose to challenge pro-life supporters to up the stakes. It called the faithful to begin "acting like you believe it is murder" by blockading clinics, or "abortion mills" as we called them, in order to rescue the innocent and make an impression on American society. In addition to ideas from Joan Andrews and Francis Schaeffer, OR drew its tactics from the nonviolent practices of Gandhi and Martin Luther King, Jr., and began billing itself as the next abolitionist movement.

I couldn't escape the logic of Randall Terry. "If you knew children were being murdered in your town, would you not feel obligated to call the authorities? And if the authorities turned a blind eye, would you not still act to prevent the murder of innocent life?"

There were biblical admonitions as well, but the logic of these simple questions burned into my conscious. That was a turning point for me. I had already been somewhat involved in the right-to-life movement, writing letters to newspapers and handing out tracts written by activist Melody Green, but had never practiced civil disobedience. That night I decided to participate in the upcoming rescue. A few weeks later, I also participated in another rescue as a sidewalk counselor. Yet years later I would regret involvement in this controversial organization and be repelled by some of the statements and actions of its founder. I failed to discern the lust for control and lack of compassion for human frailty within much of the pro-life movement, Operation Rescue in particular, and within the growing political activism of evangelicals.

THE POLITICS OF RELIGION

That night inside James Dobson's church I didn't know the whole picture of Randall Terry. It wasn't until ten years later that I would learn his true colors. Around 1999 I was doing a major rethinking of the evangelical world I was still a part of. I was reading a book by Philip Yancey, a more progressive evangelical I deeply admired. In it, Yancey quoted Terry making radical statements that revealed the core rationale behind the religiously-motivated wing of the pro-life movement. On one occasion Terry called on Christians to become "intolerant zealots" in the face of "baby killers, sodomites, condom pushers, and that pluralism nonsense." He demanded that Christians needed to clean out "the moral cesspool this nation has become" and make this a Christian nation once again.[91] In more recent years I read statements of his that appeared to justify Kansas obstetrician and abortionist George Tiller's murder. He called pro-choice politicians "child killers," including Barak Obama. In light of this, I began to wonder how much of his fiery rhetoric, like what I heard inside the Sierra Madre Nazarene Church back in 1989, had influenced anti-abortion extremists like Shelley Shannon, who attempted to kill George Tiller in 1993. And more recently, the impact it had on Scott Roeder, who did kill him and was convicted of murder in January

2010. Did their twisted thinking merely take his challenge to "act like abortion is murder" to its logical conclusion? What was it that was wrong about this absolutist way of looking at abortion?

Only after years of reflection and the advantage of hindsight did I gain a fresh perspective and begin to discover how *black-and-white* thinking was at the root of the problem. As I tried to navigate the abortion issue through the years, I often felt as if I had no place to call home. Both sides were pushing the extremes, and I bought into one extreme for a time. On the pro-life side, there was no space to permit abortion in the early stages of pregnancy, even when a 13-year-old girl faced a troubled pregnancy, or in cases of rape or incest. No one could acknowledge that a fertilized egg is not a person, nor permit a description of abortion that didn't imply it was anything less than a cold-blooded murder.

On the pro-choice side, there could be no recognition that perhaps it isn't a moral position to insist on a right to abortion in the later stages of pregnancy. Any resistance to the illogical notion that a six-month-old or older unborn baby is merely "part of a woman's body" was considered treason. Any limitations on late-term abortions cannot be tolerated because they would erode a woman's constitutional right to control her own destiny.

Frank Schaeffer, who lived to regret his part in establishing abortion as a fundamental issue among the Religious Right in the 80s, suggests that the absolutist position on both sides only fueled the fires of a cultural war where everyone is forced to choose sides. Pro-life zealots, who insisted on ideological purity, pushed morally sensitive moderates to the pro-choice side. Pro-choice adherents, who defended language about the later stages of the fetus and the abortion procedure that defied common sense and science, pushed others to the pro-life side. Meanwhile, moderates, who saw the inconsistencies on both sides and tried to forge a middle way, were labeled as traitors by everyone.

Dr. Tim Johnson, a medical commentator for ABC News and an evangelical, argued for the necessity of abortion in certain troubled circumstances, while deploring the cavalier attitude that defended abortion always as a fundamental right. He didn't exactly win any evangelical fans. Tami Bruce, former President of the Los Angeles chapter of NOW, spoke out against the *group think* attitude among her pro-choice colleagues, who derailed her for questioning their extremist party line and eventually gave her the boot. Ironically, as Frank Schaeffer points out, our American *all-or-nothing* mindset is extreme when juxtaposed with most European governments, who put limits on abortion and discourage it in the later stages of pregnancy.

This mindset created the unfortunate phenomenon of political parties demanding ideological purity on abortion and the creation of single-issue politics. Frank Schaeffer concluded, "It seems to me that by demanding ideological purity on abortion (and other single issues as well), both parties have worked to eliminate the sorts of serious, smart, pragmatic people who make competent leaders."[92] This is precisely why millions of evangelicals vote for candidates largely on how they do on a "Christian" political scorecard that measures a candidate's position on "moral" issues and not according to their level of competency, political skills, and leadership abilities. Ideology rules the day. For evangelicals, I discovered how much their ideology is wrapped up in the common perception that America is a Christian nation, the roots to which we must return.

One day in the summer of 2007, I was reading news on the Internet when I noticed a story about an interruption to an invocation in the Senate. The Senate occasionally invites a guest religious leader to invoke the opening prayer. On this day, a Hindu priest, Rajan Zed, was asked by Democratic Senate Majority Leader Harry Reid to have the honors. Upon rising to address the Senate, three protestors interrupted the Hindu cleric and declared, "Lord Jesus, forgive us, Father, for allowing the prayer of the wicked, which is an abomination in your sight... You shall have no other gods before you." The three were immediately arrested and taken away so Zed could continue. I was appalled and ashamed of this self-righteous outburst by Christian extremists. But I was doubly appalled by the reaction by evangelical Christians. "It's good to see someone who has the guts to stand up and defend the name of Christ," remarked a friend of mine. My heart sank. When I investigated more carefully, I discovered something more disturbing. The three protestors, Ante and Kathy Pavkovic, and their daughter Christen, were part of a Christian organization called Operation Save America. It's a small world after all. It turns out this organization used to be known by another name: Operation Rescue. Concerning the incident, their website proclaimed, "Have our elected officials forgotten so quickly the God of our Forefathers, the God who has blessed America and made her the mightiest nation in the world?"

Ever since Jerry Falwell established the Moral Majority in the 1970s, evangelicals are fond of this line of thought. We are a Christian nation, and a prayer offered in Congress by a Hindu or Muslim would be tantamount to idolatry. Moreover, it is a Christian's duty to combat contemporary trends that threaten the foundations of our Christian heritage and God's blessing on our country. Furthermore, they are to fight them through our political system. In other words, to win at the polls and push for legislation that reflects Christian values. In the 70s and 80s these threatening trends were the removal of prayer from public schools, the *Roe v. Wade* ruling on abortion, the prevalence of pornography and sexual immorality in popular culture, the erosion of family values, and the rise of secular humanism. Today, it is more of the same with the added threat of the gay rights agenda and the cultural shift to accept gay marriage.

Over the years, I found three serious problems with this thought process. First, we are not a Christian nation. Second, even if we were, the Bible does not teach that social change comes from top-down political activism, legislation, or forcing one's hand. And third, due to abuse of the Bible, the evangelical position that our societal trends are negative is a half-truth.

What struck me about the prayer in the Senate episode was the gross intolerance of the protestors. Here is the question that must be asked: Why not allow people of other faiths, who are citizens of our country and equal in the sight of law, to express themselves spiritually in a non-sectarian political meeting? Last I checked, the Senate chamber is not a place of worship representing Christianity.

When Lori and I were in a church-planting ministry among Muslims in Malawi, we had no problem allowing a Muslim to pray in our gatherings. It's called tolerance, love, and respect for freedom of religion to permit people to pray to their God or gods the way they perceive the Divine. Even in a church. Even if you consider a worshiper of a non-Christian deity an enemy, which I certainly do not, didn't Jesus tell us to love our enemies and not disgrace and mock them? The irony of it all is how innocuous Zed's "Hindu" prayer was. It was respectful of an overall Creator, asked for a blessing on the nation, and did not push a polytheistic view.

THE MYTH OF CHRISTIAN NATIONALISM

When Dan returned from the restroom, I switched from my Operation Rescue déjà vu scene and other recollections and got back into watching the game. "Yes!" I exclaimed as Ray Allen sank a three-pointer after getting a pass from Kevin Garnett. It was the beginning of the third quarter, and Celtics were on a roll. Both Dan and I still had one third of a glass of Pumpkin Ale. Normally, at this point in a game, I would be fixated on the screen overhead watching my hometown Celtics, but with our engaging conversations and my reminiscing, I was starting to tune out the game. I turned to Dan.

"Our talk about the church reminded me of something," I told him as he gulped his brew.

"What's that?"

"My experience in the right-to-life movement in the 1980s. Did you read that chapter in my book?"

"Are you kidding? I read the whole damn manuscript, Mike. I remember thinking that must have been a difficult chapter to write. I mean with all the emotional triggers the subject of abortion brings.

But I wanted to ask you—there was something that seemed like it was missing. I always hear people at church make statements that America was founded as a Christian nation, but you objected to that. What do you base your position on?"

I started to tell him about a book I had read by Mark Noll, called *The Search for Christian America*. I explained when I sat down with it a few years ago, I didn't know what to expect. Here was a card-carrying evangelical and a professor at conservative Wheaton College. Was he defending the evangelical status quo that Dan was talking about? No, he couldn't be, I surmised, since he had also written a seminal book called *The Scandal of the Evangelical Mind* that lambasted the movement for its anti-intellectualism. What would Noll and his co-authors Nathan Hatch and George Marsden conclude? It didn't take long to find out. The introduction summed it up: "We feel that a careful study of the facts of history shows that early America does not deserve to be considered uniquely, distinctly or even predominantly Christian..."[93]

"I always wondered," I told Dan, "how can people claim that we need to return to our Christian moorings as a country, when the blemishes of our nation seem so obvious? I mean, our founding fathers overlooked slavery, we didn't eradicate it until 1864, and we allowed child labor for years. Umm, what else? Oh, women were treated like second-class citizens and racist laws persisted until the Civil Rights Movement. Is that what evangelical moralists wanted us to return to?"

"I see what you mean," Dan said. "I often wondered about this Christian America stuff."

"Yeah, Noll's book provides the historical facts to demonstrate its absurdity."

"I'd like to read that book," Dan exclaimed. "But I have a hard time with the opposite position, too. You know, that America, with its so-called-mandate-by-God-to-dominate, is responsible for worldwide oppression."

"The book goes into that too, encouraging readers not to go to extremes. Not only is there widespread belief that we have this pure and holy Christian heritage, from which we fell away, but also the equally inaccurate view that everything America touched it exploited and oppressed. It's wrong to paint America as either a pure chosen country blessed by God or the epitome of arrogance and greed. Let's get it straight. America is a mixed bag."

"That sounds like a more realistic picture," Dan agreed.

"Yeah, take the Massachusetts Puritans for example," I said. "Coming to America to pursue religious freedom, they saw themselves building a 'city on a hill' that God ordained as an example for other nations. But were they really a positive model for Christ?"

"I've heard they were really legalistic," Dan offered.

"That's an understatement. They took the Bible as their comprehensive guide for everything done under the sun. The governor of the colony, John Winthrop, set up a system that equated ancient Israel with the Massachusetts Bay Colony. As a result, there was no separation between church and state. It was a theocracy, with a philosophy similar to today's hyper-conservatives, you know, the Reconstructionists."

"Aren't they the ones who want Old Testament law incorporated into our legal system?" Dan asked.

"Yes, that's them. In addition to murder, the Puritans made idolatry, blasphemy, adultery, and homosexuality punishable by death. Oh, and witchcraft. The Salem witch trials were the most famous miscarriage of justice under them."

"Talk about extremists," Dan said.

"They were obsessed with imposing a very strict morality. They made church attendance and keeping the Sabbath mandatory and prohibited stuff like entertainment, public displays of affection, and gossip. Guilty parties were whipped or put in the stockades with the community invited to pelt them with food! Can you imagine?"

"Now that's legislating morality! Incredible," Dan lamented.

"Their notion that New England was the New Israel was a very dangerous idea. Puritans treated Native Americans like crap. Since they considered themselves God's chosen people, they concluded that they had the right to take their land."[94]

"If that's the Christian nation conservatives want us to return to, I want no part of it!" Dan concluded.

"But there was another side to this coin," I told Dan. "Ironically, the chief example of Puritan positive influence on American culture was a Puritan dissenter named Roger Williams who was banished from the colony! He's the guy who developed the original system of separation of church and state. He understood that even the church could have a corrupting influence.[95] His colony in Rhode Island was a model of religious toleration and admirable treatment of the Indians. He actually purchased land from the Narragansett chiefs."

"Buying land instead of stealing it," Dan said. "What a concept."

"Yeah, really. He became known for his peacemaking between the colonists and native Americans."

"Sounds like Williams was no fundamentalist," Dan added.

"You got it," I responded. "And neither were the overwhelming majority of the founding fathers. They were liberals. Benjamin Franklin, George Washington, John Adams, Thomas Jefferson, and others believed in 'Divine Providence,' but as Noll concluded, very few believed in the orthodox teachings of Christianity."[96]

"So, what was their faith like?" Dan asked.

"Franklin saw Christ as a good moral teacher and example to emulate but was a far cry from an evangelical. Washington's faith was moral and humane, but not particularly orthodox. He was an Episcopalian who didn't even attend church. I think Adams respected the Bible but only read it upon occasion."

"I seem to remember reading Adams was Unitarian," Dan interjected.

"That's true. He and his wife Abigail were Universalists, not exactly a popular doctrine among traditionalists."

"And wasn't Jefferson known for being a Deist?"

"Right," I answered. "He believed in a benevolent God but not in the deity of Christ, the resurrection, and the divine authority of

Scripture. He even re-wrote the New Testament twice to remove 'the unreasonable parts.' James Madison followed his predecessor, Jefferson, in declaring the government should *not* sanction national days of prayer. It was only a handful of secondary leaders who had what we might call an evangelical faith."

"Who were they?"

"Let's see, what were their names?" I tried to recall. "They weren't the Revolution's most important leaders. Oh, John Witherspoon and Roger Sherman were two. The only founders well known today who remained devoted students of the Bible were Patrick Henry and Alexander Hamilton."

"I didn't realize most of this," Dan said. "So America's founding fathers, for the most part, did not fit the Christian image that evangelicals today are fond of claiming. These are very important details that defenders of Christian nationalism fail to mention. Like you said, today's evangelicals would consider most of the founders liberals."

"Yeah, it's ironic. They wouldn't accept them as true believers!"

"Okay, what are the lessons in all this? What did you conclude from your studies?"

"Well, the politics-of-religion mindset that has saturated evangelicalism ever since the founding of the Moral Majority is still alive and well in groups like Operation Save America, American Family Association, a host of evangelical churches, and many a Republican candidate for public office."

"Michelle Bachman and Rick Perry come to mind," Dan said.

"This mindset has an us-vs.-them and all-or-nothing mentality, which creates the monster of heavily financed political activism. One that's based on the myth that America is a Christian nation, and that we need to return to that, or else."

"Yeah, but you have to admit, us-vs.-them attitudes are on both sides of the aisle."

"I agree. Conservatives don't have a monopoly on all-or-nothing attitudes. They can also be present in left-wing politics. Hence, a smart, young feminist like Tami Bruce is driven out of the Los

Angeles NOW branch because she asks the hard questions about abortion."

"She's the one who stood up to the far-left *group think* mentality, right?"

"Yes. But my major critique is within evangelicalism where *group think* is pervasive. The attitude is one of drawing lines: Republican over Democrat, pro-life over pro-abortion, religious America over secular America. Cal Thomas has a quote I'll never forget: 'power is the ultimate aphrodisiac.'"[97]

"Who's that?"

"One of the founders of the Moral Majority. He wrote a book about how he changed his mind about the Christian Right. You see, evangelicalism within the Christian Right has always been about taking control, getting the right candidates in, overcoming the enemy, legislating the right laws, forcing an abortion clinic to close, and reclaiming America for Christ. And it's all done by manipulating the masses through fear and demonization of opponents."

"Kind of reminds me of the dark side of the Puritans," Dan offered.

"Sure," I agreed. "When you think God is on your side, anything can be rationalized, including fear-mongering propaganda. One of my pet peeves that drives me berserk is that the church loves to threaten disaster if you don't pursue their agenda. If we don't clean up the moral cesspool of liberalism, you know, things like sexual immorality, homosexuality, and secular philosophy, and return to our Christian roots, God will judge us, our country will go down the tubes, and we won't be ready for Christ's return."

"Right," Dan agreed. "And never mind that our country's 'Christian roots' are way more theologically liberal than conservative."

"Or that our roots have their own moral flaws like justifying slavery and racism. In religious politics, there are the same threats. If you don't vote Republican or for this candidate or support this bill, all hell will break loose. A contemporary example is Obama's health care legislation."

"Don't get me started on that," said Dan. I knew he was an avid Obama supporter.

"You'll like this one," I said. "I saw a prayer cast on the Internet broadcast from Washington, D.C., during the 2009 health-care debate in Congress. My old pastor friend, Lou Engle [from ALCC, the PDI/SGM church], was among the presenters. In it, another pastor named Jim Garlow claimed the health care bill currently being deliberated in the Senate violated just about every one of the Ten Commandments! Can you believe that? If we pass it, he said, the government will take over your life and God will judge us for funding abortion and disobeying the Bible. His reasoning flabbergasted me."

"He tried to make the healthcare debate about obedience to the Bible?"

"Yes! Now, there's nothing wrong with disagreeing with such legislation. But making it into a matter of obedience to God is pure spiritual manipulation."

"That's incredible," Dan responded. "We live in a pluralistic society. Good politics is about compromise, not taking control, as you said the Puritans tried to do."

"Absolutely," I agreed. "Real influence comes through open-minded persuasion and loving others, not by winning at the polls or banning abortion or suppressing gay rights."

Our remaining conversation was a summary of the lessons I had learned: Democrats, as much as Republicans, care about decency and values. God works through more than one political party, outside of evangelicalism,[98] and in people of other faiths. Fair-minded evangelical historians have corrected their brethren through sound research and concluded the historical record is clear that America is not a Christian nation.[99] Christianity has had both positive (abolition, social reforms, and civil rights movements) and negative (legalistic Puritans, oppressing native Americans, justifying slavery, and racism) influence on our country.

"Dan, I think the major lesson in all this is don't allow

black-and-white thinking to draw us into a moral, religious, or political power trip."100

"I think you're right. Seems like we evangelicals has been guilty of that."

Dan and I finished the last of our ales. It was my time for a break. As I walked away from the bar toward the restrooms I remembered where evangelical black-and-white thinking comes from. Its source, I concluded, is a literalist approach to the Bible. Dan and I had already touched on this. I recalled it had taken me years to uncover it, but I had finally discovered the Bible was routinely misused and abused, although mostly unintentionally, and even mistranslated. To arrive at this position, I had to overcome much inner conflict. I also remembered all too well what that conflict was like. Memories began flooding my mind. One day stood out.

CONFESSION #7

CONFRONTING BIBLE ABUSE

"Read the Bible like drinking beer, not sipping wine."

– N.T. Wright

Circa 2000

On a typical Pacific Northwest Sunday afternoon—that is, rainy—I decided to wrestle with theology. It's not as bad as it sounds. I lounged on my favorite couch engrossed in R.C. Sproul's book *The Last Days According to Jesus*. The issue at hand was Sproul's interpretation of the book of Revelation and the Olivet Discourse, a portion of the book of Matthew containing Christ's own prophecies about His return. As the author's arguments sank in, I sat up. Suddenly, I was angry. *You mean to tell me all these years I thought these "end-times" passages referred to the return of Christ in a far-in-the-future generation, and now you're telling me they don't?* The author was doing more than making an off-the-cuff statement. He was making a sound case, based on the meaning of New Testament Greek and its first century historical context. When Jesus predicted "the end" in passages like Matthew 24 He said, "This generation will certainly not pass away until all these things have happened." Moreover, the writer of Revelation prefaced his predictions by saying God gave the vision to "show his servants what must soon take place." Concluding *all* these "end times" events occurred in the first century made perfect sense. *Why had I not heard of this interpretation before?*

Every Bible teacher or preacher I had ever heard speak on the Olivet Discourse[101] had taught there was a double meaning to Christ's prophetic words. He was talking about some events that would occur in his own generation, but largely about what would unfold in the distant future, possibly in our lifetime, or so they said. But this author argued that the evidence doesn't support this standard evangelical view. "I am convinced that the substance of the Olivet Discourse was fulfilled in AD 70 and that the bulk of Revelation was fulfilled in that timeframe,"[102] Sproul concluded. This was no small distinction. In my mind, if correct, there was little, if any, scriptural support for the traditional belief that the return of Christ the way most evangelicals envision it is still to come. It would mean one of two things: either Christ was wrong about His return, or He had already returned. Whichever way, it would mean any "end of the world" scenario tied to this infamous passage and the book of Revelation is a myth.

While this specific possibility was new to me, the fact that our popular understanding of the Bible may be at odds with the Bible's own words was not. By studying the original language and culture of the Bible, and the conclusions of biblical scholars who had done so, I had made many similar discoveries. Over the years the number of revelations increased until they encompassed a variety of subjects, including the nature of the Bible, the church, divorce, sexual immorality, homosexuality, salvation, heaven, hell, and the kingdom of God. I found that popular evangelical teaching often contradicted a studied interpretation of the words of Christ and the biblical authors.

At first, these revelations were occasional and isolated, and I didn't necessarily believe them. *That's ridiculous*, I would think. *If that's true then most evangelicals are wrong.* But over time, as I learned more details, these discoveries began to make so much sense I couldn't ignore them. They also weren't isolated anomalies. They were piling up to form a *pattern* of misinterpretation. And it wasn't just progressives or liberals exposing them. Conservatives like Sproul were too.

What was at the core of these revelations? That the Bible is often abused.

Bible abuse occurs when someone uses the Bible for a purpose for which it was not intended. It happens when an original Hebrew or Greek word is mistranslated or when a passage is misinterpreted due to misguided theology or ignorance of the cultures of antiquity or manuscript errors. Throughout history the Bible has been abused to hurt, oppress, and mislead people. Satan did it to try to trick Jesus, the Roman church to control the masses and fill its coffers, greedy landowners to defend the slave trade, Afrikaners to justify apartheid, and sexists to subordinate women. What shocks me is how prevalent it is today.

Is Bible abuse deliberate? My experience indicates that the majority of the time it is an unconscious act. The average churchgoers are unaware they abuse the Bible. Why? They themselves are victims of Bible abuse. They are merely parroting what they've been taught by those they trust to know the truth more than they. Although it happens more often among conservatives, liberals are also susceptible to abusing the Bible.

I, like others, misused and abused the Bible for years because I didn't know how to use interpretive tools. I didn't realize modern Bible translations and church traditions often reinforce the misinterpretation of Scripture. "Truth" is often based more on the tradition of the church or whatever position is being promoted than on what the original biblical writers meant.

This is not to say the Bible is dangerous and irrelevant. Quite the contrary. One needs to expose the Bible's misuse in order to promote its healthy use and discern what it means for 21st century readers. "The Bible may be dangerous in unworthy hands, but that same book leads nations to overthrow tyrants and colonialists to demand liberty and justice for all."[103] As many people as have abused it because of literalism or control (consciously or unconsciously), all the more have drawn inspiration from it. Throughout history, within its pages people have found spiritual solace to encourage hearts and motivation to fight injustice, from abolitionists to civil rights activists to a most unlikely political/spiritual leader, Mahatma Gandhi, a progressive Hindu influenced by Jesus' teaching on nonviolence and love.

What are the major ways the Bible is abused? What misguided fundamentalist and evangelical teachings are derived from its abuse? Over the years, I discovered the answers to these questions. For literalists, what I uncover below may rock their world. Skeptics might come to realize that the Bible, absent faulty interpretive grids, is a much more progressive book than they ever imagined.

THE ROOTS OF BIBLE ABUSE

"I know this sounds strange, but it was like they worshiped the Bible, not God," my friend Cheryl told me. It was 1980. I was a senior at UMass Amherst and a brand-new believer in Jesus. Cheryl, a friend from Intervarsity Christian Fellowship, was telling me about her visit to a club on campus called The Way, a religious movement that evangelicals considered a cult.

"Why do you say that?" I asked.

"I guess because they seemed to put more focus on the literal words than on the spirit behind the words." As she explained this, I remember thinking, rather indignantly, that this would never happen in an evangelical church. Years later, I realized I was wrong. It is not only possible, but very common for fundamentalist and evangelical churches to worship the Bible over and above God. It is called bibliolatry,[104] and it is one of the problems that plagues modern organized religion. Because every passage is considered the Word of God, a person who reads the Bible devotionally and literally and without analysis can easily attribute to God something that isn't from God. This person doesn't attempt to discern the original intent or context of the author,[105] nor weigh that intent in light of other biblical themes, let alone consider whether what he or she is reading is a correct translation and based on the best manuscript copies.[106]

I was taught to read the Bible devotionally as a new believer. Without understanding the Bible's surrounding cultural context or its origin, I frequently became confused and concerned over certain themes: the vengeful God of the Old Testament, his unreasonable punishments for certain violations, Jesus' hard stand on divorce and remarriage, his teaching about eternal punishment in hell, the catastrophic events surrounding the return of Christ, and Paul's statements against women teaching and leading in the church, to name a few. I also wondered where certain beliefs in the church came from, since I couldn't see them clearly taught in Scripture. Preachers condemned masturbation, even though it wasn't addressed in the Bible.[107] Biblical moralists forbade all pornography and narrowly defined it even though some passages (the Song of Solomon for example) contained blatantly erotic descriptions.[108] *What was I missing?* I often thought when encountering these concerns. *Could we be misreading the Bible? Aren't our modern translations accurate? How could a reader today, especially church leaders with a theological education, read the Bible wrong?* The answer, I discovered, has to do with a clash of cultures.

ILLUSTRATIONS FROM CULTURE

Most of us take culture and language for granted. I remember when our kids were about two or three years old they had no concept of measured time. What road trip doesn't have the question inherent to all children, "When are we gonna get there?" Realizing they didn't know how to interpret the answer "In about an hour and a half," Lori and I devised a translation solution. We compared the travel time with the time it took for them to watch their favorite television shows. So when one of us replied, "The time it takes to watch one *Sesame Street* and one *Mr. Rogers*," they immediately got it!

Similarly, people often read the Bible without the knowledge or tools to fully understand the words used therein. Frequently, there is no equivalent English word or phrase that matches the original Greek or Hebrew. An explanatory phrase is necessary.

A second illustration comes from my experience in Africa in the 1990s. Sara and her husband, fellow missionaries with whom Lori and I worked, had just arrived in Lilongwe, Malawi. A long-term Canadian aid worker drove them in his four-wheel drive Toyota Hi-Lux to their destination five hours away on poorly paved roads. An hour into the drive Sara was worried.

After glancing at the speedometer where the needle pointed to 80, she reasoned they were going way too fast. Trying to trust her experienced new colleague behind the wheel, and noticing her husband didn't seem too concerned, she kept her thoughts to herself.

Shortly she noticed people standing on the side of the road motioning to the car with their right hand as it went by. They held their outstretched hand out in front of their face with the palm of their hand facing down. A moment later they began waving their hand in a downward motion. Every few miles she saw other people do the same.

She thought perhaps they were trying to get him to slow down. Too mentally and physically exhausted to cause a stir, she again kept it to herself.

In her mind, she observed "facts" that were obvious. They were traveling upwards of 80 miles an hour, and people on the side of the road were motioning them to slow down. But was she interpreting these "facts" accurately? Later, she learned that the driver was in fact only going 50 mph and the people weren't concerned in the least he was driving too fast. So what were her interpretive mistakes?

First, the needle pointing to 80 indicated 80 kilometers per hour, not miles per hour. Translation: In a place like Malawi, 80 is the new 50. But Sara had never been inside a vehicle that did not have miles indicated on the speedometer at all.

Second, the people motioning with their hands were actually

hitchhiking. They were doing their culture's equivalent of holding out their fist with their thumb extended upright. Sara had the basic facts right; she just misinterpreted those facts. She wrongly assumed the practices in our culture were the only way for people to operate. Everyone who lives abroad for any length of time can attest to this faulty thinking.

So it is with people reading the Bible or any ancient or foreign literature. They interpret what they are reading through the lens of their own culture and can easily miss what is really going on, not only related to social and cultural cues but also due to a lack of knowledge about the historical events of antiquity. As a result, they come to faulty conclusions.

TWO STEPS TO ASCERTAIN THE BIBLE'S MEANING

By 1982 I'd been reading the Bible devotionally as a follower of Christ since college. But something was missing. At the point when I became perplexed about certain biblical passages, what the church taught, and how they clashed with my sense of reason, I wondered: how could one cut through difficult passages and get to the truth? It took a young seminarian I met from Gordon-Conwell Theological Seminary and an author named Gordon Fee[109] to provide me with the right tools. These sources showed me the answer was found in the hard work of biblical interpretation, not the casual devotional reading that was so common. I soon learned there are two key skills that are essential to sound Bible study.

Two fancy words represent these skills. First, one must discover what a passage meant to the original author and audience by learning its historical and cultural context. Scholars call this exercise *exegesis*. Then, and only then, one can attempt to determine what it means for us today. This second step is called *hermeneutics*.

Principally, the Bible is a compilation of historical documents, whether one believes they are accurate history or not. "Even the parts of the Hebrew Bible that seem more disembodied, such as the law, the statutes and the legal formulations still belong to the history. The law is never eternal or absolute. It is bound to a given history."[110] Without knowledge of Jewish history (and culture, since history is bound within culture), the Bible is easily misunderstood. *Exegesis* traces this background and includes acquiring knowledge on translations, and when necessary, learning the original Hebrew or Greek words in the text to clarify the meaning.

Hermeneutics is the activity of interpreting what the passage means for the modern reader. Simply put, one must have the facts surrounding the written word and then rightly interpret those facts to apply them to today. Slowly, over the years, I began to read the Bible more and more in this fashion and began to see how easy it is to misinterpret the Bible—a compilation of books written over thousands of years in ancient languages among cultures vastly different from modern Western culture.

In 25 years in evangelicalism, with the exception of some studies at Fuller Seminary, there were only three times that I recollect where a church leader accurately and thoroughly taught Bible study skills that included sound *exegesis* and *hermeneutics*. All three of these times, the teacher was not the senior pastor, and the church did not actively practice them. I was one of those teachers years later, when I spearheaded an adult Sunday School class on the topic. Over those years, I slowly came to believe that the evangelical church has misread the Bible. Author Gregory MacDonald admits this possibility. He wrote:

> I have very gradually and reluctantly come to the view that there is a serious conflict between traditional interpretations of the Bible and reason. I ought to restate that by reason I do not refer to human autonomous reason but reason informed by the self-revelation of God testified to in the Bible. We must be open to the possibility that we have misread the Bible.[111]

FOUR WAYS THE BIBLE IS ABUSED

(1) The Problem of Translation:

Translation work is not straightforward, especially for languages greatly separated in culture or time. When I lived in Africa, I experienced some of these translation hazards firsthand.

In the Chiyao language of southern Africa (Malawi, Mozambique, and Tanzania), people do not *live* in their house, they *sit* in their house. So, if you want to ask someone "Where do you live?" you say "Where do you sit?" or to be perfectly literal, "You are sitting where?" (*Aku tama kwapi?*). In the Somali and Oromo language and culture, as I learned earlier, the core of human emotions is the *liver* not the *heart*. You don't share feelings with *all your heart*. You share them with *all your liver*. One can imagine how this could create confusing translations if one always insisted on literalism.

This is why some translators advocate a translation style that finds a *dynamic equivalent* term rather than using a literal translation. For example, a *dynamic equivalent* approach would not translate the Chiyao question above literally as, "You are sitting where?" but "Where do you live?" so the English-speaking reader would hear the question in the ordinary way it is said in English. Likewise, the word *liver* in Somali or Oromo, would not be translated literally, but in the *dynamic equivalent*, which would be *heart*. In studying this, I learned that The King James Version (KJV) is particularly problematic because it uses both a literal translation and archaic language no longer in use today.

I also discovered that some Bible translations use a more literal approach (KJV) and some use a more *dynamic equivalent* approach (NIV). A third approach is a "free" translation (The Message Bible), which is more like a paraphrase and can come close to being a commentary and therefore read more into the text than is really there. Although it is by no means foolproof, the *dynamic equivalence* theory of translation best follows sound exegetical and hermeneutical practice and has the least chance of misleading the reader.[112] The average Bible readers are not aware of these different types of theories and the inherent problems in translation.[113] It's easy for them to be misled and go beyond the original intent of the authors, sometimes due to a word for which there is no direct translation and other times because of a translator's theological bias. They are also misled if Bible editors don't include footnotes (or if they are included but ignored) that are necessary to explain disputed or variant translations of words in the original language.

(2) Misinterpreting Passages:

The most common way I saw Bible commentators misinterpret a verse or passage is reading it out of context. Devotional reading of the Bible encourages reading and quoting isolated verses[114] without taking into account the context surrounding it. In other words, people sip the Bible like a glass of Port rather than drinking in whole sections as one would a pint or two of Guinness.

Ideally, the epistles (letters) of the New Testament should be read as a whole, not selecting sentences out of context of the larger point the letter is making. Without a straight read-through, it's too easy to misinterpret what the writer is saying, especially Paul with his long-winded arguments. Unfortunately, it is all too common for Bible readers to only read small portions of the epistles of the New Testament or small portions of other parts of Scripture, taken out of context of the full narrative.

Another reason for misinterpretation is misunderstanding the history, culture, and literary style behind the text. As my friend Sara misunderstood the Malawian sign for hitchhiking, people misread cultural cues, historical context, and literary styles, such as Hebrew parallelism (when the same thing is said in two different ways) and hyperbole (when exaggeration is used to make a point). To reiterate, they don't do the hard work of discovering what a passage meant to the original author and audience (*exegesis*) and then, and only then, attempt to ascertain what it means for us today (*hermeneutics*).

Misinterpretation can also take the form of selective reading. It's textual abuse when one quotes an Old Testament verse as authoritative for today (e.g., a command to tithe income), which is part of the Law for the Israelites, and ignores the New Testament principal that in Jesus, believers are not under the supervision of the Law (Acts, Chapter 15).

Finally, the Bible can be misinterpreted when people don't leave room for interpretation at all but insist that the text is always clear. They push inerrancy to its limit, and real study of the Bible ends. It's the "God said it, I believe it, that settles it" attitude. "It [the Bible] is no longer open to interpretation. Dogma replaces study, because scholarship can only be meaningful when you are allowed to ask real questions and let the chips fall where they may."115

(3) Misusing the Claim to Authority:

The Bible is not a compilation of timeless axioms that are to be strictly obeyed to the letter. It never claims to be such. "...there is no biblical doctrine of the authority of the Bible. ...the Bible itself is much more concerned with doing a whole range of other things rather than talking about itself."116 The Bible is simply the history of God's relationship and communication with the chosen Jewish nation and humankind from creation up until a generation or so after the life of Jesus. Whatever authority one attributes to it, its authority is limited and is not made up of arbitrary "thou shalt nots." For example, the stipulations in the Torah were specific to the Israelites within the timeframe they were given and were not meant to apply to all of humankind for perpetuity. When people use such commands to try to control society, they abuse the Bible, as they do when they insist that every belief and practice be proven by reference to the Bible.

The Bible's authority is in the fact that as a whole—with some exceptions, I daresay—it recognizes the importance of rationality, and it expounds a remarkable dose of wisdom and moral inspiration. Who can doubt the inspiration of Jesus when he asks us why we think we're morally good if we only greet our friends? We should be indiscriminate like the Creator, Jesus tells us, who "lets the sun shine and rain fall on the evil and the good." We should "love our enemies and be kind to those who persecute us." Who can fault him when he says love is the greatest commandment? Who can argue with Paul when he states, "Love is patient, love is kind. It does not envy, it does not boast, it is not proud." Most readers find profound wisdom and authority in such passages, but not an authority to crush, control, or manipulate.

The Bible at its core is a history book rather than a handbook. It never claims to be a complete authority over human life. Those who use it as a handbook for themselves and others can end up worshiping it over and above God. In making decisions or evaluating what's true, they discount the role of personal responsibility. What they read in the Bible trumps individual conscience, common sense, science, and the spirit of a God of grace who leads a soul.

It took me years to recognize this because the ingrained culture and tradition of evangelical and fundamentalist churches is one of total acceptance of the Bible as infallible and authoritative for our lives today. This notion is accepted as true without any solid evidence to back it up, except one or two proof texts that are stretched beyond reason, such as I Timothy 3:16.[117]

When people insist the Bible is the "Word of God," that insistence is based on tradition rather than an intrinsic claim within the text itself. The Gospels only claim Jesus Christ is the "Word of God."[118] Nowhere in the Old or New Testament does it claim that the whole Bible is the "Word of God." Yes, it is sometimes called "Scripture," but this is merely a word that denotes a set of writings about God's story.[119]

I often wondered where this notion came from that everything written in the Bible was "God's Word," because I never found it stated in Scripture. But I never questioned it seriously until I began noticing Bible abuse. Well-meaning Christians begin to follow the Bible rather than follow Christ; the consequences become an absence of grace and a presence of legalistic religion. "Biblicism becomes bibliolatry, the actual *worship* of the Bible by assigning it the same status as that which is accorded to Jesus Christ. The Person is replaced by the proposition: flesh by words; the Word of God [Christ] replaced by written, and much-disputed text."[120]

Whereas the Bible does claim God sent Jesus to bring good news to the Jews and the human race, it never claims its stories of the early church or Paul's advice to local first century churches are a timeless model to be followed to the letter by all believers throughout history. If it were, Christian abolitionists might not have fought the battle over slavery. In the New Testament, although Paul humanizes slavery, he tolerates it and in no instance is there any proactive stand taken to abolish the practice. Following the New Testament to the letter does not produce an abolitionist theology. It must be reasoned from other biblical principals.

Moreover, would Christian American Revolutionists have fought for independence from the British if they followed the New Testament to the letter? Most likely not. They would have strictly followed Paul when he said in Romans, "obey the governing authorities" and "...if you owe taxes, pay taxes...."

(4) Mislabeling Authenticity:

Another way that evangelicals misuse the claim for the Bible's authority is by overlooking obvious errors and inauthentic passages. They ignore or downplay the science of biblical scholarship called *textual criticism*.[121] According to Bart Ehrman, a biblical scholar and former evangelical who wrote *Misquoting Jesus* and *Jesus Interrupted*, the practice of ascertaining the ancient texts closest to the originals is nowhere near as straightforward as the average evangelical is led to believe. Those who hand copied the Bible changed the New Testament texts over the years, either due to human error or their own theological bias. Finding the original manuscripts is impossible. Finding the texts closest to the original is sometimes possible but no means straightforward. This doesn't mean the majority of the Bible is suspect. Ehrman concedes that most of the changes that copyist made are immaterial to the general historical and theological pronouncements. Nevertheless, there are several instances that reveal the problematic nature of the doctrine of the authority of Scripture. These cast doubt on certain cherished doctrines. If we are uncertain what the original text was, how can we say what we have in our hands today was preserved by God and is authoritative? How can we really know what to trust in the Bible? The answer, I believe, is to couple our study of Scripture with the best available biblical scholarship and a healthy dose of common sense.[122]

There are five examples of scriptural portions considered inauthentic. First, the end of Mark has a section that scholars agree was not part of the original.[123] It is set apart and footnoted in the NIV and other translations but is still printed as part of the Gospel of Mark. Second, the story of the woman caught in adultery in the Gospel of John[124] is almost universally agreed to be inauthentic. This is set apart and footnoted similarly. Third, there is a verse in I John that reinforces the doctrine of the Trinity that is not genuine.[125] Today, it is not included in modern translations, although it was in earlier versions of the King James Version. Fourth, two verses in I Corinthians that forbid women from speaking in church are considered to be inauthentic and added by later copyists (These verses are not indicated as such in modern translations). Finally, a consensus of modern scholars is in agreement that the apostle Paul did not write I Timothy, II Timothy, or Titus, and that II Thessalonians is not altogether genuine.[126] Apart from these instances there are other smaller portions of Scripture scholars are not sure about. "There are some places in which modern translations continue to transmit what is probably not the original text. There are other places where our best trained textual critics continue to disagree which texts should prevail."[127]

For me, these examples revealed a much more human Bible than I ever imagined. But there's an irony to this new awareness. When the practices and beliefs based on misuse were revealed, I discovered the Bible to be much more progressive than expected.

BREWS AND EXAMPLES OF BIBLE ABUSE

By the time I returned from the restroom, Gina was about to take my seat next to Dan.

"Can't stay away from this place, huh?" I said.

"Yeah, I finished shopping. I just couldn't resist coming back for a Pumpkin Ale." Gina smiled. "And your conversation was so interesting, I guess I was hoping to get in on it again."

"We were just talking about the problems of mixing religion and politics," Dan said to Gina. "But there's something else I want to ask Mike about that you might be interested in."

Brett the bartender interrupted. "Ready for another round, guys?"

"Hmm...," Dan mused. "Seeing how it looks like we'll be here for awhile more, I think I'll take a break on the brews. Ice water with lemon is fine for now."

"Me too," I told Brett.

Gina, on the other hand, had only had one beer and ordered the Ale she tasted earlier. I glanced up at the basketball game. The Celtics were still in the lead with five minutes left in the third quarter. After Brett served our drinks, Dan started in. "So, listen Mike. Your chapter on the Bible didn't go into specific examples of how people abuse it."

"I'd like to hear about that too," Gina said.

Man, I love these guys, I thought. They aren't afraid to address controversy. Dan and Gina had their backs to the bar, and I stood in the aisle, which was still full of a standing-room-only crowd. My "congregation" was all ears. Historically, I told them, the church abused the Bible by using it to justify slavery, racism, and the oppression of women. In contemporary conservative churches, the Bible is used to justify a litany of unfounded practices and beliefs. I reminded Dan we had already addressed how the concept of "church" is misunderstood due to Bible abuse. And there were other examples as well.

Controlling People

"Well, first the Bible is used to control behavior," I began to explain. "By insisting Christians believe in the inerrancy and unlimited authority of the Bible, teachers can use the Bible, consciously or unconsciously, to try to control people's lives. Since it is God's Word, if you don't obey it, you are rebelling against God, the reasoning goes. This teaching prevents people from interpreting the nature of God's revelation for themselves and coming to their own conclusions. I don't think anyone should ever insist that people accept things in the Bible that violate their sense of justice or reason," I concluded.

"Amen to that," Dan said. "I think this is exactly what many churches and teachers do. It's like they place the Bible over and above an individual's conscience."

"Right," I said. "I saw that happen at almost every church I ever attended to a degree, but especially at ALCC. Gina, that's a church in California Lori and I attended for five years. At that church, if people voiced disagreement over what the Bible said or the church's interpretation, they were often judged to be disobedient to the Word and accused of 'not taking the Scriptures seriously.' Remember what we discussed Dan. When taken to extremes, there can be serious emotional and psychological abuse of members."

"That sounds manipulative, sure," Gina said. "But I need more specifics. What practices or beliefs are you talking about?"

Enforcing Tithing

"Okay, let's start with tithing," I said. "The overwhelming majority of evangelical churches teach their members to tithe to their local congregation, you know, donate ten percent of their income to the church, based on Old Testament passages and at least one New Testament verse. A fair historical study of tithing, however, reveals it's not mandatory for Christians. Therefore, it's entirely optional. It should not be a measuring rod for spiritual maturity."[128]

"What's the history behind it then?" Gina asked.

"Well, it originated as a part of God's covenant with Israel and is not relevant to people under the new covenant of Christ. Also, tithing was technically the practice of donating a portion of one's harvest, not money. Claiming authority for an Old Testament passage like that one in Malachi[129] to teach people to tithe to their local church is abusing a time-specific command."

"Wait now," Gina said. "Jesus said somewhere that people shouldn't neglect tithing."

"That's the verse where he tells the Pharisees they should have tithed their herbs and spices without neglecting justice and mercy,"[130] I said. "You have to take it in context. Jesus was addressing people of the Torah and not establishing a tithing law for all time. When you take the New Testament as a whole, the major admonition about giving was to give to the poor. Paul never says tithe to the church."

"Okay," said Gina. "I can see that. You're saying tithing had a different function originally, one that really doesn't apply to the modern church."

"Yeah, that's it. If it's presented as an option, that's one thing. But it's usually taught like a command from God." I explained how some churches I attended were so legalistic about tithing, they taught that God would bless you materially if you tithed and withhold blessings if you didn't. So people became bound to a man-made religious duty for fear of losing out on God's provision.

Dan agreed. "I've heard pastors say something like that."

"Okay, that's a good example. What else?" Gina took a sip of her ale.

Misconstruing Divorce

"Probably one of the most divisive examples in the evangelical church is divorce," I said. "Mostly because of the widespread confusion over what Jesus and Paul taught. Some fundamentalists see no biblical basis for divorce and remarriage at all, while most evangelicals see the only basis for divorce and remarriage as physical abuse, adultery, or if an unbelieving spouse insists on leaving the marriage. And then there's the bias against divorced people."

"True enough," said Dan. "I've heard of churches that forbid divorced people from remarrying or at least from being leaders in the church."

"Right," I agreed. "But what if someone actually did the hard work of exegesis and hermeneutics on this issue? What would they conclude?"

"Exa Jesus? Herman who?" Gina asked.

Dan and I laughed. "I'm sorry. Those are scholarly terms from my book. I mean if someone studied the first century and Jewish context of divorce before applying it today. Recently I read about a theologian of Jewish literature who described what it is like to misinterpret the passages on divorce and the resultant epiphany that came after doing doctoral studies."

"What exactly did he study?" Dan asked.

"Well, he read a ton of surviving writing of the rabbis of Jesus' time and 'got inside their heads.' Even though he had read the biblical texts on divorce many times before, after reading the rabbis, the texts took on a new slant. The texts hadn't changed but his understanding of the language and culture in which they were written had. He was reading them like a first-century Jew, and the confusing passages made more sense."[131]

"That's cool," Gina said. "What did he discover?"

"That Jesus addressed a common practice in New Testament times called 'any-cause divorce,' which allowed men to divorce their wives for something as benign as burning dinner."

"So what are you saying?" Gina asked. "That he was only addressing casual divorce by men?"

"Basically. See, Jesus wasn't saying that divorce is always wrong with the exception of adultery. He was saying the practice of casually divorcing or accepting 'any-cause divorce' was wrong because it abused a woman's rights and left her abandoned. He wasn't saying there is only one just cause for divorce, adultery, nor that remarriage after legitimate divorce is wrong. This author wrote a whole book explaining this."[132]

"Sounds like you have another book to read," Gina told Dan.

"Well, the real kicker, Gina, is something else. It turns out the word 'divorce' is routinely mistranslated. There are two Hebrew and two Greek words that are commonly translated as 'divorce.' These two terms don't mean the same thing even though some conservative scholars claim they are synonymous."

Gina's eyes seemed to widen as I spoke.

"One word, whether in Hebrew or its Greek counterpart,[133] means a legal divorce with a certificate, which allowed a woman to remarry. And given the status of women in those days, she had to be married to survive. The other word[134] just means 'to put away' or abandon someone. So in Malachi,[135] God didn't say, 'I hate divorce.' He said he hates when men 'put away' women. The word is *'shalach,'* and refers to when men desert women without giving them recourse to remarry."[136]

"I'd say that's a very important piece of information that we don't hear in churches," Dan said.

"I really want to accept what you're saying," Gina told me. "It would clear up the narrow assertions about divorce. But I have hard time believing this distinction hasn't been made in the church all these years. Maybe there's a good reason they always translate those words as 'divorce.'"

"Maybe, but not according to people who study this. The traditional translation is problematic, and the distinction has the ring of truth. It puts a new slant on what Jesus taught. He taught that when a man 'puts away' his wife, he causes her and whoever subsequently marries her to commit adultery. Jesus was protecting women's rights, not legalistically condemning all divorce across the board. Have you heard of Don Francisco?"

"Can't say that I have," Gina answered.

"Isn't he some Christian musician from back in the day?" Dan asked.

"Yeah. But it's his wife Wendy who has an excellent study on this topic on her website. She makes the point that the divorce passages address a completely different situation for which we have no modern equivalent. Jesus did not say that if a man marries a divorced woman he would be committing adultery. He said that if a man married a 'put out' woman he would be committing adultery. This is because she was technically still married!"[137]

"Sounds like most Bible teachers have screwed up the meaning of these texts," Dan said.

"I think that's right," I said. "As Wendy Francisco says, probably millions of people have been negatively impacted by errant doctrines that come out of these misinterpreted verses. When I finally saw these facts for the first time, it was a great relief, since I had always struggled with the traditional interpretation of Jesus' teaching about divorce."

"I know what you mean," Dan said. "The church has a history of being dogmatic about divorce—condemning all divorce or allowing it only under one or two conditions."

"Or, like you said, treating divorcees like second-hand citizens and disallowing remarriage," Gina added.

"Yeah, and it's all based on Bible abuse, either done callously or from ignorance," I said.

"So why doesn't the church teach this stuff?" Dan asked. "You'd think with all these professional clergy going through seminaries supposedly designed to train them how to rightly interpret the Bible, they would know this."

"Good question, Dan," I said. "As far as the church goes, it appears that tradition trumps truth in the issue of divorce. Unfortunately, that's not the only issue where this occurs."

"I have to admit," Gina said. "These examples are pretty serious misuses of original Bible language. Still, I'm not entirely convinced. Like Dan said, if this is true, why is it not taught? I'd like to read for myself what scholars say on this. What other examples are you thinking of, Mike?"

Misunderstanding Heaven

"Right." I said. "Here's another one. A mistranslated phrase— 'kingdom of God' or 'kingdom of heaven.' 'Kingdom of heaven' is not referring to a blissful place in the afterlife. In Matthew, the author is addressing first century Jews, who wouldn't say the name of God out loud. Consequently, he replaces 'God' with 'Heaven" to be sensitive to this custom.[138] So Jesus is *not* talking about the afterlife when he mentions the Kingdom in his teachings. Author N. T. Wright also exposed this misinterpretation. In one of his books, he says 'kingdom of heaven' has been long misunderstood by Christians to be a place where saved souls go after death. It meant nothing like that in Jesus' world, but was rather a Jewish way of talking about Israel's god becoming king."[139]

"I've never heard of this," Gina said. "This seems weird. How can 'heaven' not mean what it says?"

"Because we don't understand real meanings in Greek. There's another one, the word 'kingdom,' which is the Greek word *basileia*. It isn't a place or political framework or *the church*; the more accurate translation is "reign."[140] Jesus announces the 'reign of God' is 'in your midst' (Luke 17:21). The kingdom or reign of heaven is actually wherever Jesus is present, and remember, he said he is present in spirit wherever two or more are gathered in his name."

"Like us right now," Gina said.

"Yeah, even in a microbrewery," Dan added.

"Absolutely," I agreed. "And his other teaching says in effect that one enters this reign only by love."

"You know," Dan said. "These facts also put a different slant on other passages. For example, 'You must be born again to enter the kingdom of God.' Sounds like Jesus wasn't saying you must become a born-again Christian to enter a place called heaven, but rather you must have a spiritual awakening or epiphany to recognize or enter into the reign of God."

"Yes!" I exclaimed. "By definition, this would make someone like Mahatma Gandhi, who remained a Hindu but respected all religions, one who is born again, since he perceived the reign of God in the person of Christ."

"Now that is fascinating," Dan said. "It helps resolve the problems with a narrow view of salvation."

"That does make sense," Gina agreed.

Once I got started, my list of examples just seemed to keep flowing as if a floodgate—locked up by my own fear of negative reactions—had at long last been opened. Dan and Gina's curiosity to know more kept it going.

Judging Jesus

"Bible abuse is an equal-opportunity activity, you know. Liberals are also susceptible. The team of scholars that are called the Jesus Seminar are famous for whiting out certain words of Jesus in the Gospels as inauthentic. They printed a Bible that displays the sayings or deeds of Jesus in various colors, representing which parts were genuine and which were concocted by the biblical authors or other sources. After all is said and done, only one fifth of the Gospels are retained."

"I'm glad you brought that up," Gina said. "I've heard of the Jesus Seminar and wondered what it was."

"Well, I have mixed feelings about it. Not all of the members are biased toward abusing the Bible. For one, I find Marcus Borg to be fair-minded in his conclusions. Nevertheless, liberal Catholic historian Garry Wills calls the Jesus Seminar the 'new fundamentalists' because they approach the New Testament with a pre-determined assumption that anything odd or supernatural cannot be historical."

"That's a huge bias, I'd say," Dan said. "It discounts miracles without being open to their possibility."

"Sure," I agreed. "Just like the old fundamentalists Jerry Falwell, Pat Robertson, and James Dobson, some, not all, on the Jesus Seminar start from a position of closed-mindedness, so are unable to arrive at an objective conclusion or fairly analyze historical evidence. Wills says, even though some people have called them radical, they are actually very conservative. They tame the real, radical Jesus. It's like they take him down a notch or two.[141] To the extent this happened in the Jesus Seminar, the members were guilty of abusing the Bible."

Subordinating Women

"Okay," Gina started. "What have you found about the way the church interprets passages on women. There are major problems with the traditional view."

"Gina, you're right. The evangelical church is still bound to legalistic interpretations of New Testament passages about women. Look, based on Paul's admonitions to first century churches, we know conservative churches don't allow women to be Pastors or elders. They base this on a literalism that must accept the entire Bible as God's Word for today. Unfortunately, their cursory reading of Scripture doesn't usually take into account the Greek and Jewish cultural setting of the first century or the extraordinary ways that Jesus honored women to the dismay of the disciples and the Pharisees. You know, Paul was the one who said there is 'no male or female' in Christ [Galatians 3:28]. He even mentions a woman, Junia, as among the apostles [Romans 16:7]. The early believers in Jesus were the most socially progressive groups of their time."[142]

"I get that," Gina said, "but there are still those controversial verses about women submitting and being silent. What about those?"

"Well, literalists refuse to consider the implications of discrepancies in Paul's writings on women. Like when Paul states women can pray and give prophecies in gatherings in I Corinthians 11 and that they should remain silent in I Corinthians 14."

"How in the world do you remember this stuff?" Gina asked.

I laughed. "I guess I've had my head in this stuff with the book research, I just retain it. Anyways, because of contradictions like that and other internal problems with the Greek text, a large number of scholars have condemned the verses on women's being silent as an interpolation later added to the original letter.[143] This includes one evangelical who I've admired for years, Gordon Fee, but didn't learn his view on this until recently.[144] If you read the passage without the verses in question [I Corinthians 14:33b to 35], it makes so much more sense. Those verses about women don't fit the surrounding context of the passage."

"Really?" Gina seemed pleasantly surprised. "That's encouraging! To think that sexist verse that always drove me batty may not even belong in the Bible. It clears up a lot of confusion about women's roles. But then, you get the problem Lori brought up. How can there be errors in Scripture?"

"Because people are human," Dan said. "We shouldn't worry so much about how the Bible can be fallible, but follow where the evidence leads."

"Think about it, Gina," I said. "Isn't it more encouraging to discover that Paul wasn't the woman hater he appeared to be, even if that means the Bible has been tainted? There's also another similar verse in I Timothy,[145] but many scholars don't think Paul wrote that book."

"I'll have to think about this," she said. "It's just such a different way of looking at the Bible than what I've been taught."

"Gina, let me give you an example of what happens when we don't look at the Bible more critically," I offered. "There's this columnist for the conservative Christian magazine *World,* named Adrée Seu. In 2007 she wrote an article called something like "A Symbol of Glory; One Woman Says Yes to God." In it, she announced that she has begun wearing a head covering during worship based on that verse in 1 Corinthians."

"Oh, the one that says women should cover their head,"[146] Gina remembered.

"Yeah. Because she's an inerrantist, and agrees with the magazine's statement of faith that the Bible is infallible, she presumed she was commanded by God to wear a head covering. She said she knows most people consider this culturally irrelevant but her 'high school literary skills tell her otherwise.' That's the problem, Gina. Literalists assume no other skills are necessary. They don't realize they must understand surrounding context and step back into the minds and lives of the original audience, or else they will misconstrue what was meant and how to interpret it for today's world."

"Right," Dan interjected. "The question is, why would Paul's admonishment to a first century church to have their women cover their heads, be interpreted as a command for women in the 21st century? It's an obscure kind of command that has no basis in Jesus' teachings. Following it doesn't make sense."

"And it's interesting that people who follow such a verse are not consistent," I added. "This journalist believes the verses about being silent or not teaching men are still authentic, but she doesn't apply them to herself. She doesn't endorse women being silent in church and actually teaches men in her column. It appears she practices what I call 'selective literalism.'"

"Okay," Gina said. "You guys have made good points. I can see if you are strictly literal about the Bible, you can come up with some crazy ideas."

Selective Literalism

Dan brought up an important point. "The most common form of Bible abuse must be taking verses out of context."

"Yes, and it's easy for any of us to do," I added. "In fact, I've been guilty of all these things I'm talking about. But, taking things out of context is what I mean by 'selective literalism.' In the book, I define it as when a reader who believes that the whole Bible is genuine chooses which parts of the Bible to accept literally and which parts to ignore."

Dan had something to say about that. He gave two examples. One was the health-and-wealth gospel proponents who focus on a verse of the Bible that says God wants people to prosper.[147] "I read about this recently," Dan said. "It's where 3 John says 'I pray that you may prosper...' But the original Greek does not mean monetary prosperity but merely wishing things go well for people. These health-and-wealth teachers ignore this and other Scriptures that talk of how to handle material wealth. They twist the text by claiming it means God wants people to become wealthy, which of course justifies their own lavish lifestyles."

"That's a good example," I agreed.

"Another good example is how popular end times 'experts' claim we are living in the generation who will see Christ's return by quoting the book of Revelation," Dan continued. "I mean, aren't there lots of verses in there that say the time is near for these things to be fulfilled?"

"Yes, there are," I said. "Like when it says the vision is about 'what must soon take place.' The original readers would understand that to mean it will play out shortly in their timeframe, not thousands of years in the future. People pushing end times theology ignore those statements."

Gina was sitting quietly but now perked up. "Okay, I see what you're saying, but what you said about ignoring Scripture got me thinking. Don't take me wrong, but don't you do the same when you say stuff like certain passages don't belong in the Bible? I mean, aren't you just choosing what to accept?"

"Great questions," I said. "I guess the issue is what is the justification for saying one portion of the Bible is true and another is not? I see 'selective literalism' as when someone claims the whole Bible is true, and then chooses one passage and ignores another to support a *pre-determined* theology. I think that's altogether different from someone who leaves the all-true Bible question open, and makes a case that a portion of Scripture was probably not in the original or wasn't meant to be a command for all time, based on textual and historical evidence."

"That's a good clarification," Gina said. "I can see that difference."

Other Teachings

Although our conversation on this particular topic was winding down, I knew this was actually the foundation for much of what I was addressing in my book. In a very short time I would discuss with Dan and Gina, and our mutual friend Steve, how the Bible is abused to misconstrue what it teaches about the return of Christ, sexual immorality, homosexuality, the age of the earth, the origin of life, and the meaning of hell.

THE FRUIT OF BIBLE ABUSE

I was finally finding some allies in Dan and Gina who were open to learning how prevalent Bible abuse is and how it is one of the major problems with religion. Gina was acknowledging the possibility, and Dan was arguing for it. They could see some of the modern consequences of abusing the Bible, the bad fruit if you will, and the importance of handling the Bible in a more responsible way.

I also knew Bible abuse could cause psychological damage. One Christian counselor reported that at least eighty percent of his clients had problems that could be traced to bad theology![148] Bad theology typically comes from those who misread, misuse, and abuse the Bible. The pervasiveness of bad theology influenced Christian psychologists Henry Cloud and John Townsend to write books like *Twelve "Christian" Beliefs That Can Drive You Crazy.* "Time and time again, we'd find that our patients—sincere, Bible-loving believers struggling with emotional issues—had a double burden to bear. Not only were they depressed... but they were handicapped by certain teachings that sounded Christian, but weren't. The ideas appeared true because those who taught them used religious language and quoted Scriptures. These ideas, however, are emotional heresies."[149]

We had only touched on one of the most prevalent cases of Bible abuse: the teaching about the "last days." That rainy day on my favorite couch came to my mind. As we concluded our latest spirited discussion, I wanted to address this example in more depth. I remembered all too well the part of my journey when I researched and confronted the "end-times" belief system. Before I began my search for a valid explanation for it, I never would have dreamed of the conclusions to which I arrived.

CONFESSION #8

LAST DAYS DELUSIONS

"Those who don't learn from the past are condemned to write end-times books."[150]

–Steve Dennie

At Explo '72 I had my first encounter with people who believed the end of the world was on the horizon—that we were living in the last days. The Bible was clear, they had said. Jesus is coming again in the future—possibly in our lifetime after a period of worldwide tribulation[151]—to judge the world, separate the just from the unjust, and usher in the kingdom of God, an inauguration of a new age. We had better accept Christ and be ready. Nonbelievers would be sentenced to eternal separation from God in hell. So much for the good news.

Like the ones I met at Explo, some of these folks believed in a two-stage return of Christ. Jesus would first come *invisibly* immediately prior to the tribulation to take his church, the true believers in Christ, to heaven during the Rapture. The rest of humanity would be left to suffer through seven years of apocalyptic trials, but still have a chance to accept Christ. Lucky for them. At the culmination of the seven years, Jesus would come *visibly* to oversee Judgment Day.

All evangelical churches I attended taught one of these two positions on eschatology (the study of the end times)—either a one-stage or two-stage return. After all, it was plainly spelled out in the Bible.

Or, so people said. What I didn't realize during my first few years as a believer was how much these beliefs are subjectively read into passages in the Bible, not objectively derived from them. There are years of traditional misreadings, translation biases, subtle half-truths, and a lack of understanding of biblical culture and literary style that contribute to the church's or any author's misinterpretations of end-times passages. Scholars and translators should really know better, but average Bible readers are typically in the dark about certain facts.

RAPTURE FEVER

Shortly after my conversion I began investigating the two-stage "pre-trib" Rapture version of the end. At first, it seemed almost every-one taught it, due to the popularity of Hal Lindsey's book, *The Late Great Planet Earth*, and its sequel, *The Terminal Generation*. I soon discovered, however, that some evangelicals disagreed. At the Jesus Festival I attended in Pennsylvania in 1979 I heard Larry Tomzcak, one of the founders of PDI/SGM, vehemently challenge the pre-trib position. He made the case for a *post*-tribulation Rapture. Jesus would return once, at the end of the seven years. In some parts of the world, people are already going through a type of tribulation, he said. Since the pre-trib view sounded bizarre and fantastical[152] and Lindsey's book didn't make sense to me, I was relieved to hear Tomzcak's argument. Still, I wanted to see for myself what the Bible actually taught. I was foggy about both these competing theories. Are we really on the cusp of the end of the world? Does the Bible really teach there will be a Rapture, regardless of the timing?

"What's with this Rapture and being whisked up to heaven before some great tribulation?" I asked Dave, an experienced believer I was rooming with in Massachusetts who also came out of the Jesus Movement. It had been a year or so since I had heard Tomzcak. "I remember Jesus talking about judgment, but not about some Rapture beforehand. Where exactly is it found in the Bible?"

"Sounds like you've read Hal Lindsey," he answered. "He comes out of Dallas Theological Seminary, which is pre-trib. You know, not all scholars subscribe to that. I have a book you should read that critiques it. You have to be careful about Bible prophecy, Mike, sometimes people twist the Scriptures to fit their pet theology." Dave was more sophisticated than the average believer. He understood Bible abuse. I was clueless to its dangers.

Although Dallas was the strongest promoter, it turns out other evangelical institutions supported this view, namely fundamentalist Moody Bible Institute and even the more moderate Wheaton College. The book Dave gave me, written by an evangelical, refuted the theological grid of Lindsey and these institutions, which was called *dispensational pre-millennialism*. Don't ask. In the grand scheme of things, it doesn't matter what that means.

Finally, after years of hearing nonsensical descriptions of the Rapture, I was reading something that spelled out the misguided source of this strange version of eschatology. This was a relief, since I had floundered between accepting and doubting the Rapture for several years after my experience in Dallas. I remember once in high school, before my conversion, coming home to an empty house when I expected my parents to be home. For a brief moment, I was gripped with fear, thinking that perhaps it had occurred and I had been left behind.

Apocalyptic pronouncements by self-assured prophetic "experts" who claim the Bible is infallible can have a powerful impression on vulnerable minds. "The Bible tells us on that day, millions of people will disappear from the face of the earth in less than a millisecond. And the purpose of that evacuation is…to avoid horrific devastation."[153] So Dr. David Jeremiah assures us and then goes on to say we too can avoid the destruction of the seven years of tribulation if we turn to Christ and begin to live pure and holy lives; if not, we will be "left behind to experience horrors worse than anything the world has yet seen." What young impressionable mind wouldn't think twice about turning to Jesus after hearing that type of warning?

After talking to Dave and reading the book he gave me, I was astonished. As a new convert, I was naïve enough to believe that not only was the Bible true, but all true Christians agreed on what it taught. Dave's book and what I'd heard at the Pennsylvania Jesus Festival opened my eyes to see how easy it is to come to different conclusions when interpreting the Bible. It also revealed how prevalent it is to misuse it because of readers' ignorance of history and culture. Dave's book made perfect sense. The pre-tribulation Rapture was a sham.

None of the early church fathers saw a pre-trib Rapture in Scripture, the author had said. They may have been futurists, but views like Hal Lindsey's or Tim LaHaye's would have been completely foreign to them. I learned the pre-tribulation view was entirely unknown until 1830, when a preacher named John Nelson Darby, who was part of the Plymouth Brethren, began teaching it. That's about eighteen hundred years after Christ. If it were true, you'd think someone would have taught it a little sooner than that!

Moreover, the Bible says absolutely nothing about believers' being rescued by Jesus from the tribulation period and then Jesus' coming back with them seven years later. It does not say someday millions of people will disappear from the face of the earth in less than a millisecond to avoid horrific devastation. That notion is not stated in Scripture but mentally inserted into a smattering of isolated verses that say things like "we will be caught up together with them in the clouds to meet the Lord in the air" (I Thessalonians 4: 17). This is classic Old Testament imagery referring to the general resurrection of believers with no mention of the tribulation period or Jesus' coming back when the period is over. Bible commentators like Gary DeMar have painstakingly exposed the fallacy of these views, calling the pre-tribulation doctrine a gigantic hoax.[154] The way verses like these are interpreted is a prime example of how the Bible is routinely abused. "These verses in I Thessalonians 4 have been grievously abused by those who have constructed out of them the big picture of a supposed rapture."[155]

The more I was exposed to sermons and Bible commentators talking on the subject of the end times, the more I realized the variations of evangelical eschatology are mind-boggling. The reason there is so much disagreement about what exactly is predicted in the Bible is because much of it is based on Jewish symbolism and apocalyptic literature, about which most people are clueless; it makes the practice highly subjective. That's why we get the pre-, mid-, and post-tribulation views on the Rapture, as well as, the premillennialist, amillennialist, and postmillennialist views on the supposed thousand-year reign of Christ. Lindsey and company are premillennialists, and non-premillenialists are either amillennialists or postmillennialists. Frankly, I never figured out which one I was until I didn't care. There seems to be no limit to the variations of these and other end-times views and the nooks and crannies one could explore. Extremely bright theologians who have the gift of investigating the idiosyncrasies of all the eschatological schools of thought, from the harebrained to the hell-bent, can fill you in on the details.[156]

Regardless, there were more discoveries that forced me to rethink whether the Bible really taught the end of the world.

THE SKY IS FALLING

The question that frames this whole subject was asked by Jesus' disciples two millennia ago in a portion of the book of Matthew called the Olivet Discourse. Addressing Jesus, they asked,

"What will be the sign of your coming and of the end of the age?"

The overwhelming majority of evangelicals believe much of his answer to that question (most notably found in Matthew 24:4-51) is a prediction of the end of the world as stated earlier—whether they believe in a pre-trib Rapture or not. What I discovered turns that notion on its head. The context of that question—Jesus' prediction that the Jewish Temple would be destroyed[157]—is vitally important.

Besides a Rapture and final judgment, most evangelicals believe other events are part of the time of the end. These include the rebuilding of the Jewish Temple (evangelical Zionism) as a necessity to fulfill prophecy, the rise of a diabolical world leader called the Antichrist, a one-world religion and government, the final battle of Armageddon, and the millennial rule of Christ, when Jesus reigns for a thousand years on earth. All of these scenarios are supposedly based on Jesus' Olivet Discourse recorded as separate accounts in Matthew, Mark, and Luke, and also other passages in the books of I John, I and II Thessalonians, Revelation, and several Old Testament books.

In my experience, most of us evangelicals believed that the signs of the contemporary times pointed to the probability that Jesus' return and the end of the world would occur in our lifetime, or at least within a generation or two. Some of us took this more seriously than others. For instance, many of my more moderate friends and I grappled with this issue and never arrived at a reasonable explanation. We still believed in some future return of Jesus at the end of history, for that did seem to be what the Bible taught. We just couldn't be sure of the details and frankly didn't care. We chalked it up as a mystery. There were other inspirational parts of the Bible that seemed more applicable to our lives, so why worry about eschatology? We would often joke, "It's too confusing for me, that's why I'm a pan-millenialist. I believe everything will pan out in the end."

What's more, moderate evangelical churches usually didn't dwell on the sensationalism of biblical prophecy. They were more apt to promote world change through global evangelism and love-in-action ministry. Nevertheless, they taught the return of Christ and escalating earthly trials in some form before the end. Its ever-present possibility helped formulate their worldview. Despite degrees of interest in the end times, its reality was rarely doubted.

For some conscientious Bible prophecy advocates, every major news story fulfilled what the Bible foretold. "We have more reason to expect Christ to return in our lifetime on the basis of fulfilled prophecy and current events than any previous generation" is a fairly typical statement one still hears in a sermon or reads in a popular book or website. Every new global calamity, major earthquake, or war becomes further evidence that this is the case. Over the last sixty years, some of the most blatant so-called signs of the end were the creation of Israel in 1948, the retaking of Jerusalem in 1967, the Yom Kippur war in 1973, the famine in Ethiopia in 1985, the First Gulf War in 1990, 9/11 in 2001 driven by Islamic terrorism, the Iraq War starting in 2003, the 2008-09 economic crisis, and various natural disasters. For believers in biblical prophecy, events such as these are part of a wider, unfolding divine plan.

A slew of Bible prophecy books (written by some "internationally recognized Bible prophecy expert"), some of them fictionalized accounts of the end, laid out the probable scenarios and implied, if not directly predicted, that the current generation would see the end. This instilled in readers a sense of urgency.[158] The time was short and the church had to be purified and ready for Christ's return. It must evangelize the lost and labor to reach the unreached peoples of the world on the mission field, as missionary zeal was often portrayed as a way of hastening Christ's return.

The urgency of the approaching end made many churches and organizations all the more resolute in countering secularism, abortion, the gay rights movements, the general moral decline in society, and reaching the lost before it's too late—partly so believers would be found doing the Lord's work when he returns. Appeals encouraged members to volunteer to act or give money to some ministry that fulfilled these goals. The more politicized and conservative messages would add one more urgent admonition to stem the tide: vote Republican.

One reason it was and still is prevalent to interpret contemporary times as the last days is because of the widespread evangelical belief that America has been torn away from its Christian foundation. This fits what the Bible says about there being "a great falling away"[159] before the end.

The end-times theme is a perfect fit for the agenda of the Christian

Right and much of the evangelical worldview. Frank Schaeffer shares his wariness over this pervasive attitude he remembered in the 1980s, when he was still an evangelical activist.

> What began to bother me was that so many of our new "friends" on the religious right seemed to be rooting for one form of apocalypse or another. In the crudest form, this was part of the evangelical fascination with the so-called end times. The worse things got, the sooner Jesus would come back. But there was another component: the worse everything got, the more it proved that America needed saving, by *us*![160]

In my experience, with a few exceptions, a sky-is-falling mentality was widespread, whether it was referring to the end of the world or the escalating immorality in our culture. The more any church hailed the sky-is-falling rallying cry, the more it emphasized the end times and promoted individual readiness through pure living and world evangelism and fostered a negligence in building a better future for this world. After all, if Jesus was coming soon, why bother preserving the environment or advocating for global justice? We best get to the business of saving souls and preparing for the end.

Within a few years of my conversion, I had uncovered the false assertions of an extreme version of this mentality. Still, nagging doubts remained about the whole concept of the last days. Did the Bible and the facts of history really support this notion that we are in the end times? In time, I slowly uncovered answers.

CLEARING THINGS UP

In 1999, with Y2K on the horizon, there was renewed interest and speculation about the second coming of Christ. For me, it led to more research on the subject. I began reading authors who laid out all the existing opposing views and offered an informed argument backed by biblical and historical scholarship. For the first time in my evangelical experience, things were becoming clear about this question. While I was reading another book, *Last Days Madness* by Gary DeMar, I had had another epiphany. One that didn't make me angry, but put me at peace. It uncovered the unhealthy obsession the church has with the end times.

I told several friends about it, but they weren't sure what to make of it. People had a fear of reinterpreting Scripture, calling it "revisionist" thinking. The prevailing view was we may not know when Christ will return—no one should set dates—but we know it will happen. Evangelicals considered precise Date Setters to be revisionists too. Jesus taught us to read the signs of the times, but also said no one knows the day or the hour.

I introduced the idea to my friends that perhaps we have misunderstood the time indicators in the New Testament. The church assumed there were double fulfillments—the near and far future—to some of Jesus' predictions, but scholars, like Gary DeMar, were saying there's no basis for that. That notion contradicts what the church has said throughout history was the typical reply. I reminded my friends that the church has been wrong many times before. *Last Days Madness* laid out a litany of misguided prophecies.

The church, starting in the second century, had sounded countless warnings that their generation was living the last days and Christ's return was imminent. It hadn't started in the 70s with Hal Lindsey. It had been going on for centuries. There is nothing new under the sun. DeMar listed at least sixteen instances before the 19th century in which leaders of the church warned that the return of Christ was at hand. They had one fascinating thing in common. They were all wrong!

The Motanists predicted the end was coming in the second century. A prophet called Novatian gathered a huge following in the third century proclaiming Jesus was coming. So did Donatus in the fourth century. In A.D. 410 the sack of Rome by the Vandals was believed to be a sign of the end. Pope Gregory in the sixth century assured the faithful that Christ's return was close, based on so many

Bible prophecies being fulfilled in his day. On the last day of A.D. 999, masses thronged St. Peter's Basilica weeping and waiting the end of the world. Some Europeans traveled to Palestine to await Christ's return. Similar mistakes in biblical prophecy happened in 1100, 1200, and 1245. Some thought the Inquisition (1209–1244) was the beginning of the end. The Black Death, which killed millions in Europe, was seen as part of the earthly trials prior to the end. Martin Luther believed the end of the world was near in his lifetime. The second coming was predicted to occur in 1533, 1734, after the Lisbon earthquake in 1755, and around the time of the French Revolution.[161] A biblical scholar, named Johann Albrecht Bengel, predicted the end in 1836.[162]

In the last 40 years, a slew of self-proclaimed Bible prophecy experts came out with predictions or probabilities on when the end would occur, especially after the creation of the modern state of Israel in 1948—a supposed prophetic milestone. Jews returning to Israel supposedly "proved" the return of Christ was near. As we learned, Hal Lindsey popularized the view that the end would occur near 1988, forty years or one generation after the birth of Israel. Edgar Whisenant wrote a book called *88 Reasons Why the Rapture Will Be in 1988*. Apparently a number of readers thought the reasons were so sound they quit their jobs.[163] Maybe Whisenant should have quit writing end-times books and promoting absurd conjecture.

Surprisingly, usually even-keeled Billy Graham got on the band-wagon and suggested that Armageddon was near in his 1992 book, *Storm Warning*. The book was released again in 2010 and used by Billy's son, Franklin, to promote end times scenarios. David Koresh and the Branch Davidians thought the end was at hand and that the FBI siege of their property in Waco, Texas, in 1993, was fulfilling their apocalyptic theory. Other cults formed over the beliefs of the return of Christ and the urgency to reach the lost. The Children of God's founder, David Berg, claimed his group was the one true remnant of believers in the last days before Christ's return. At one point, he prophesied that Jesus would return in 1993. In light of this urgency, he eventually led his members to recruit the lost into the fold by offering their sexual services! Several biblical prophecy "experts" pointed toward the year A.D. 2000 as a probable termination date for the end of days. Finally, there's the recent incident that happened years after I brought this up with friends in 1999. Harold Camping, an obscure pastor with a radio ministry, made headlines when he predicted the Rapture would occur on May 21, 2011. Misreading the signs of the times in the Bible is apparently an occupational hazard for Christian leaders—both orthodox and cultish.

Back when I had conversations with several friends on these things, I was just starting to investigate this issue in more detail. Within a few years I would come to further conclusions I never dreamed were possible.

Suddenly, my recollections were interrupted when I heard Dan shout at the overhead screen.

THE RETURN OF THE KING IN A PUB

I looked up and registered the status of the game. Eight minutes into the fourth quarter the Celtics were squandering their lead. "Man, what happened?" I asked Dan.

"Kobe Bryant is on a roll and Ray Allen is missing from the outside."

"This doesn't look good," I said. "We need someone to step up and take control of this game!"

"Yeah, like Paul Pierce," Dan said. "He was hot earlier and could be the answer if he gets in a groove." Dan wasn't from Boston but rooted for the Celtics because Pierce was from his alma mater, University of Kansas. When Bryant was fouled and went to the line, I glanced at Gina.

"You know, Mike," she said. "You're really giving me a lot to think about. One of issues I struggle with is this notion that we are in the last days. Has your research uncovered anything about that?"

Gina's interest in this subject broke my focus on the game. "I was about to bring that up," I said. "Yes, it has. I've got a whole chapter on it."

"I've read about the problems with the Rapture before," she said. "But what about this stuff about Jesus coming again at the end of the world? Isn't that pretty clear in Scripture?"

By now my interest in this part of the game had dissolved. I'd catch the very end, I told myself. As Dan continued to stare at the overhead screen, I began to share some of my findings with Gina. I told her about theologians N. T. Wright and Gary DeMar. According to them, the apocalyptic language of the Bible has been grossly misunderstood throughout church history. In our modern context it has been butchered to the point of seducing millions of evangelical Christians with the popular craze of last days theology. I knew Gina was familiar with the passages that supposedly talk about the end times, most notably the famous description of Jesus' predictions (after he announced the Temple would one day be destroyed) in what is called the Olivet Discourse.[164]

"There are some major misreadings of these passages," I told Gina. "Let me see if I can remember them." I gulped my lemon water, gathered my thoughts, and began explaining some major points.

Not the End of the World

"First, when the disciples or Jesus say 'the end of the age,'" I explained, "they do not mean the end of our space-time world. *End of the age* refers to the end of the era of the Temple system of worship. Oh, and the mention of the 'age to come' is referring to the new age of the Messiah. The Greek word for age, *aion*, is sometimes mistranslated 'world.' If the author wanted to convey the concept of 'world,' he would have used the Greek *kosmos*.[165] Still, even when it's accurately rendered as 'age,' most of us misinterpret it as the end of the world."

"That's so true," Gina said. "Everyone I hear teach on that says it's the end of the world as we know it."

"But careful study reveals that it's not. This is unconscious abuse of the Greek text."

"Hmm... I'll have to think about that," Gina concluded.

Jesus Talks to His Contemporaries

"If you pay attention when you read these passages about the end," I told Gina, "you'll notice how Jesus addresses his disciples and says things like, 'Watch out that no one deceives *you*,' or 'Then *you* will be handed over to be persecuted...' His explanations about the end are directed to his contemporaries."

"Okay, I see that," Gina responded. "I remember once he said, 'So *you* also must be ready...' And didn't he say something like that at his trial?"

"Yes, before the Sanhedrin, he said, '...*you* will see the Son of Man sitting at the right hand of the Mighty One and coming on the clouds of heaven.' You see, Jesus is clearly not referring to some future audience. People read into these verses a futuristic scenario."

"I never noticed that, but it's clear, when you explain it," Gina agreed. "We're so used to reading the Bible like it's addressing us today—we forget that."

The Return of Christ is Not a Worldwide Event

"This is a big one," I said. "In most Bible translations, when Jesus refers to the coming of the Son of Man—I think you know that's an Old Testament term for Messiah—he says 'all the nations of the earth will mourn' and will see him coming on the clouds. DeMar reveals how the phrase 'nations of the earth,' is better translated 'tribes of the land.' Most Bible translations do not capture the true meaning of the Greek. Their choice of 'earth' shows their bias."[166]

Gina leaned forward. "Really? I always figured translation work was straightforward. I never pictured translators being biased."

"You'd be surprised."

"So you're saying it only speaks of a smaller region that will see Jesus coming?" Gina suggested.

"Yes. In the context, the phrase 'tribes of the land' makes sense. As I just said, Jesus addressed his hearers in his presence, like when he said in Luke's version 'When *you* see Jerusalem surrounded by armies.' He wasn't giving a message to the whole world, but to the peoples of the region, that their city and Temple would be razed, which would produce great mourning. You see, the context of the disciple's original question, 'what will be the sign of your coming and the end of the age?' is Jesus' prediction that the Temple was to be destroyed. That's not a worldwide event."

The Gospel Preached in the Region, Not the Whole World

We had talked about this earlier. Since I had been a missionary, this point was of particular interest to me, and I wanted to reinforce it.

"Most Bible translations render that famous verse in Matthew[167] as 'This gospel of the kingdom will be preached in the whole world as a testimony to all nations, and then the end will come.'"

"Yeah, that's the verse we hear in churches that says the gospel must reach all the ethnic groups of the world before Jesus returns," Gina said.

"And many teachers claim it means we can actually hasten the return of Christ by participating in missions to 'unreached' peoples," I added.

"Oh, yeah, I hear that a lot at Christ Memorial," Gina said, referring to the church she and Dan were currently attending.

"This view is based on a faulty translation," I told Gina. "Again, the Greek word *oikoumene* is routinely mistranslated as 'world,' but should be rendered *inhabited earth* or *land*. It's the same Greek word used in Luke when referring to the census that Augustus ordered at the time of the birth of Christ. Obviously, that wasn't a global census. It was restricted to the *Roman* world. So, Jesus' prediction was correct. The gospel message did reach the extremes of the

Roman Empire before A.D. 70, and there's historical evidence for it.[168] What's more, Paul states this in Colossians[168] when he said the gospel had already been proclaimed to 'every creature under heaven.' He didn't mean throughout the whole world, but the Roman world."

"Wait a minute," Gina said. "Are you implying the end occurred in 70 AD?"

"Yes, I'm getting to that."

"You're blowing me away," Gina responded. She touched Dan's arm. "Are you listening to this?" she asked him. Dan turned his attention back to us.

"Yes, I've got one ear on it. Remember, I read his manuscript and picked his brain before. Why don't you tell her about when Jesus spoke of the end coming within one generation?"

"Right, that's key," I said.

Everything Happens Within One Generation

"Okay, in Matthew 24, at the end of describing the long list of cataclysmic events—you know, wars, earthquakes, signs in the heavens, presence of false Messiahs, his return—not to mention the destruction of the Temple—Jesus said, 'Truly I say to you, this generation will not pass away until all these things take place.' To a first-time reader who has no preconceived ideas on eschatology, it would be plain that Jesus means the people with whom he was speaking would live to see and experience the events he just described."

"I can see that," Gina said. "But..."

"So, you see, he was saying the generation alive who heard his words would not die out before these 'end-times' events took place. Sound scholarship reinforces this meaning."

"Yeah, but I've heard some teachers say that word doesn't mean 'generation.'"

"I know, I know. But really, that's twisting the term to mean something entirely different. Some claim it should be translated 'race,' meaning the Jewish race would not pass away until these things occur."

"Right, that's what I've heard."

"But that's a gross error. It's a faulty *dispensational* interpretation that has had so much power and influence it has resulted in being placed as a footnote in major translations. In the New Testament, the word translated 'generation' is never used in any other way but to mean the contemporaries living in that day. In his book, Gary DeMar forcefully made this point, and others have too. This is another good example of selective literalism. In this case, conservatives don't accept the plain meaning of the English or Greek text."

I was suddenly reminded of Bertrand Russell, the renowned atheist. I had read his book *Why I am Not a Christian* as a new believer and concluded he was biased against Christianity due to the hypocrisy he saw in the church. *He should reject the church but not Christ,* I had thought. But now I realized he was right about one thing. His historical examination of the New Testament revealed the authors and Jesus himself expected the end of the age and the second coming of Christ to occur within the timeframe of their generation. Others agreed. "Jesus never indicates that he has a distant coming in mind. There is nothing in the Olivet Discourse that would give the reader the impression that a distant event is in view."[170] This was one of the stumbling blocks that convinced Russell the Bible was not trustworthy. How could Christ be a wise man when he thought his second coming would occur before the death of his followers? If he was wrong about this, how can we trust anything he said?

I didn't mention Russell's doubts, but I briefly made this point to Gina, and also Dan, who was now listening. "You see, the New Testament writers portray the early church as thinking the end was near, in their lifetime."

"But the end didn't happen in their lifetime," Dan interjected. "Isn't that a prophetic problem?"

"Sure, it causes a dilemma for the church," I said. "If Jesus, Paul, and the book of Revelation are taken at face value as far as time indicators are concerned, then Jesus would have returned, and the end would have come within a generation of the time he gave the Olivet

Discourse. Therefore, since as you said, that did not happen—at least according to traditional eschatology—it begs the question: How can the Bible and the Jesus portrayed in it be trustworthy? This is the challenge of most liberal scholars." I was also thinking of Russell. It was the same point he had made. "In order to circumvent that claim, the traditional view must show that the biblical events describing the end are referring to a time in the distant future and that they do not occur shortly or within a generation. They must insist that the time indicators surrounding last-days prophecies are not to be taken literally."

"So you're saying," Dan said, "the literalists can't take part of the Bible literally, or it will jeopardize the reliability of the Bible!"

"You got it!" I said.

"So how can they justify that?" Gina asked.

"Several ways," I said. "First is the claim that the word 'generation' means 'race,' as you've heard. Second, they claim that the time indicators are from God's perspective of time, not man's, so therefore they refer to distant events. Conservative commentators admit that some predictions Jesus made were fulfilled around the time of the destruction of Jerusalem. But they also claim that other forecasts he made refer to the last days that would occur in the distant future."

"Yes," Dan said. "Isn't this the dual prophetic time-period theory?"

"Right," I answered. "The NIV Study Bible states it in footnotes. They flatly claim Jesus was talking about both events: the first century fall of Jerusalem and Jesus' return at the end of the world.[171] Careful study contradicts this popular view."

More Predictions Jesus Made

Right then Dan piped in. "Actually, I can remember other places where Jesus equated his return with the first century. Didn't he say to the disciples, something like, 'Some who are standing here will not taste death before they see the Son of Man coming in his kingdom?'"

"Yes, that's right," I agreed.

"And I think it was to the twelve apostles he said, '*You* will not finish going through the cities of Israel before the Son of Man comes.'"

"This is what I mean!" I exclaimed. "His coming again was always explained as soon-to-occur."

"I don't get it," Gina said. "Jesus didn't return in the first century. If what you're saying is true, then the Bible is wrong!"

That's what Bertrand Russell concluded, I thought to myself.

"There is an explanation, Gina." I said. "Jesus' coming did occur, but in a way we don't recognize." I told her I'd explain after a few more points that will make it clearer.

History Confirms: It All Happened by 70 A.D.

"Look, we assume Jesus didn't return and his apocalyptic predictions haven't yet occurred—with the exception of the destruction of the Temple—because we are ignorant of history," I said.

"What do you mean?" Gina asked.

"Well, secular historians, such as Josephus, Eusebius, and Tacitus, tell us the events that Jesus described did in fact occur! They happened in the years prior to and surrounding the siege and destruction of Jerusalem by the Romans."

Should I tell them about the details of first century history? I asked myself. *I've already been too academic. And, we are in a bar after all. Ah, what the hell. I've already played the historian for Dan.* I then explained some first century events as best as I could remember. During that period, false Messiahs appeared, Christians were persecuted under Nero, earthquakes were prevalent, famines occurred, comets were sighted (Haley's Comet appeared in 66 AD), civil wars were fought, the Roman army took siege of Jerusalem, and the city, Temple, and Jewish way of religious life were destroyed. A million Jews died at the at the hands of the Roman legions.

I remembered quotes from historians and paraphrased them for Gina and Dan. In the *Anals of Imperior Rome*, Tacitus explained conditions in 51 A.D. He said there were many omens like earthquakes, a shortage of corn that led to famine, and insurrections and wars. Then there was Josephus. In *The War of the Jews*, he reported a famine associated with the Roman siege of Jerusalem and a star, which resembled a sword, which stood over the city.

"I've never heard those details," Dan said after I finished my brief history lesson. "I mean about the famines, earthquakes, and wars, in the first century—and a heavenly sign."

"I never did either, until I did my own study. We don't hear this because the church doesn't study that history—or conveniently ignores it. It contradicts their eschatology. Now remember, the Temple's destruction was the context of the question the disciples asked Jesus: When will this happen and what will be the signs of your coming? Historical evidence makes it clear. It all happened by 70 AD. Not just the Temple's destruction, but also the tribulation period."

"What books did you get this from?" Gina asked. "I gotta check this out."

"Then you really must read Gary DeMar's *Last Days Madness*. He gives the details of a ton of documented happenings.[172] Even though he's a conservative, he argues for it because the evidence is so compelling. Other conservative scholars agree, like R.C. Sproul.[173]"

"Who's he?" Dan asked.

"He wrote *The Last Days According to Jesus*—another one you should read." I went on to another point.

The Book of Revelation Written Before 70 A.D.

"You two will be interested in my new position on Revelation. Most conservative scholars believe Revelation was written in the 90s A.D., while many liberal scholars say it was written before 70 A.D. If the late date is accurate, then its prophecies are still in the future and are not regarding the destruction of Jerusalem, for that would have already occurred."

"So a late date would be evidence for the traditional end times view," Dan said.

"Right. But if the pre-70 A.D. date is accurate, then there is a strong case that it describes events that occurred prior to and during the fall of Jerusalem. This is the conclusion I came to when I read conservative scholar Kenneth Gentry's book, *Before Jerusalem Fell*. It makes a solid case that Revelation was written around the early to mid 60s. For me, this solved a long-standing puzzle. The confusing book of Revelation only makes sense if it allegorically portrays the tribulation and cataclysmic events that occurred in the first century 60 to 70 A.D."

"I have never even heard of this possibility," Gina said.

"I'm not surprised. Gentry's case, which has since been accepted by a minority of conservative scholars as well, is not generally accepted by evangelicals. It exposes the fallacy of trying to give a late date for Revelation in order to explain away the apparent contradiction that Jesus didn't return quickly, which the early church thought he would."

"Tell me more about that," Gina said. "About how the early church thought he would come back soon."

Early Church Expected a Timely Return of Christ

"Well, that's another thing we overlook. We were talking about this before. While claiming that Revelation is talking about events in the far future, such as in our lifetime, we evangelicals conveniently overlook all the times the book directly states that what it describes will soon take place."

"Yes, I see what you mean," said Dan. "The New Testament never says it will happen in the distant future."

"Right," I continued. "In fact, Revelation states at least eleven times that the events described in it would occur shortly and that Jesus was coming quickly. I might have said this earlier, but the first verse in Revelation says it's something that 'must soon take place.' A couple verses later it says, 'the time is near.' Later it says an hour of testing is coming and is about to come upon the whole land—not the whole world, but the Greek, *oikoumenes,* which means *land.* Finally, at the end of the book, Jesus says, 'I am coming quickly.'"

"That's amazing," Gina said. "Like I said before, it's like we're programmed to overlook those statements. But I always wondered why the author said them."

"Because that's what he meant." I didn't mention it, but I remembered what one scholar lamented in the 19th century and how true it is today: "Yet in the face of these express and oft-repeated declarations, most interpreters have felt at liberty to ignore the limitations of time altogether, and to roam at will over ages and centuries..."[174]

"And it's not just Revelation. The other New Testament books are the same. Peter said in I Peter, 'the end of all things is near,' and that Jesus appeared 'in these last times.' The writer of Hebrews said the current time is the 'last days' and exhorted his audience 'as you see the day drawing near.'

"Now that you're bringing them up, I'm starting to remember some," Dan said. "Doesn't I John say that in his day it was 'the last hour?' And in Acts, it quotes the Old Testament Joel as predicting 'the last days' in the disciples' day?"

"Right. And Paul says 'The Lord is near,' in Philippians. And James says something like 'the coming of the Lord is at hand.'"

"You know, it's remarkable," Dan said. "If you put yourself in the shoes of the original audience, it's clear they are speaking about the first century."

Old Testament Cosmic Imagery

"Okay, Gina. This is where I answer your question. Jesus taught with the Old Testament history and figurative literary style in mind. Sound study would insist we read his words in this way. For instance, Old Testament prophets often associated clouds with God's glory and his intervening in the affairs of humankind. When Isaiah said 'the Lord rides on a swift cloud and is coming to Egypt'[175] and somewhere else it says 'God makes the clouds his chariot,'[176] the Jews knew the prophets didn't mean it literally. I think it is in Ezekiel where it says, the 'day of the Lord' is 'a day of clouds.'[177]"

"Yeah, I can see how those are obviously figurative," Gina said.

"Right. So the question is, why don't we take them figuratively in the New Testament?"

"Good question," Dan piped in.

"Okay, there's more," I said. "When Daniel says 'there before me was one like a son of man coming on the clouds of heaven,' he then states this son of man approached God and came into his presence. His coming was up to God, not down to earth!"

"Isn't that the passage that Jesus refers to when he said he would be seen on the clouds?" Dan asked.

"Yes, that's where he says '...you will see the Son of Man sitting at the right hand of the Mighty One and coming on the clouds of heaven.'[178] First, this isn't physically literal, and secondly, it's Jesus coming up to the throne of God, not down to earth!"

"Wait a minute," Gina interrupted. "It clearly says Jesus *coming* in those passages, not going."

"Actually, *coming* is not a good translation. The Greek word means *going* as well, depending on the context.[179] N.T. Wright argues the *coming* is an upward, not a downward, movement, and his *coming* is not to earth but into God's presence."[180]

"This is a whole other way of thinking about this," Gina said.

"Yes, and Jesus' words confirm it," I explained. "He said once, 'At that time the *sign* of the Son of Man will appear in the sky...' It wasn't Jesus who would appear to them on the way to earth but the 'sign of the Son of Man' that would appear. In other words, a sign that would prove Jesus is in the presence of God, sitting at the Father's right hand. DeMar also gives a rationale for this that holds up."[181]

"I don't know what to say," Gina said. "This is so contrary to what I've been taught."

"I know," I said. "It floored me when I saw it for the first time." I gave Gina another example. It was the way the Old Testament described the heavens when a prophet was predicting a change to a socio-political system. In Isaiah 13 there is a judgment against Babylon and the prophet warns "a day of the Lord is coming" when "the stars of heaven... will not flash their light; the sun will be dark... and the moon will not shed its light" (13:9-10). This is not literal but a way of describing the downfall of a nation. Jesus quotes part of this passage when describing his coming in the Olivet Discourse. His disciples would have recognized the imagery and understand that his coming is associated with Israel's coming under a judgment similar to that of Babylon. Jesus' coming wasn't a return the way we think of it, but a vindication.[182] A *coming* in a first century judgment. I made one final point as Gina's jaw kept dropping further and further. I thought it might touch the floor. "It's fascinating to note when Jesus said that the coming of the son of man would be like the days of Noah, he referred to the people who were not saved from the flood. They knew nothing of what would happen 'until the flood came and took them away.' In this parallel story, it wasn't the saved who were taken away but the unsaved. The righteous ones— Noah and his family—were the ones who were left behind, not the unrighteous!"

"Aha!" Dan exclaimed. "So it's the good guys who are left behind after all."

"Wait, wait," Gina said. "Back up. Let me get this straight. You're saying Jesus already returned but not the way we've been taught."

"Well, yes, Gina. That's what I've been saying. Haven't you been listening?"

"Well, yeah," Gina said, "but I guess it's hard to swallow given what I've been taught."

"I know exactly what you mean," I said. "But the evidence says Jesus came back *figuratively* in judgment on the corrupt Jewish religionists—not all Jews, but those who rejected him and his love-over-law ethic. He destroyed the Temple and its socio-political system of sacrifices, and, well, was ushered into God's presence to receive his reign, that is, his kingdom. A reign, remember, that is centered on love. This also clears up liberals' objections. Christ did what he had predicted before the death of his followers."

"Okay," Gina responded. "What about the resurrection? When does that occur?" Gina had asked a good question. Frankly, I wasn't sure how to answer it.

HERE COME THE PRETERISTS

"Okay, before I get to that, there's one last thing I have to explain. When I read that R.C. Sproul book, I learned a view of eschatology I had never heard before. It's called *preterism*. Preterists believe that the return of Jesus and judgment already occurred in 70 A.D.—in the manner I just laid out. Then Jesus replaced the old system with the good news of God's reign of love for everyone—Jews and Gentiles. The end of the age was the end of the Jewish sacrificial system of worship."

"You know, this is starting to make sense to me," Dan said. "It makes clear a lot of what Jesus taught."

"Right," I agreed. "The prevailing evangelical view of the last days is nonsensical. I mean, why would Jesus talk about a future occurrence within forty years in one sentence, and without explaining the difference, talk about another occurrence thousands of years in the future in the next sentence?"

"Good question," said Gina. "Like you said, he did make it clear that the events he spoke of would happen within a generation. But still, the resurrection..."

"Yes, Gina—I'm coming to that. The preterist view solves the dilemma over how to explain the return of Christ. Jesus plainly spoke of events that would all happen before the contemporary generation died off."

If I had his book with me open to the right page, I would have read this quote by Sproul: "The preterist is a sentinel standing guard against the frivolous and superficial attempts to downplay or explain away the force of [time-frame] references."[183]

"But there are two types of preterists—*partial* and *full*. Partial *preterists* believe that there are still some New Testament prophecies that haven't taken place, like the resurrection and last judgment. A *full preterist* sees all biblical prophecies as having already been fulfilled by 70 A.D. An increasing number of evangelical scholars in our day, such as N. T. Wright, R. C. Sproul, and Kenneth Gentry, are *partial preterists*. In a sense, they believe in two second comings, or returns, of Jesus. Once in 70 A.D. to judge the Jewish religionists and again a second time at the end of history at the resurrection and final judgment."

"Two second comings?" Dan asked. "That does seem weird. Where does the Bible say that?"

"That's the right question, Dan. The answer is, it doesn't. And that's why, to me, the position of *partial preterists* is problematic. There was a day of judgment when Jesus came in A.D. 70, but the New Testament gives no direct reference to a second day of judgment at the end of the world to occur centuries later. None of the authors make it clear that Jesus returns twice and that the general resurrection and ultimate judgment is a completely different event than what Jesus described in Matthew 25.

"In other words, the New Testament does not differentiate clearly between the end of the age and the end of human history, or between the judgment on the Temple system in 70 A.D. and the ultimate judgment of humankind. The partial preterist appears to arrive at his or her position, not because the Scripture explicitly teaches two returns or two judgments, but because there is no other explanation given his or her theological grid."

"I'm still waiting for your explanation of the resurrection," Gina interjected.

"Well, Gina, I'm not entirely sure. It appears to be a mystery. But the point is that *full preterism*—you know, that all biblical prophecy has already been fulfilled—makes the most sense. With it, there is no need to explain multiple comings and judgments, because there is only one to explain; time periods are easily understood in plain language, and the Old Testament figurative language explains the descriptions of clouds and signs in the heavens. As for the later resurrection of the dead, it would have to be explained as a spiritual event, much like what we propose happens to people upon death. But if that is where the evidence leads, so be it."

"I don't know about that," Gina said. "I'd like to look into this more. But, I have to admit, you have uncovered problems with the traditional view."

"Look, I'm not saying the *full preterist* position clears up everything, just that it appears the least problematic and should be considered a perfectly legitimate view. I prefer it, but I'm not entirely satisfied with the way the resurrection must be handled as a result."

"You know," Dan said. "N.T. Wright has a good book that might shed light on this."

"Do you mean *Surprised by Hope*?" I asked.

"That's the one."

"I admit, that book gives me reason to rethink full preterism, the way he makes a case for bodily resurrection from New Testament teaching. But the problems with partial preterism are too great in my mind."

I sensed Gina was still processing this new way of looking at the supposed end times, and for a moment she was quiet. She then posed a question that surprised me.

"So, how do these new perspectives impact how we follow Christ?" It was an important question.

"Well, the most obvious thing is we should expose people who twist the Scriptures to promote some pet 'last-days' theology," I said. "You know, how books and ministries push sensationalistic end-of-the-world scenarios that seduce and manipulate people to convert, donate money, or support political views and conservative agendas. Then I think we can focus on making the world a better place, rather than obsess over and fear the end of the world. The dire global warnings of the New Testament belong in the first century. Its core message is not an inevitable doom-and-gloom ending but a hopeful, new beginning. What we do to improve the world today will remain."

"I like that," Gina said. "We can be more positive about caring for the environment and building a brighter future for everyone."

"Yes," agreed Dan. "And I think both of these preterist views would support that."

"Right, but for the church, looking at the world with more hopeful eyes—it's not about to end, I mean—is easier said than done. An end-times belief is entrenched in the evangelical mind."

"You're right about that," said Dan.

"Most evangelicals would consider the *partial preterist* view as suspect and the *full preterist* view as heretical," I said. "The notion that practically all biblical prophecies—and possibly all—have already been fulfilled in the past is largely perceived as revisionist thinking."

"Ain't it the truth," said Dan. "That way of looking at it is the realm of organized religion."

"Right," I responded. "Draw boxes, in this case beliefs about biblical prophecy and the return of Christ, and make sure people's beliefs fit inside the lines."

"Yes," Dan agreed. "There's little freedom to think outside the box, even if that thinking actually fits better with what the original biblical writers meant, like you've been explaining."

Finally, our long conversation on this topic wound down. Dan mentioned it was time for another round. All this talk reminded me where my journey had taken me. Around the year 2000, I had overcome another hurdle in my quest for a reasoned faith. Yet there were still more religious barriers to reason to breech. In my next adventure, I learned how the problem of religion had infected an issue even more controversial than the end times: sexuality.

Gina has a hard enough time with this last days stuff, I thought. *How would she or Dan or Steve respond to some of my other views?* Right then Steve walked into the pub. *Yes, Steve! How would he handle my new views on sexuality? Do I dare bring them up?* I tried to mentally organize my evolution on this topic in case Dan brought up the remaining chapters of my book with Steve. With Steve, I'd need to have all my ducks in a row. But were we really ready for something a tad uncomfortable? A candid discussion about religion and sex? I wasn't sure I was ready to talk about it.

CONFESSION #9

THE SEX GOD

*"Religious leaders have labored long
in the development of their additions
to what the Bible says about sex."*

– *Philo Thelos*

Hot, pink, enticing, and intoxicating. As a young teen, sexual stirrings were inside my body as raging hormones surged through my veins. Suddenly the sight of a shapely young woman was inexplicably pleasurable. Whether I eyed a girl at school or the image of soft skin, alluring curves, striking poses, and magnetic eyes leapt off the pages of *Playboy* magazine, it was the same feeling. I was obsessed with sex. I wasn't the only one. My friends felt the same way.

We shared our magazine collections under our beds and read the sex scenes from *The Godfather* with wide-eyed fascination. In ninth grade, Matt Nolan and I shared fantasies about getting laid by gorgeous bikini-clad women from the latest James Bond movie, or at least making out with Lisa Borders from history class. The urges were more than raw physical desire. We were enamored by being in the presence of girls we liked and enjoyed getting to know them. Eventually in high school, for some of us more than others, those fantasies came true. Sure, maybe the women weren't exactly Halle Berry types, and the *coming true* part was sometimes exaggerated.

Okay, mostly exaggerated. But sex was on our minds, and it all seemed so normal.

In another context, I was hearing other impressions in evangelical churches and youth groups about human sexuality that conflicted with these natural tendencies. These voices were suspicious, saying sex was dangerous and dirty unless strictly tamed and kept under the umbrella of marriage. Masturbation, pornography, heavy petting, and pre-marital sex were painted as immoral, unnatural, or simply prohibited.

By the time I was 22 and a new "born-again" believer, I really wanted to do the right thing in my sex life. I began to consider these voices. In high school and most of college, prior to "accepting Christ," I had been fairly promiscuous. I confess I was largely selfish in my sexual pursuits. Now with a more loving spirit in my heart, I wanted to change. As with other issues, my thinking was that there were only two ways to approach sex. Either pursue "free love" like the "world"—meaning anyone outside the church, particularly the hippie culture and Hollywood—or abstain until marriage and live a "pure" life. It never occurred to me that a middle way was possible; that one could view masturbation as a gift from God to relieve sexual pressure; that there was an ethical way to be sex-positive; an unselfish way that would treat women respectfully, not as I had treated Kathy or other girlfriends—that one could be free to choose sex when ready, in a responsible and loving way, and not necessarily wait until marriage.

I listened to what the evangelical church said. Teachers insisted that God's way is abstinence until marriage and controlling sexual urges through prayer and small group accountability. Most condemned masturbation. All warned against pornography and pre-marital sex. I talked to God about it. *Lord, I need your help, otherwise, I'll think about sex all day long.* I think He helped me. I still thought about sex all day long. I guess I just felt better because I was at least being honest with God.

When I decided to read the Bible for the first time cover to cover,

I was in for a shock. I discovered many things I was hearing in church about sex didn't line up with what the Bible said. In some ways the Bible was incredibly strict; in other ways it was extraordinarily permissive.

THE BIBLE AND SEX

Delving into the Bible, I found a fascinating array of mixed messages: implicit and explicit positive and negative references, long lists of sexual taboos and punishments, and seemingly unbridled sexual exploits.

In the Holiness Code—what scholars call the list of laws in Leviticus—the God of Israel mandates specific laws against men having sex with women in their extended family, spelling out every conceivable sexual liaison. The law of Moses condemns a man who has sex with another man's wife, a woman having sex with anyone other than her husband, and a man having sex with another man ("Don't lie with a man as one lies with a woman"). Bestiality, rape, and a man having sex with any woman during the "uncleanness" of her monthly period are condemned. There is an obvious double standard. The prohibitions for a man implied he might have sex with women outside of marriage. It wasn't the same for women. Also, women are expected to be virgins at marriage with no such insistence for men.

The punishments for disobeying are steep. The death penalty is proscribed for many sexual and some non-sexual sins, even for cursing one's father or mother. In other cases, the penalty is receiving the curse of being childless or being "cut off from your people," as is the case for couples that have sex during menstruation.

Damn! I thought. *The God of Israel was serious about enforcing sexual prohibitions.*

Then I would turn the page and see it was fine for a man, even if married, to sleep with a woman who is a slave girl[184] as long as she belonged to him. It was also perfectly acceptable for men to have more than one wife and have sex with concubines, those women of a lower social status who for various reasons weren't allowed to marry certain men. They were almost like wives, having voluntary ongoing relationships with men, often for reasons of economic security, and even with some marital rights.

Incredible. Despite strict enforcements, these men have remarkable freedom, I mused.

Since childlessness was such a devastating curse, it was also not uncommon for legitimate wives to allow their husbands to sleep with their maidservants to solve the problem of their own barrenness. Thus, I read about Sarah giving Hagar to Abraham, Leah giving Zilpah to Jacob, and Rachel (Jacob's second wife and sister of Leah) also giving her maid Bilhah to Jacob. In fact, the whole nation of Israel (Jacob was also known as *Israel*) was derived from the twelve sons of Jacob, who became the twelve tribes of Israel, and were children of a polygamous and non-monogamous marriage! Not once did God condemn any of these relationships with wives, concubines, maidservants, and slave women, as long as they fit the limitations of the Holiness Code. It was obvious these biblical characters were operating within a vastly different worldview than ours.

Before long I became intimately familiar with a long list of bigamists, many of them heroes of the Judeo-Christian faith. People like Lamech, Esau, Abraham, Jacob, Gideon, Elkanah, David, Solomon, Ahab, Jehoiachin, Hezron, Asher, Izrahiah, Rehoboam, Abijah, and many others. They all had multiple wives and usually a few concubines. Solomon topped them all with 700 wives and 300 concubines. The list of women who apparently had no objections to their polygamous or matrimonial-like relationships, and the wives who occasionally initiated new relationships for their husbands, were equally impressive. Sarah, Hagar, Rachel, Zilpah, Bilhah, Tamar, Michael, Bathsheba, and many others. Incredible. My mind couldn't grasp it. Shirley Dobson or Ruth Graham would never do such a thing.

Aside from God's warning Israelite kings to beware of acquiring great numbers of horses, wives, and riches (Solomon's downfall wasn't polygamy but excessive polygamy, particularly marrying pagan women who turned his heart against God), there is not one word of correction against the polygamy and concubinage of these men and women, nor a word about monogamy being strictly endorsed.[185] The law found in Deuteronomy 25:5-10 commands a man to marry his brother's wife if his brother dies childless,[186] even if he is already married. Moreover, God has specific provisions for men with two wives.[187] He spells out rules for treating a firstborn fairly in the case when a man loves one wife over another. I realized when David committed adultery with Bathsheba, if Bathsheba had not been married to Uriah, the already-married David would not have been accused of adultery. Furthermore, through Nathan the prophet, God forgives David and ignores the death penalty stipulated in Leviticus for such an act. God then tells David He was the one who gave him his many wives, and if they weren't enough, he would have given him more![188]

About smack dab in the middle of the Bible after the Torah, the history of Israel, the Psalms, and wisdom literature, came the erotic: the Song of Solomon. Its words are sensual and graphic. Suddenly, I was imagining a tan and beautiful woman with nothing on but sandals. She's kissing an unclothed sleek young man as the imagery of flowers, fruit, and fragrances fill my senses. They both step back and describe each other's physique.

How beautiful your sandaled feet...Your graceful legs are like jewels...Your navel is a rounded goblet that never lacks blended wine. Your waist is a mound of wheat encircled by lilies. Your breasts are like two fawns, twins of a gazelle...How beautiful you are and how pleasing, O love with your delights! Your stature is like that of the palm and your breasts like clusters of fruit. I said, "I will climb the palm tree and take hold of its fruit."[189]

My lover is radiant and ruddy...His eyes are like doves by the

water streams...mounted like jewels. His lips are like lilies drip-
ping with myrrh. His arms are rods of gold...His body is like
polished ivory...His legs are pillars of marble...His mouth like
sweetness itself; he is altogether lovely. This is my lover, this my
friend...[190]

They describe each other's delights and invite each other to
partake.

Your lips drop sweetness as the honeycomb...milk and honey
are under your tongue...You are a garden locked up...a spring
enclosed...Your plants are an orchard of pomegranates with
choice fruits.

Blow on my garden that its fragrance may spread abroad. Let
my lover come into his garden and taste its choice fruits.[191]

Then friends encourage them to enjoy their lovemaking.

Eat, O friends, and drink; drink your fill, O lovers.[192]

I was enthralled. It read as if they are illicit lovers, stealing away
time together; the man knocks at her door in the middle of the night
and the woman yearns to openly embrace him in public. For centuries the obvious acceptance of sex and sensuality in the book was
explained away as allegorical by the church. Today, the argument is
whether the relationship described is purely marital or not and what
sexual acts all the poetic language describes.

There were other references to sex. For instance, in the Book of
Esther, the "lovely and beautiful" Jewish woman Esther was one of
the many virgins that King Xerxes slept with to determine whom
he wanted to replace Queen Vashti. I was struck how matter of fact
the text put it. When the king summoned a virgin candidate, she
would go to be with him in the evening and return to the harem in
the morning. He wasn't just giving each one a quick viewing; he was
obviously having sex with each one. The girl who pleased the king the
most would become queen. Esther had no qualms about performing
this task. Why didn't she refuse and say that participating in this

promiscuity was against her religion? That's what would be expected of a young Christian woman today. But Esther was voluntarily engaging in pre-marital sex.

In another bizarre story, Judah had sex with Tamar, thinking her a prostitute.[193] She was actually his daughter-in-law disguised as a prostitute and trying to trick him into impregnating her. Her husband had died, and Judah initially told his son Onan to impregnate her to produce offspring for his dead brother (later this became known as the Levirate law in Deuteronomy 25:5-10). Judah's son Onan purposely practiced *coitus interruptus* with Tamar, spilling his seed on the ground. Later God struck him down for refusing to carry on his brother's line (this story is used by some to condemn masturbation).

Judah refused to provide another of his sons to marry Tamar, so she devised the scheme to get pregnant by Judah himself. Judah was not rebuked for visiting who he thought was a prostitute. Tamar was excused from acting like a prostitute under the circumstances and even praised by Judah, after she confronted him, who said, "She is more righteous than I." It appeared that commercial prostitution was allowed for men and only restricted to women who were still under the "ownership" of a Jewish family.

In another story, Samson had been set apart by God from birth as one who would deliver Israel from the Philistines. God blessed him and on several occasions "the spirit of the Lord came on him with power." Once he visited a prostitute in Gaza. There was no censure from God.[194] In fact, the morning after spending a night with her, he was delivered from an angry mob of Israel's enemies who wanted to kill him.

The book of Hebrews in the New Testament honors "Rahab the prostitute" for helping the Israelite spies. Yet there is never a word about her leaving her profession. It was striking to me that she wasn't referred to as a "former prostitute." I thought, *Funny. What church would honor a convert by calling her a title that represented her former sinful lifestyle? Would a pastor stand up and say, "Folks, we really appreciate drug addict Sheila, because of her service for the church?"*

I had also noticed when God specifically spoke of prostitution in Deuteronomy, he spoke of "shrine prostitution." *What was that?* I wondered. "No Israelite man or woman is to become a *shrine prostitute.*"[195] In the New Testament, Paul condemned prostitution in his letter to the Corinthians, a city with a pagan Temple dedicated to the goddess Aphrodite. Later I learned this Temple had 1000 sacred female prostitutes.[196] Did all this mean only some forms of prostitution were condemned, e.g., *shrine prostitution*? It seems prostitution to other gods was the sin.

Premarital sex was treated in a way that seemed very foreign. Examples given always involved a young woman living within her father's household. If the father wanted the male culprit to marry his daughter, the penalty for premarital sex was indissolvable marriage! However, if the father didn't want him to marry his daughter, the man had to pay the father the bride price, and that ended it. Clearly, the Israelite culture was such that young unmarried women were like family property. Women were not free to have relationships or arrange their marriages on their own.

In the New Testament, there wasn't much material related to sex. Adultery is condemned, but Jesus' forgiving attitude toward all is reflected in the story of the woman caught in adultery. He exposes the judgmentalism of her accusers more than the woman's sin and refuses to condemn her or carry out her stoning, which was what the Holiness Code commanded. He forgives her and tells her to "go and sin no more." In fact, Jesus is very inclusive of women, exposing the sexist attitudes of men, particularly the Pharisees.

Paul did put limitations on polygamy in the New Testament by stating that any elder of a local gathering (church) should be the husband of one wife. But nowhere is the practice condemned across the board. Jesus never addressed it. It was still permitted in first century Judaism. Later I learned that monogamy was the law of imperial Rome—a fact I never heard taught in churches. Was this why Paul admonished Jesus gatherings in the Roman world to select monogamous elders?

There was one phrase I encountered in the New Testament that seemed to lump all sexual sins together. In the New International Version it is translated "sexual immorality," while in others it is sometimes rendered "fornication." Later I learned the Greek word is *porneia*. The term is never specifically defined, but I noticed how Bible commentators often claimed it represented a whole range of sexual sins from masturbation to pornography to pre-marital sex to adultery to anything considered deviant. This, despite the fact that masturbation and pornography aren't referred to in the Bible, and pre-marital sex, the way we envision it, isn't addressed.

I was surprised when *porneia* was mentioned in the book of Acts[197] in the list of recommended (not commanded) prohibitions for Gentile believers. The more orthodox Jewish believers in Jesus thought Gentile believers should be required to be circumcised and to obey the whole Law of Moses. The apostles met to discuss the issue. They decided that Gentiles should not be required to obey the Law because that would be testing God by "putting on the necks of the disciples a yoke (the Law) that neither we nor our fathers have been able to bear." They agreed not to make it difficult for the Gentiles. They decided to not burden them beyond four points of the law especially important to Jewish believers in order to promote peace in the Jesus community. These were abstention from (1) food polluted by idols, (2) sexual immorality (*porneia*), (3) the meat of strangled animals, and (4) partaking of blood. The conclusion in a letter written to Gentile believers was "You would do well to avoid these things," in other words, this was a concession not a command.

This was confusing to me. "That's all they have to obey in the Law of Moses?" I wondered. "What about 'do not lie,' 'do not steal,' and 'do not murder?'" Three of the stipulations on the list were not moral laws but had to do with Jewish purity (food polluted by idols, meat of strangled animals, and partaking of blood). Wasn't "sexual immorality" obviously sinful? If purity was the concern, it seemed like *porneia* didn't belong on the list. It was tucked in between obvious ceremonial laws. Unless it means something other than what we think it means. I filed this additional disconnect away in my mind.

When I completed reading the whole Bible, the overall impression I got was that the regulations for sexual practices are confusing, complicated, and often overkill. They rarely match the circumstances of our modern culture. Even the contemporary church doesn't follow the stricter codes. Although a few loony fundamentalist groups might, evangelicals generally don't call for the death penalty for adultery or for cursing parents. Nor do they insist that couples that have sex while a woman is menstruating should be "cut off" from the community. Kind of makes one glad most of us evangelicals aren't consistent literalists.

Other times, the Bible is surprisingly open or supportive of a variety of practices, such as polygamy, concubinage, forms of open marriage, the pre-marital sex and promiscuity in the book of Esther, overlooking certain forms of commercial prostitution (as opposed to *shrine prostitution*, prostitution by a woman who still belongs to her family, prostitution by the daughter of a high priest, or forced prostitution), and publicly celebrating nudity and the sensuality of illicit lovers in the Song of Solomon. Yet the church roundly condemns all these things. The inconsistency was confusing. Kind of makes one mad we evangelicals aren't more understanding of people who choose alternative sexual lifestyles.

Then there was obvious and disconcerting double standard against women, especially in the Old Testament. Men had more freedom than women in sex. On the other hand, Jesus openly promoted women's rights and generally treated women as equals. New Testament authors portrayed women positively as Jesus' legitimate disciples, financially supportive of his mission, and among those who did not abandon him in the end.

Amazingly, despite the fact that what the Bible proclaimed was not entirely congruent with what the evangelical world taught, as a young believer I concluded the church was basically right to prohibit things like masturbation, fantasies, pornography, and pre-marital sex. If the majority of evangelical authors and teachers were against these practices, who was I to question their authority? Their voices were louder than my personal observations. In the back of my mind, I wondered about the disconnects I saw, but I wasn't ready to make waves or risk censure.

Years went by before I realized the church spoon-feeds members its teachings on sex. We aren't encouraged to think and decide for ourselves about sex and how to reconcile the conflicting sexual messages in the Bible. We are hypnotized by groupthink. Gradually, I changed. I became willing to address the contradictions I was seeing. What I discovered rocked my worldview.

SEXUAL OPENNESS

Ole (pronounced "Oh-lee") Anthony, editor of the religious satire magazine *The Wittenburg Door*, once appeared on Pat Robertson's television show *The 700 Club* when he was a younger man. He told co-host Ben Kincheloe that he had prayed to God to either send him a wife or stop making him so horny. He was permanently banned from the show.[198]

At least in public, there is no subject that makes fundamentalist and evangelical Christians so nervous as the subject of sex. With some notable exceptions, the church exudes an attitude about sexuality that often communicates virtually everything sexual (outside a narrow window of acceptable marital sex) as taboo. And, when someone promotes any open honest discussion about the topic, his or her spirituality becomes suspect, hence the censure of Ole Anthony.

One of the few exceptions to this general rule is when Christian authors write marriage manuals on sex. More moderate evangelical authors have contributed some excellent and less-narrow material on sexual intimacy for the married Christian couple.[199] Yet my experience has been that open attitudes about sex and sexual practices are, by and large, limited to confined and controlled environments, such as the marriage manual market. If you talk about sex in the evangelical world, it generally must be done the right way with particular attention to the boundaries of acceptable sexual practice.

During the stage where I was beginning to question the church's attitude about sex, I began reading some books that explained sexual morality in ways contrary to evangelical tradition.[200] One of those books was entitled *The Poisoning of Eros* by Raymond Lawrence. He wasn't talking about liberal heresies poisoning sex. He was talking about conservative poisons squelching sex! Normally, I would never read a book like this because it was not written or endorsed by an evangelical. However, I was beginning to outgrow that "us vs. them" way of thinking.

A commonplace notion in the modern world, one promoted by numerous Hollywood films, is that the Roman world at the beginning of the Christian era was marked by uninhibited sexual promiscuity and that the Christian religion introduced and promoted sexual restraint. Nothing could be further from the truth.[201]

Lawrence made a solid case that today's church views on sex have more to do with Greco-Roman Platonism and Augustine's warped perspective (despite his wisdom on other topics) than a rational reading of Scripture. For instance, the Jewish tradition from which Christianity arose was sex-affirming as evidenced by some of the Old Testament passages cited above. Contrary to popular belief, the Greco-Roman world, in which the early church grew, was not wholly a debauched sexual culture. The sex-negating Platonists and Stoics, who had fearful attitudes toward "irrational" sexual pleasure, influenced early church fathers like Augustine and Tertullian and later Bible commentators.[202] It was Greek syncretism that regarded the flesh as evil and only the soul as divine that tainted the church's attitude about sex. Greek philosophy, not the Bible, was responsible for some of the hyper-sex-paranoid, early church views that carried on through medieval Europe, influenced groups like the American Puritans, and are still with us today. "Hence, the uniquely Hebraic way of seeing and valuing sexuality has been obfuscated by subsequent [faulty] translation and interpretation. The biblical texts are commonly viewed through the distorting prism of Platonism."[203]

One specific instance of how these sex-negative Greco-Roman values influenced the English translation of the Greek New Testament is the word *porneia*. Lawrence calls it "perhaps the most deliberately mistranslated word in the biblical literature,"[204] when it is rendered "fornication," and I would argue when it is also translated "sexual immorality" (as in "flee sexual immorality"[205]). Conservative Biblicists have condemned a host of sexual behaviors under that one word without understanding what it meant to the original audience. One scholar believes a better translation is "harlotry,"[206] for the connotation of *porneia* is selling oneself to break covenant. Moreover, it is not always about sex, as is evidenced by the number of times it or its Hebrew equivalent is translated as "idolatry." The context in which it was used often determined what the meaning was.

These facts shed new light on that passage in Acts. Now it made sense to me. *Porneia* was a range of unacceptable sexual and covenantal behaviors within Judaism. It was to be avoided by Gentile believers because of its ties to breaking covenant and idolatry. In the case in Acts, some scholars believe *porneia* refers to *shrine prostitution*, when men or women either dedicate themselves to prostitution in a pagan temple or visit prostitutes in such a temple.[207]

These types of discoveries led me to refine my views. They revealed how evangelicalism has inherited a sex-negative religion and developed a case of *erotophobism*—the fear of sexuality.[208] More importantly, they helped me see how critical it is that one use the one "law of love" as the guiding principle in matters of sex.

LOVE OVER LAW IN SEX

By 2003 I still counted myself an evangelical, although I was moving toward the fringes and was beginning to explore what would become the *emergent church* movement. At the time, I was a writer for World Vision, the largest Christian and evangelical aid agency in the world. That year they sent me to Washington, D.C., to report on an international AIDS conference convened by evangelical organizations. Many perceived this event as a huge breakthrough for the evangelical world.

Although a small minority, progressive evangelical groups, such as Sojourners and Evangelicals for Social Action, had been involved in social justice issues for years. Moreover, evangelical relief and development agencies such as World Vision and Food for the Hungry had been working for decades serving the poor worldwide. But a gathering of hundreds of evangelicals to strategize about how to fight the AIDS pandemic? This was unprecedented! Particularly because AIDS is linked to perceived sinful sexual promiscuity and homosexuality. I was surprised when I heard mega-church pastor Rick Warren among the conveners and speakers at this conference. In his message, he admitted that the church was "late to this fight" and admonished evangelical churches to go to war against this deadly disease.

World Vision had developed a strategy to fight AIDS similar to the Ugandan government's that gained worldwide recognition in the late 1990s. The approach is sometimes called the ABC strategy, with A standing for a̲bstinence, B for b̲e faithful, and C for the use of c̲ondoms. Education is geared around teaching young people to be abstinent, married people to remain faithful, and for those who are unable or unwilling to do A or B, to use condoms. Although it shouldn't be an oversimplified correlation, Uganda's drastically decreased HIV/AIDS rate from 18 percent in 1992 to 6.2 percent in 2002 is usually attributed to this comprehensive ABC strategy.

I was glad that World Vision was one of the few evangelical

organizations that wasn't afraid to encourage condom use in certain cases. On the other hand, they were a bit paranoid that conservative Christian supporters might perceive them as promoting promiscuous sex. As a stopgap, President Richard Stearns often stated they preferred people follow the A and the B of the strategy and have the C not be a capital letter but a small "c." Despite their concern over people suffering from AIDS at this conference, particularly the endemic rates of HIV infection in sub-Saharan Africa, most evangelicals were still suspicious about the role of condoms to effectively prevent HIV and concerned that their promotion would encourage promiscuity.

On the first day of the conference I sat down to interview an HIV-positive Anglican priest from Uganda who was a leader in a World Vision HIV/AIDS project. His perspective fascinated me. He wasn't your typical Western evangelical thinker. Suddenly we heard a commotion across the hall. The conservative evangelical group called Concerned Women for America (CWA – including, Beverly LaHaye, wife of Tim LaHaye, coauthor of the *Left Behind* series) had entered. They were protesting World Vision's acceptance of condoms as part of an AIDS-fighting strategy and began passing out literature condemning it on moral grounds. I grabbed the flier and quickly skimmed it. To CWA, condoms should have no role in preventing HIV. Abstinence and faithful monogamy were the *only* solutions. I brought the flier to the attention of my new acquaintance. After the bishop read it, I expected him to react as I had. To me, they were just another misguided fundamentalist group. I was stunned when he laid his head down on the table and began to weep. I didn't know what to do.

Finally, he looked up and turned toward me. "Don't they see how unloving this is? What about women who are married to someone who they suspect may be HIV positive? Or those who feel they must resort to prostitution to feed their children? These people shouldn't use condoms?" To him, this was an affront to his sense of Christian compassion and justice. Their message wasn't just wrongheaded. It was patently unloving. It was un-Christian.

I tried to console him. We talked a bit about the callousness of people who have no understanding of human frailty in dire or imperfect circumstances. CWA had a nicely wrapped, black-and-white, "biblically-based" morality, but one that ignored the realities of human conditions. Although uncomfortable with some of its ramifications, at least World Vision was trying to accommodate for those conditions and trying not to cram an abstinence-only message down people's throats (In retrospect, I think World Vision shouldn't downplay condom use as a last resort but as an essential part of a three-prong strategy; a big C in other words).

"Even if the church considers it an immoral lifestyle, where is the compassion in withholding information that could save a life?" I asked myself later. In the face of an incurable disease, CWA's and many evangelicals' attitude is one of "accept our standards or else." There is no room for different views or for allowing someone time to change his or her behavior. It is the familiar all-or-nothing, our-way-or-the-highway mindset. Love isn't ruling. Law is.

MASTURBATION AND LUST

The condemnation of masturbation is a favorite of fundamentalist and evangelical moralists. It was at ALCC in Pasadena where my pastor Che Ahn often preached against masturbation, calling it *self-abuse*—a term that he or someone else apparently created, since there is no reference to it in Scripture. There is a wealth of Christian materials on sexuality that also condemns masturbation, typically on the basis of its being an impure and selfish act.

Ironically, one of the leading Christian moralists on the Religious Right, James Dobson, doesn't condemn masturbation! In a family-values film he produced in the early1980s, which I saw when attending an evangelical church in western Massachusetts,

Dobson shared how he changed his view after trying to help a young man overcome masturbation through counseling. He confessed he sees no basis for its condemnation from Scripture. Apparently, he acknowledges that the story of Onan in Genesis is not regarding masturbation, but about a man refusing to impregnate his dead brother's wife, as family convention expected.

I'll never forget hearing the tense discussion that ensued in my church at the conclusion of that film. A prominent member stood up and passionately countered Dr. Dobson's opinion. The church was split on the issue. Having been indoctrinated by mostly anti-masturbation literature, I was conflicted. Later church leaders who preached against the practice, like my pastor in California, would solidify my own negative attitude toward it. Imagine that. For a time, I was more far right than James Dobson.

In later years after realizing my own indoctrination, I concluded since there is no command against masturbation, there is freedom for individuals to govern themselves, either choosing to practice it or refrain from it, based on their own conscience. The only moral basis for any type of censure is a situation where masturbation either dishonors a spouse—when one uses it to avoid meeting the spouse's sexual needs—or when it becomes an obsessive, out-of-control habit that negatively affects other responsibilities. Both of these would violate the principle of love and respect for another.

But what about lust? When people masturbate, view pornography, or indulge in fantasies, aren't they lusting after someone to whom they are sexually attracted, and isn't that sinful? After all, Jesus did say "anyone who looks at a woman lustfully has already committed adultery with her in his heart."[209]

That pesky verse always bothered me and appeared to be another disconnect. If Jesus was right, then lust and "adultery in the heart" was an unavoidable sin for every testosterone-filled male on the planet throughout all of human history. That was my conclusion before I made a couple of discoveries.

First, the Hebrew and Greek words for *woman* are often

synonymous with *wife* depending on the context.[210] In the Jewish worldview, a female is either unmarried, that is, a virgin, or she is married and now considered a *woman*. In keeping with the Old Testament Scriptures that allow men to have sexual appreciation for single women they deem beautiful, even considering them a potential wife (Deuteronomy 21:11), Jesus was probably referring to *married women*. As we shall learn shortly, adultery was considered a property issue in the Jewish mindset, not sexual betrayal as it is in Western culture. Therefore, it wouldn't be sinful for a man to look at a *single woman* with sexual appreciation or desire, because she doesn't belong to another—or at least she is eligible to pursue through seeking permission from her father—whereas a *married woman* does belong to another.

Second, it turns out the word translated "lust" in English is the same Greek term that is translated "to covet" in the Greek Septuagint (the Greek translation of the Old Testament).[211] Substituting "to covet" for "lust" puts a whole new spin on it. *Covet* in the Old Testament, referred to the desire to deprive another of his property. In Exodus 20:17 God told the Israelites, "You shall not covet your neighbor's house. You should not covet your neighbor's wife, or his manservant, or maidservant, his ox or donkey, or anything that belongs to your neighbor." In this context, *to covet* was not merely having awareness that something is desirable—either practically or sexually. It was an inward desire that mirrored the external act of stealing. It seemed more likely that Jesus wasn't making adultery an inescapable sin for all men, but rather was showing how coveting another man's wife—desiring to possess her for oneself—mirrors the sin of adultery. As was his custom, Jesus was exposing the nature of sin. It originates in the heart and not in the physical act itself. It wasn't sinful to look at a married woman (one who belongs to another) and be aware she is sexually desirable, but only sinful to look at her with desire or intention to possess her for himself.[212] It's possible to appreciate someone sexually without wanting to possess her or take her away from her spouse. This is a perfectly reasonable interpretation based on the original language, culture, and teachings in the Torah.

ORAL SEX

In the early 1980s as a young believer trying to sort out a sexual ethic for myself, I picked up a book popular among the Christian group I was part of at the time, InterVarsity Christian Fellowship (IVCF), a college ministry and evangelical publishing house. The book was *Eros Defiled*, by John White. White spoke of liberal heresies tainting God's ideal of sex. Using strange and murky logic, he discouraged the practice of oral sex, saying it was "subnormal"—a practice not part of God's design. In fact, he decried *any* erotic stimulation that did not lead to sexual intercourse as subnormal.[213] The implication was intercourse was the only acceptable way for a man and a woman to reach orgasm.

I confess I was disappointed. Prior to my conversion, I hadn't exactly run from sexual experimentation. In my experience, oral-genital stimulation was a natural sexual practice adding variety to a sexual relationship. I assumed, as a Christian, it would be part of my sex life when I was married. But White's claim made it sound like it was wrong, out of God's perfect will, and a sign of the world's twisted influence on sex. Moreover, who was I to disagree with a major evangelical IVCF-approved theological expert like John White? My indoctrination into conservative evangelicalism was strong at this juncture. I sincerely believed the author spoke the will of God. Oral sex was subnormal at best and sinful at worst. Damn.

Yet the jury was still out on oral sex. A few years later I noticed a shift. Many evangelicals began to lighten up over this practice and accept it as a legitimate sexual technique for lovemaking (within the confines of marriage). One of my conservative Pastors admitted in private he accepted it. This was no small shift. I came to realize an IVCF-endorsed theologian's position on oral sex was, frankly, legalistic bullshit. Oral sex isn't even condemned in Scripture. I just hope all those couples that read John White's book and others like it got the revised memo. Of course this begs the question. Who really speaks for God on the subject of sex?

PRE-MARITAL SEX

Abstinence—the notion that God calls single believers to remain sexually pure until marriage—is the universal, unquestioned position within evangelicalism. Except for renegades.

"Actually, the Bible doesn't specifically condemn singles having sex," Susan declared. A group of my evangelical friends were having a discussion in the living room of a house some of us rented near the campus of UMass Amherst. It was 1980. I had only been a "believer" for one year.

"What!? How can you say that?" I replied.

"Well, there's a school of thought that says when Paul condemns 'sexual immorality,' the Jews of his day did not envision that to mean all sex outside monogamous marriage. In other words, we read into that term a definition that wasn't conceived by the original audience."

The thought of this was extremely uncomfortable to me. I was in my naïve stage. (I also had not completed my cover-to-cover reading of the Bible). Susan was challenging a largely unanimous church teaching. That struck a chord in several of us. The discussion that ensued was animated. It wasn't that we were afraid of sex (I'm sure most of us were attracted to the implications for freedom her view had). It was the idea that the church could be wrong about interpreting Scripture. That was disconcerting for people who sincerely believed we evangelicals had the truth.

In the next few months, I searched the Scriptures to gain some clarity. I had to admit there was no verse in the New Testament that clearly promoted abstinence. I finally found the passage in Deuteronomy that said if a man had sex with a single woman, the penalty was to either marry the woman or, if the father didn't approve of him, to pay her family the bride price. I concluded this proved that the evangelical teaching on abstinence was correct.

But I was wrong. I had not read the passage in its own historical and cultural context. If I had, I would have realized that the passage does not address our modern phenomenon where single women eventually become independent and free from their family's authority—a modern family that has no concern for pure lineage. I had searched for a proof text to prove a position and stuffed a preconceived view into that passage. Years later, after learning how to do sound exegetical studies with an open mind, I realized the Bible does not specifically condemn all pre-marital sex.[214] My friend Susan had been right. Was I detecting a pattern of misinformation?

Something else dawned on me. Our evangelical paranoia about sexual experimentation for singles and our teaching that "God will bring you a spouse in His perfect time" encourages passivity in relationships. This attitude spawned the "courtship" movement and popularized books like Josh Harris's *I Kissed Dating Goodbye*."[215] In attempting to obey the perceived law of abstinence for the purpose of pleasing God and maximizing the joy of marriage in the future, Christian singles often lacked practical experience with authentic romantic relationships. They may also have delayed marriage against their will and their own emotional and physical longings.

If another evangelical teaching is emphasized, such as the Scripture "it is better to marry than to burn with passion,"[216] Christian singles may marry prematurely before they are financially and mentally prepared because their bodies are telling them they want sex now, and the church is saying the only way to have sex is within a marriage covenant.

As for abstinence, teaching it hasn't proven to be as effective as proponents claim. For instance, numerous studies have shown that young people who sign a "virginity pledge" may delay the initiation of sexual activity but are less likely to use condoms when they do engage in single sex[217] (think Sarah Palin's daughter, Bristol). They also tend to marry at younger ages. I ultimately learned our evangelical system of morality doesn't make a real difference. The divorce rate for evangelical Christians is the same or higher than for those who aren't trying to obey the Bible. Atheists and agnostics have a significantly lower rate.[218]

PORNOGRAPHY

One day in 2002 Lori and I were attending a marriage conference sponsored by Family Life, a division of Campus Crusade for Christ. There we sat inside an enormous conference room in a hotel in Bellevue, Washington. In the evangelical world, this was one of the few venues where the faithful felt safe to hear candid talk about sex—at least during the one session on the subject. But I knew from experience I shouldn't expect anything too erotic or brazen.

During one session, Dr. David Allender, a professor at a small evangelical seminary in Seattle called Mars Hill, began talking about the Song of Solomon, that sensual book in the Bible that fascinated me the first time I read it. What I didn't realize, until I heard Dr. Allender speak, was it is more than sensual. It is unambiguously pornographic.

Allender dropped a bomb. There are two Hebrew words in the Song of Solomon that are euphemisms for male and female sex organs and have been mistranslated. In Song of Solomon 7:2, the two words translated "navel" or "waist" are really Hebrew slang words for the English term "vulva." And, in 5:14, the word often translated as "body" or "abdomen" is really Hebrew slang for "penis." Knowing how scandalous this sounds to many evangelical ears, Allender insisted he had thoroughly checked this out with biblical scholars. You could hear some uncomfortable shuffling in seats. He made the point how this demonstrates God's acceptance and even promotion of enjoyment of the human body and sexual intimacy. I was dumbfounded. Campus Crusade let this guy talk? Don't get me wrong. I was pleasantly surprised.

As I later shared with Lori, I started my own fantasizing. Maybe Christians could start plastering these verses with their newly discovered "truth" on refrigerators, nature photographs, and T-shirts! I envisioned the infallible Word of God preached to the world: "Your vulva is a rounded goblet that never lacks blended wine,"[219] and "His penis is like polished ivory decorated with sapphires."[220]

As I reflected on this, I was struck how an important element went over most people's head. Apparently no one wanted to announce this to the world and reveal the "inerrant" genital descriptions to the masses. They wanted it to stay in the married-only conference session (there was a separate session for engaged singles that didn't include this material), sheltered from innocent ears, and maybe just acknowledged so good Christian married couples could enjoy each other's bodies more. That may be a good start, but why not share the joy? Both of those passages of Scripture were actually in the conference booklet encouraging such enjoyment, but guess what? They were written in the traditional way. Or I should say they were false translations!

The truth is Bible linguists and evangelical scholars have deliberately mistranslated these words in our Bibles for years, even centuries. And, even with the truth of it known, apparently no one is planning on doing a mass Bible recall to correct the errors or at the very least throw in a footnote that spells them out. And I thought the Word of God was infallible and not to be changed by man? If liberals try to change the Bible, e.g., to make it gender neutral, there's a sense of outrage in the conservative evangelical community. But if conservative translators purposely mistranslate to protect our sexual queasiness, aside from a few brave souls like Dr. Allender, there's deadening silence. There is no evangelical call to correct translation errors in the Song of Solomon.

What does this have to do with pornography? Everything. The images in this book of the Bible are clearly pornographic. Lovers are admiring each other's naked bodies and genitals. Even some evangelical sex therapists admit there are references in the love poem to oral sex. The question is, if it is acceptable to *write* such graphic erotic descriptions of sexual love, why isn't it acceptable to *draw, photograph*, or *film* such descriptions?

One only has to take a trip to Western Europe and visit any major museum to know that historically pictorial portrayal of the naked human body has always been acceptable among Christian artists (think Michelangelo's *David* or Alessandro Allori's *Sussana and the Elders*). The reason pornography is condemned across the board among American conservative Christians is because the term has been falsely defined. The term pornography comes from that now familiar Greek word we have learned, *porneia*. Technically, pornography is the graphic (written or displayed) depiction of *porneia*, which we have learned means *elicit sexual and covenantal behavior*. Tracing the term back to its Old Testament Holiness Code roots, it means things like incest, rape, adultery (as defined by the Torah), bestiality, shrine prostitution, idolatry, male homosexuality[221] (female homosexuality is nowhere mentioned), premarital sex for women (not men), and sex during a woman's menstruation. It does not mean erotic literature, as we have seen, or the portrayal of naked bodies or people engaging in sexual activities that are not condemned by the Holiness Code.

Biblically, today's definition of pornography must be ascertained according to the love ethic that Jesus taught. Does its production and consumption violate the law of love? For purveyors of porn, it's obvious that child pornography, depictions of rape, and portrayals that blatantly demean women (or men) as sex objects violate love. Likewise, much of the multi-billion dollar porn industry is driven by lust and greed and may inadvertently condone or explicitly spur sexual exploitation and trafficking. This male-dominated "business" ends up using and discarding women as products for consumption marketed to men. Using sex to physically and economically exploit others is a form of control on par with slavery. For consumers, it isn't loving to exhibit addictive patterns of behavior with pornography that negatively infringe on other relationships and responsibilities.

Yet extremists on the right and the left paint pornography with a broad brush. In particular, fundamentalists and evangelicals push polarized views of sexuality calling anything erotic pornographic. The church condemns anything outside a narrow range while ignoring the Bible's sexually affirming material. Pornography as I've outlined above does not follow the New Testament's love ethic. But what of uses that don't fit those obvious categories? Could it be the Bible affirms responsibly portrayed and enjoyed erotic images and literature? I came to the conclusion that it does, and that there is room for the erotic in the lives of adults following biblical love.[222]

I hoped I could keep all this straight as I saw Steve approach.

SEX IN THE PUB

Steve spotted us and came over. "Well, fancy meeting you here," Gina said. "Are you out carousing around all by your lonesome?"

"Actually, I tracked you down through Lori."

"Yeah, he had called me on my cell earlier," I informed Gina. "We were expecting him."

Inwardly, I was wondering if we would continue talking in the same vein as we had been and how Steve would respond.

"I'm glad you came," Dan said. "We need a break from talking pub theology."

Good, I thought. *Maybe we won't talk about my book anymore.*

"Steve, sit here," Gina said. "I'm ready to leave anyway." She explained how she came in a separate car, had been shopping, and it was time for her to call it a night.

Our friend Steve always struck me as an even-keeled evangelical. He was perfectly comfortable drinking a couple of beers on occasion. He had a loving heart and always showed concern for his friends. What set him apart from Dan and me was that he was still very theologically conservative. He hadn't made much of a shift in that area—nowhere near what I had. Of average height with short black hair, Steve took Gina's seat.

We all chatted a bit as Gina lingered, standing there. She sat her glass on the counter with about a half-inch of beer left. "Okay, I'm heading out," she announced. Then she caught my eye.

"Thanks for explaining all that," she leaned in and said to me. "I'm not sure what I think, but I'd like to read that book you mentioned."

"I'll lend it to you later," I said. She was referring to *Last Days Madness*.

Gina said goodbye, and right then another seat opened up at the bar so I grabbed it. With Steve here, it was time for another brew. We all ordered. I noticed our game. It was winding down with four minutes on the clock and the Celtics ahead by six. Of course in basketball, the last four minutes is an eternity. I was thinking how this game could go either way.

"Pierce is hot. He's carrying them this time," Dan observed. "It'll be interesting." Right then the Lakers took a time out.

Dan turned to Steve and began explaining what we'd been talking about—that we'd discussed the issues in almost every chapter of my book. "We didn't plan it, we just started going through the whole thing. Let's see..." He looked at me. "What haven't we covered?" That's when he brought up the topic of sexuality. "He's got some controversial takes on it," Dan said.

Thanks, Dan, I thought. I wasn't in the mood to open up a can of worms. But I was glad I had reviewed things in my mind. Right then, Brett the bartender placed our tall mugs on the counter—a Panther Lake Porter for Steve and two Belgium Blonde Ales for Dan and me.

Steve, sitting between us, turned to me, "So, what's so controversial?"

Okay, here goes. I took a deep breath. "Well, for one," I began. "I conclude that we evangelicals tend to create a set of rules about sex. It's like, uh, we're stuck in a law-based approach to God. As a result, more conservative churches mimic some of the sexually repressive ideas of people like Augustine, who believed sex was only acceptable for procreation and not for pleasure."

"Yeah, that only-for-procreation view is pretty extreme," Steve agreed. "God obviously created sex for more than propagating the human race."

"Right," I said. "That is a biblically Jewish perspective." I knew we could at least agree on that. "But the concept of sex as good beyond procreation was lost in Western society for centuries."

I paused and took a sip of my ale. "More moderate churches are more accommodating and have a shorter list while emphasizing the basic goodness of sex. But really, I think the approach of the church making rules and denunciations about sexual practices is not in line with what Jesus and Paul taught." I was thinking of John White's take on oral sex and others' hard-line stance on premarital sex.

"Really?" Steve appeared surprised, but I wasn't. I was bracing myself for his reaction. "But aren't you ignoring some of their teaching?" he objected as he straightened up. "Don't we still have laws to obey, like 'thou shalt not commit adultery.' What are you saying?"

I took a deep breath realizing I had touched a chord already. "Steve, I don't mean *anything goes*. Don't misunderstand me. Adultery, the way we think of it, is wrong because it is deceptive and breaks an agreed marriage bond—not to mention the pain it causes. I'm saying the Christian perspective ought to make *love* the ultimate authority on what is right and wrong sexually, not a list of laws."

"Oh, you mean 'love is the fulfillment of the law,' as Paul said. Since adultery is obviously not loving, it is wrong."

"Yeah, that's it, if we have the right definition of adultery. The real test is whether an act is unloving toward others or not. In other words, I think the New Testament teaches a 'love ethic,' and that should guide individuals in how they pursue their sex life. I don't think there is a 'sex ethic,' in the sense that there's a list of rules."[223]

"I'm not sure where you get that," Steve said. "It seems obvious there is a sex ethic."

I knew this was a tall order—trying to explain to someone like

Steve my views on sex. I wasn't sure I wanted to respond. During an awkward silence between us, I began to ruminate. Without his hearing the background of where I got my ideas, a straightforward rejoinder felt like jumping into a cold lake without testing the waters. All I wanted to do was be true to what the Bible *really* taught. So much of what the church teaches on sex is just man-made religion, in my mind. It focuses on external rules that are read into the Bible not derived from it. Whereas, Jesus—and even Paul—had a radical new way at looking at morality. It wasn't obeying laws that made one righteous but one's heart attitude. Dan and I had discussed this earlier. The new way of following God was through love. Love is the guiding principal for us to follow. What Garry Wills wrote was in the back of my mind:

> Religion took over the legacy of Paul as it did that of Jesus—because they both opposed it. They said the worship of God is a matter of interior love, not based on external observances, on temples or churches, or hierarchies, or priesthoods. Both were at odds with those who impose the burdens of "religion" and punish those who try to escape them...They only saw two basic moral duties, love of God and love of the neighbor. Both were liberators, not imprisoners—so they were imprisoned. So they were killed. Paul meant what Jesus meant, that love is the only law.[224]

When I first read Wills' words they jumped out at me. *That's exactly the conclusion I came to!* I had thought. For in any issue I faced—even sexuality—I was just trying to be true to this principle. That love is the only law. That by applying the principles of love for others and personal responsibility, one can set their own boundaries on sexual conduct.

Steve broke the lull in conversation, interrupting my internal reverie. "By the way, what do you mean having the *right* definition of adultery? Isn't that obvious?"

"Well, no. The Bible defines adultery differently than we do today. Partly because of the Jewish obsession with pure lineage. I mean, in biblical times adultery was a violation of another's property. To protect his lineage, a man needed to ensure that his wife was a virgin and had never slept with another man. Today, adultery is more of a betrayal of personal trust for both spouses. When we assume our modern definition of adultery is the same as the Bible's, we inevitably misunderstand the issues around marital faithfulness."

"I don't know, Mike. I've never heard of that," Steve confessed. "It sounds suspicious."

"Maybe that's because we're programmed to read things into the Bible that aren't there and ignore things that are there."

"What are you talking about?" Steve asked.

"Well, in the Old Testament, a man only committed adultery if he had sex with another man's wife. If he had sex with a slave, prostitute, concubine, or one of his other wives...oh, or a divorced or widowed woman, it was not considered adultery.[225] This was the case because those relationships didn't jeopardize family lineage. However, a woman committed adultery when she had sex with anyone outside her marriage, because a man's and a family's lineage was at stake. This was why the woman was considered property of the husband and the husband's family."

Steve squirmed in his seat. "Honestly, I think that's ridiculous. You're forgetting Genesis. It's clear that God's model for marriage was for one man and one woman to become *one* flesh." He emphasized the word *one* as he pointed his index finger toward me. "You can't become one flesh with a harem! Anything outside the 'one flesh' bond is adultery."

"But, Steve," I insisted, "the Jews never understood that Scripture[226] as excluding polygamy or endorsing monogamy. A man could become one flesh with more than one woman. How do you explain all those Old Testament heroes—you know, like Gideon and David—who practiced polygamy and concubinage with no condemnation? Or the passage[227] where God has stipulations for men with two wives? Or when Jacob slept with his wives' maidservants?"

"What? Are you condoning men owning women and using them sexually?"

"Of course not! I'm just saying we are obligated to know the Bible's original definition of sexual prohibitions, like adultery and fornication, before we make judgments about what the Bible teaches on sex."

I delved deeper into what I meant. "Jesus' teaching on love and his defense of the rights of women, and Paul's bold statement—for his day—that 'there is no male and female in Christ,'[228] circumvents the sexist patriarchal system of the Old Testament. Look, I don't think polygamy is a good idea and I'd never endorse it, but biblically and practically, it's not wrong in and of itself."

"Really now, where do you get that?"

"Well, like I said, it's not specifically condemned in Scripture. And, having lived in two polygamous cultures in Africa—Somalia and Southern Malawi—I know there are some cultures for which polygamy works, however imperfectly. I even became friends with several polygamists and their wives."

"Then I'd imagine you would have seen how oppressive it is."

"Okay, it's true women's rights are suppressed in many traditional cultures, such as fundamentalist Islam—and you know Steve, they're also suppressed in conservative Christianity too, and yes, in certain polygamous societies.[229] But in other polygamous cultures, when men treat their wives equally, it need not be exploitive. For example, John Stott's independent studies of polygamous communities in the western U.S. bear this out,[230] as well as what I know of some African cultures."[231]

"Oh, I'm sure I could find research that goes against that."

I realized this was the first time Steve had heard my new position. I wasn't surprised at his reaction. "But biblically, in and of itself, polygamy is not sinful," I continued. "Neither is pre-marital sex or any human sexual practice. These things are wrong only when they violate the new love ethic. Individuals and couples can decide their own sexual restrictions as they follow the law of love—as they treat others as they would like to be treated."

"Mike, you've lost it," Steve insisted. "I can't believe you're saying this. You can't throw out clear laws. Yes, love is the cornerstone, but we have to adhere to what the whole Bible teaches. After all, 'all Scripture is profitable for correction.'"[232]

"Well, which Scripture are you going to obey? The church is not consistent. There are some practices we don't follow that the Bible commands and others we condemn that the Bible permits."

"Huh? Like what?" Steve probed.

"Well, on the one side, we don't execute people for adultery, for cursing one's parents, or a woman for not being a virgin when she marries. Let's see…oh, we don't care if couples have sex during menstruation. Um…we allow farmers to plant more than one type of seed in the same field. And then on the other side, we condemn polygamy, concubinage, and arranged marriages for women, even though the Bible permitted them."

"Okay, it seems to me," Steve said, as a realization came to him, "That we choose what Scripture to obey according to whether it's in the New Testament. Sure, lots of those Old Testament laws are obsolete. But not all. If Old Testament law is reinforced in the New Testament, it's binding."

We both took a break from the spirited discussion and sipped our microbrews, oblivious to the boisterous noise all around us. The game was blaring, and Dan and a few others were rooting for one of the two teams. I knew I wasn't going to win any arguments with Steve, but I was glad he at least was open to hearing my views. Still, I wondered if it would affect our friendship.

"To me," I began again, "We need to be very careful not to make any part of the Bible into a set of binding laws. The Bible was not meant to have that much authority. Also, I think the evangelical church misses a major point the apostle Paul makes. That the new covenant that Jesus brought means 'we have been released from the law'[233] and are 'no longer under its supervision,'[234] or any law-based approach to God.[235] See, what the church tends to do is make the new covenant into a new set of laws to replace the old covenant."

I was on a roll. Steve let me go on. "Look, we know from the first eleven chapters of Romans that the Law was meant only as a temporary system to reveal to God's chosen people that they—and all humankind—fall short of His ideals. What really counts to God is faith, or more accurately, trust. That's why the father of the Christian faith is not Moses, who brought the Law, but Abraham, who '*believed* God and was credited with being righteous.' And remember, he was alive during a day when there was no such thing as the Torah or the Ten Commandments."

"Where are you going with this?" Steve asked.

"Here me out, now, I'm getting to it. So, when Jesus came, he showed how evil it is to follow the letter of the law, which the Pharisees did, and as a result oppressed the poor and disenfranchised. Jesus kept making exceptions to the law, e.g., working and healing on the Sabbath, declaring all foods clean, ignoring Temple regulations to meet human need. Um, what else? Oh, forgiving the guilty without insisting on the law's punishment; all in the name of a higher principal—love. He also exposed man-made law that squelched concern for people. That's what we need to do. Circumvent law in the name of love. 'Love is the fulfillment of the law'[236] and as Jesus said, 'All of the law hinges on love.'"[237]

"Yeah, but, Mike, if you took that view," Steve said, "to ignore the law, you'd end up condoning things like pre-marital sex. Mike, without law, people are free to sin!"

"Not if the law of love truly rules," I insisted. "And of course, how do we define what is sinful? The Bible really doesn't condemn pre-marital sex across the board. So, why doesn't the church let single people decide for themselves based on being loving and responsible?"

"Not so fast," Steve interjected. "Of course the Bible condemns pre-marital sex. Paul addresses fornication in Ephesians."

Again, without explaining background information first, it was difficult to make my points. "Actually, the word 'fornication'

Holiness Code to Israel. Even with the training I received on how to interpret the Bible in its cultural context, this appeared straightforward to me. Although it was a specific law to the people of Israel, the mention of homosexuality in the New Testament seemed to reinforce this Old Testament command. At least the part that said it was detestable.[241] With the exception of a fringe group called Christian Reconstructionists, mainstream evangelicals are not calling for the death penalty for homosexuals. (Lucky for us. If they did, to be consistent with other commands in the Holiness Code, they would call for the death penalty for teenagers who cursed their parents and adults who commit adultery—a hefty chunk of Americans.)

"Do not be deceived: Neither the sexually immoral nor idolaters nor adulterers nor male prostitutes nor homosexual offenders nor thieves nor the greedy nor drunkards nor slanderers nor swindlers will inherit the kingdom of God," the Apostle Paul warned the Corinthians (I Corinthians 6:9-10). That was straightforward too. Homosexuals won't inherit the kingdom of God. Because evangelicals interpret "inheriting the kingdom of God" as going to heaven,[242] that meant homosexuals supposedly wouldn't go to be with God when they died unless they repented of their sin.

Jake and I talked further about his family's dilemma. Little did I know how soon my thinking would change. Less than two years later I began to look at homosexuality and passages like these with a new set of eyes.

STRANGER AT THE GATE

By the time I sat down with Jake at that restaurant booth inside Reagan National Airport, I was already moving to the fringes of evangelicalism. Over the years I had gravitated away from conservative teachers like Pat Robertson, James Dobson, Larry Tomzcak, and Randall Terry, preferring the more moderate voices of Tony Campolo. Brennan Manning, and Mike Yaconelli. Another of the moderate voices I liked was an influential author named Philip Yancey who wrote the book *What's So Amazing About Grace?*

Once in an interview with *Sojourners Magazine* Yancey said, "I myself have been surprised at what I can get away with. When I sent off the manuscript of *What's So Amazing About Grace?* I said to my wife, Janet, 'That's probably the last book I'm going to write for the evangelical market.' It's got a whole chapter on Mel White, who's now a gay activist..."[243]

Yancey pushes the envelope. Some evangelicals tolerate him because he doesn't go over the top. In the chapter on Mel White he encouraged readers to read White's exposé and memoir, *Stranger at the Gate: To Be Gay and Christian in America*, without endorsing its conclusions about homosexuality. When I took up Yancey's challenge, I didn't realize where it would take me.

Mel White's story gripped my heart. A devout evangelical Christian, he struggled all his life to change his same-sex orientation, a compulsion he could not explain by attributing it to an absent father, domineering mother, or childhood sexual abuse. He had no such background. As a youth, he pleaded with God to change him to be like the other boys. Although I couldn't relate, I empathized with him. In his twenties, he denied his orientation, married, and had two children. His marriage didn't fix his "problem." He was still inexplicably drawn to men. He experienced intense temptation and guilt every time he saw an attractive man.

White was an extraordinarily creative individual. After Bible college and later seminary, he became a writer and producer of evangelical books and films. In the midst of his internal struggle, he ghostwrote for the likes of Francis Schaeffer, Jerry Falwell, Pat Robertson, and Billy Graham. With sermons, Bible verses, and evangelical dogma ringing in his ears, he became convinced if he succumbed and pursued a homosexual lifestyle, he would be utterly ruined. His marriage would end, his family would despise him, his career would derail, and God would reject him forever. Fear paralyzed him.

Not until his thirties did he tell anyone of his internal battle. His myriad desperate attempts to change into a heterosexual man escalated. Ongoing prayer, Christian counseling, radical therapy, electric shock, exorcism, and monastic retreats all failed to make a fundamental difference. Nothing worked. Devastated, he contemplated suicide.

Ultimately Mel White found peace. But not as an "ex-gay" heterosexual. Nor through the means that evangelicals insist work: homosexual ministries, church accountability, and supernatural intervention. No, he eventually embraced his own homosexuality as a gift of God to be practiced responsibly in a faithful, loving relationship. Although it was a painful transition, his wife Lydia came to terms with her husband's sexual orientation and they divorced amicably. I was impressed with her courage to accept him the way he is.

Was White's experience representative of homosexuals? How could he remain a Christian in light of what the Bible teaches? These questions sprang into my mind. I was familiar with those who claimed to be delivered from a homosexual drive. I had to dig deeper. In light of Mel's story, were these people truly "cured," or were they merely masking their homosexuality as Mel had all those married years?

I surfed the Internet looking for testimonials written by gays and lesbians who claimed to reconcile their Christian faith with their sexual lifestyle. Their stories paralleled Mel White's journey. Despite well-meaning efforts and a commitment to reparative therapy, these gay men and women were not overcoming their compulsions. After years of trying, often within an "ex-gay" ministry such as Exodus or Love Won Out, they gave up. Some of them decided the only way to reconcile their faith with their sexuality was to become celibate.

Celibacy as a pastoral answer for homosexual Christians is a middle course that some evangelicals like Tony Campolo recommend. Yet testimonials showed that few are able to achieve that goal. I sympathized with these people and wondered, if the majority of heterosexual Christians aren't willing to be celibate, how can we insist that homosexuals be? I realized there is a serious pastoral problem with homosexuality. The platitudes and easy pat answers to life's problems we evangelicals often spout are not adequate to this quandary. Love and reason demand an alternative response.

I read about many other Christian gays and lesbians. They believed God isn't concerned about the gender of the person they sleep with but rather how responsible and loving they are in their relationships. Today, I can't argue with that. Often after years of trying to change, they embraced their homosexuality as a mystery of life that they could affirm with God's blessing as long as they focused on Christ's law of love for others. If this was the appropriate alternative response, what is a person to make of those Bible verses that seemed to scream that homosexuality is detestable? Was the Bible irrelevant on this issue? Or was it mistranslated and misinterpreted?

GAY WRONGS

In the evangelical world, most things are already settled. There aren't many gray areas. The Bible is the Word of God, you must be born again to go to heaven, and Jesus is definitely coming again. And of course, homosexuality isn't just sinful, it's an "abomination." My indoctrination into evangelical theology taught me that well.

As a heterosexual man who couldn't comprehend how two men could be sexually attracted to each other, it wasn't hard for me to accept this teaching. I had a little harder time accepting the condemnation of female homosexuality. Okay, a lot harder time. Admittedly, the thought of two lesbians getting it on is an enticing turn on, at least for most heterosexual guys I know. Yet nature does appear to favor heterosexual couples; they are the only ones who can reproduce through the sexual act. Until my encounter with Mel White and the testimonials I found on the Internet, I had no reason to doubt the standard evangelical fare about homosexuality. I really hadn't thought it through.

So I delved into another Bible study project. My first lesson was a reminder. Sound exegetical studies insist that the Bible can't mean today what it never meant to its original audience. The key to interpreting the Bible for modern readers is putting it in its proper context—both cultural and literary. "The Biblical text does not come to us in the form of timeless axioms."[244] The texts were created in a particular time-space environment. To understand the Bible, the reader must put himself or herself in the original situation in which it was written as much as possible. I especially understood this in recent years after studying the phenomenon of Bible abuse.

Starting to study homosexuality, I immediately noticed the bias of evangelical authors. Most of them made blanket statements against all homosexual acts. But the truth, I discovered, was not so cut and dried when taken in the context of when and why passages on homosexuality were written. Liberal authors helped me see this.[245]

As we have learned in an earlier chapter, biblical authors related their ethics concerning sex to *property rights*. Certain sexual liaisons were wrong because they violated another's right to their property, e.g., a family, father, or husband had a right to demand sexual exclusiveness for women who "belonged" to him to ensure a family's lineage wasn't mixed with an outsider's blood. If one's culture is not concerned with pure family lineage, then sexual exclusiveness for women is not important.

Regarding sexual ethics, another phenomenon I had not considered was Israel's *purity code*, which defines animals, people, and actions, as either *clean* or *unclean*. Although every culture has a purity code (to Americans, e.g., eating insects is unclean, whereas for Africans, it's not), Israel's was particularly important. It was one of the principal forces that kept Israel separate from the pagan nations surrounding them. Purity means avoiding dirt. The Holiness Code of Israel[246] specified the dove as clean and the pig as unclean (dirty); a woman with no discharges as clean and one who is menstruating or recently given birth as unclean; a man with no discharges as clean and one with a recent semen discharge as unclean; a healthy man with rights of descent to the priesthood as clean, but one with an injured body part as unclean; the act of sewing one fiber into cloth as clean, but combining two varieties as unclean; planting one type of seed into a field as clean, mixing varieties of seeds as unclean; meat drained of blood as clean, meat that wasn't as unclean.

It was complicated but had a particular rationale. People who are partially leprous (actually not just with leprosy but a variety of skin diseases) are unclean, but one who is totally leprous is clean![247] It is the attention to wholeness that counts. A person should be of a single kind and hue, not have blotches or blemishes mixed with healthy parts. Or have discharges mixed with none. Or be dedicated to both the true God and idols. Or intermarry with non-Israelites. There should be no mixing of kinds.[248] "This is the reason for the condemnation of homosexual acts [by men], as the phrasing of the rules makes clear; the offense is described, literally, as a man lying with a male 'the lyings of a woman' (Leviticus 18:22; 20:13). The male who fulfills the 'female' role is a combination of kinds and therefore unclean, like a cloth composed of both linen and wool..."[249] The man in the "male" role is participating in this unclean act.

Understanding the purity code of Israel puts a new light on the issue. If one's culture or convictions are not concerned with purity the way Israel defined it, then the admonitions associated with that code are not morally binding. For instance for Israel, not only was male homosexuality an "abomination" (*toevah* in Hebrew) but so was having intercourse with a woman while she is menstruating (the penalty for such an act is for the couple to be cut off from their people).[250] For that matter, so was eating pork and a host of other unclean foods![251] Why are we evangelicals so concerned with homosexuality and couldn't care less about these other "detestable" things? I pondered. And why do we ignore other purity rules? Because we view purity differently, I realized. Evangelicals have no purity concern with female discharges and thus no problem overlooking the command and penalty about having sex during menstruation. Nor with the penalty for eating certain foods. To be consistent, shouldn't we lighten up regarding the command about male homosexuality? I also wondered why is only male homosexuality addressed in the purity code? Lesbianism is not addressed in the entire Old Testament!

In the context of purity, *toevah* (translated *abomination* or *detestable*) refers to something that makes one ritually unclean.[252] For the Hebrews, these were any defiling behaviors that the surrounding pagan nations practiced. Israel was commanded to set themselves apart from these nations by following a specific code. I knew from my own study of the New Testament that Israel's code of conduct was not relevant to Gentile believers or Jews under the new covenant. For instance, Jesus had declared all foods clean,[253] and as we learned earlier, Paul had vehemently argued that believers in Jesus were "no longer under the supervision of the law," had been "released from the law [the written code],"[254] and in fact, Jesus "was the end of the law."[255]

Jesus taught purity of the heart, not physical purity. The new way of being right before God was by following Christ's one law of love, denying one's selfish nature, and being led by the spirit, not obeying a set of laws and stipulations.[256] Was it possible to fulfill Christ's law of love as a practicing homosexual? Certainly one could do so and ignore other purity laws. Why not stipulations against homosexual behavior originally directed toward ancient Israel?

Finally, there was the question of what types of homosexuality were common in the culture in which the Holiness Code and purity rules were written. My study led me to determine there were only two types: homosexual rape, often inflicted by soldiers to humiliate prisoners of war,[257] and *shrine prostitution*, referred to many times in the Old Testament.[258] This type of prostitution entailed male or female prostitutes servicing worshipers of foreign gods, particularly the god of Baal.[259] These were the kinds of behaviors the pagan nations surrounding Israel practiced. If the original authors and audience of the Holiness Code had only these types of behaviors (exploitive and idolatrous homosexuality) in mind when homosexuality was mentioned, then modern readers misinterpret Old Testament admonitions against homosexuality. This was a revelation for me.

I then turned my attention toward the New Testament passages that supposedly referred to homosexuality. The first one is in the book of Romans, where Paul speaks in the context of idolatry. Here are the verses immediately before the controversial passage:

> For although they knew God, they neither glorified him as God nor gave thanks to him, but their thinking became futile and their foolish hearts were darkened. Although they claimed to be wise, they became fools and exchanged the glory of the immortal God for images made to look like mortal man and birds and animals and reptiles. (Romans 1: 21-23).

The people Paul is talking about were not glorifying God or giving Him thanks. They were worshiping false gods and graven images made to look like humans or animals. Historical studies revealed that this type of idol worship was common throughout Israel's history and into the first century. Paul continues:

> Therefore God gave them over in the sinful desires of their hearts to sexual impurity for the degrading of their bodies with one another. They exchanged the truth of God for a lie, and worshiped and served created things rather than the Creator— who is forever praised. Amen. Because of this, God gave them over to shameful lusts. Even their women exchanged natural relations for unnatural ones. In the same way the men also abandoned natural relations with women and were inflamed with lust for one another. Men committed indecent acts with other men, and received in themselves the due penalty for their perversion. (Romans 1: 24-27).

Again Paul is referring to people who "worshiped created things rather than the Creator." These people go beyond worshiping idols to doing something that is sexually impure, that entails women and men exchanging natural sexual relations for unnatural ones. It sounds like the passage is referring to homosexuality. But the critical question is what was Paul thinking about when he wrote this, and what did his audience perceive when they read it? Were they thinking about homosexuality the way we view it or something altogether different?

In the city of Corinth, where it is speculated Paul was when he wrote this letter, there was a temple dedicated to Aphrodite, the Greek goddess of love, beauty, and sexuality. One method of worshiping this "idol made to look like a mortal woman" was through fertility rituals, including having sexual intercourse with her priestesses. At one point, this Corinthian temple had 1000 sacred prostitutes living on its grounds.[260] When Paul talks of "women exchanging natural relations for unnatural ones," I realized it is far more likely he is referring to women who dedicated their life to sacred prostitution, and not to lesbian women in general. The context supports this argument. Lesbian women can still worship God and give thanks to him, whereas Paul was speaking of women who were committing blatant idolatry.

Of the many varieties of idol worship in the Greek and Roman world, Cybelene worship in Corinth, Athens, Ephesus, and Rome included castrated male priests who would have sex with other men as an act of dedication to an idol.[261] Again, I realized that this religious context meant the likelihood was high that Paul was thinking of these male priests (and probably others referred to in the Old Testament as male prostitutes and part of the fertility rites of Israel's pagan neighbors) and not homosexual men in general. The evidence was overwhelming that Paul wasn't addressing homosexuality across the board but the abandonment of natural sexual activity for unnatural activities that included the recruitment of cultic priest and priestess prostitutes, idol worship, and castration of males. "Paul condemns the 'unnatural' act of abandoning true worship of God and using sex in worship of idols, and pursuing such treatment of others as degraded them through exploitation and violence."[262] This was another world-rocking revelation.

The most shocking discovery for me was when I learned that the word translated "homosexual" in our modern Bibles is incorrect! When it is used in the Old Testament (typically in modern or paraphrased versions), the passages can't be referring to all homosexuality because, as mentioned, only male homosexuality is addressed as part of a purity rule in the Holiness Code.[263] The fact that female homosexuality is not mentioned at all in the Old Testament is remarkable. If God was so against all forms of homosexuality, why doesn't the Old Testament condemn lesbianism?

Secondly, the one word in the Greek New Testament commonly translated "homosexual," is the word, *arsenokoitai* (I Corinthians 6:9), which is rarely found in ancient literature and whose meaning is uncertain.[264] To translate it "homosexual" without at least including a footnote about its ambiguity is irresponsible. When scholars analyze its use, they conclude it's unlikely it refers to homosexuality across the board but rather to some type of sexual exploitation that could be homosexual but not necessarily so. It is more likely that *arsenokoitai*—literally meaning *male bed*—refers to men who engage in economic exploitation by sexual means, i.e., rape, coerced prostitution, or pimping.[265] The English word *homosexual* wasn't even coined until the early 20th century and never appeared in the Bible until a 1946 Revised Standard Version."[266] Prior to that, *arsenokoitai* was translated "abusers of themselves and mankind" in the King James Version.

As I studied the cultural setting of the New Testament, I discovered another common form of homosexuality of the day was *pederasty*—the oppressive male-initiation practice in the Greco-Roman world of men having sex with young teen or pre-pubescent boys. Although I remember a few Bible commentators mentioning *shrine prostitution* when discussing passages like Romans, Chapter one, I have no recollection of any evangelical pastor or teacher mentioning *pederasty* in all my years in the church. If *pederasty* was common in the Greco-Roman world, then certainly New Testament writers like Paul would probably have referred to it.

Pederasty was sometimes consensual and sometimes forced. There were brothel houses filled with young boys, whose existences were devoted to being the passive partners in pederast relationships with a man. Beautiful boy youths were sometimes castrated to prolong their feminine-like features. The most famous example was when the Roman Emperor Nero castrated his slave-boy Sporus, dressed him in women's clothing, and married him.[267] In the instances when it was forced, it is likely the exploitive man would have been called *arsenokoitai.*

Another term that is often associated with homosexuality in the New Testament is *malakos* (translated "male prostitutes" in I Corinthian 6:9-10 in the NIV). Scholars are certain this term means something like our term "effeminate." It is sometimes associated with male homosexuality but not always. Other uses in Greek literature reveal that it primarily means a male who is "soft," overly feminine, or controlled by women, and could even mean laziness or coward-ice.[268] One commentator makes a strong case that the combination of terms, *pornoi* (from the term we discussed earlier *porneia,* which one scholar translates *harlotry*), *malakos, arsenokoitai*, and another term translated "slave traders" found in lists of behaviors that Paul condemns in I Corinthians and I Timothy refers to the practice of *pederasty.* The young boys are the male prostitutes (*pornoi* or *mala-kos*), the men who "bed" them are *arsenokoitai,* and the ones who gain economically are the slave traders.[269] In fact, the New Jerusalem Bible translation supports this view. It translates *malakos* as "cata-mites," a term that refers to the boys kept by a pederast.

The overwhelming conclusion of this study was that the verses normally used by evangelicals to condemn both male and female homosexuality are talking about certain forms of homosexuality common in biblical times into the first century. They are not talk-ing about consensual homosexual relationships not associated with temple prostitution or exploitation. In other words, the Bible doesn't address the modern concept of gay and lesbian relationships based on one's sexual orientation. The Holiness Code condemns male homosexuality (not female) on the basis of obsolete purity rules within cultures where soldiers raped men as a way of humiliating their enemy and Baal worshipers dominated males sexually during sacred orgies. The New Testament condemns exploitive sexual relationships and those associated with idolatry. If this is the conclusion of the best biblical scholarship, why are evangelicals still insisting gays and lesbians repent of their sin and transform into practicing heterosexuals or remain celibate? Why do they cast scorn on the LGBT community? Could my friend Steve ever see the logic of these facts? I was about to find out.

GAY TALK AT THE PUB

My Belgium Blonde Ale tasted good. I placed it on the counter as an attractive, brown-haired woman with a Silver City nametag that spelled *Brenda* walked up to Steve and me. Her words interrupted my thoughts about Jake and my evolution on homosexuality. "You guys need a menu?"

"I don't. Steve?"

"I'm alright."

Earlier, while Steve and I were engrossed in our intense discussion about sex, Dan was watching the Celtics game and had started a conversation with the person to his left. The game had about 50 seconds left. Kevin Garnett had just hit a 17-foot jumper, putting the Celtics ahead by four. *It still could go either way*, I thought.

"Okay, Mike," Steve started again after taking a gulp of his Porter. "Since we've been talking about sex, I've been meaning to ask you. What do you say in your book about homosexuality?"

Oh well. I've already swum in the deep end. I might as well dive off the high dive.

"Well, in a nutshell, I say Scripture only condemns certain forms of homosexuality—the same way it does some forms of heterosexual-ity. The church has mistranslated and misinterpreted many passages."

"Why am I not surprised?" Steve responded. "I think you've read too many of those Bible revisionists. They've clouded your thinking. When I hear this stuff, what I don't get is this idea that suddenly someone today has figured out the church has misread Scripture. Like, how could the church be wrong all these centuries?"

"Yeah, but don't forget, the church has been wrong many times. It was wrong on discrimination against women, slavery... things like that. In fact, the church really didn't start its bias against homosexu-ality until the 12th century."

"Where did you get that?" Steve probed.

"From church history. Before that period, the church was indiffer-ent to homosexuality and occasionally supportive of a gay subculture among clergy and nuns.[270] But that's beside the point. What counts isn't what the church or the apostolic creeds teach, but what the orig-inal biblical authors meant when they wrote the passages in question and whether their teaching passes the tests of love and reason."

"I'm not sure where you get your history, Mike. But regarding meaning, it seems to me that's pretty obvious. I mean, Moses in Leviticus and Paul in the epistles were not ambiguous about this." Steve was referring to places in the Bible where both of us knew homosexuality was addressed. "I mean, really. Aren't those passages pretty clear?"

"Well, on the surface, but looking deeper, no. The writer of Leviticus was writing the Holiness Code for the people of Israel. He wasn't writing a law to apply to the whole human race for perpe-tuity. I mean, we just talked about this. We ignore tons of stuff in Leviticus." I also reminded him of Paul's astounding statement that believers are no longer under the supervision of the law or Torah.

"Sure, the Torah included a lot of ceremonial law." Steve conceded. "The ceremonial stuff isn't for all mankind, but moral laws are. Leviticus speaks of homosexuality as sin and makes a moral rule against it."

"Well, no," I countered. "It doesn't speak of all homosexuality but only the behavior of males. Female homosexuality isn't mentioned in the entire Old Testament. The questions are what type of homosexuality was common in antiquity? What exactly was the author referring to? And is it relevant to our modern concept of homosexual orientation?"

I explained to Steve about the discoveries I had made about homosexuality in Israel's history and the surrounding culture. In other words, homosexual rape, humiliating one's enemies after a battle, and shrine prostitution, which included when males became involved in ceremonial orgies that were dedicated to foreign gods. This is why passages[271] in I Kings and Hosea refer to "male prostitutes," "shrine prostitutes," and "male shrine prostitutes," I told him. "You see," I said, "all of these facts strengthen the case that only certain forms of male homosexuality were condemned in the Torah, and that did not include responsible, loving relationships between people with a homosexual orientation."

"Okay, the Leviticus passages aside, Paul's letters in the New Testament are very clear that homosexuality is a sin. They confirm it was abhorrent to God throughout Israel's history." Steve countered.

"Wait a minute," I said. "You have to answer those same questions I referred to before coming to a conclusion. What did Paul originally mean and does his teaching pass the test of love and reason?"

"You keep saying that—passing the test of love and reason. That sounds like an excuse to justify anything. How do we know our concept of love and our reasoning are correct? Doesn't the Bible say the human heart is desperately wicked? Isn't that why we need the Bible to be our guide?"

"Your questions imply we're not able to think for ourselves," I said. "Maybe we need both the Bible *and* our reason. Like, if it weren't for love and reason, the church would still be condoning slavery by applying the Bible literally. If Christians hadn't employed reason during the American Revolution they would have remained British loyalists. They would have blindly believed those verses in Romans

and be compelled, you know, to 'submit themselves to the governing
authorities' and 'pay taxes' or else be 'rebelling against what God has
instituted.'

"It's love and reason that leads us to ignore some of the radical
laws in the Bible. We evangelicals don't stone our kids for cursing
us, as Leviticus commands. Even though most churches don't allow
women to be pastors, we at least permit women to speak in church,
even though Paul supposedly commanded they be silent in congregations.[272] Finally, contrary to popular opinion, the Bible doesn't
claim it (a written code) should be our guide but that the Spirit and
love should be our guide, which is Paul's argument in the book of
Romans." I paused and lifted my glass to my lips. "No, the Bible isn't
the ultimate guide. The Spirit and love is."

"Just because love is our guide doesn't mean we can ignore what
Scripture teaches," Steve said. "You're taking extreme license to toss
away parts of the Bible."

"I'm not tossing them away. I'm trying to get at what they really
mean and how they apply to us today," I explained. "For example, the
word *homosexual*. In modern translations it's a mistranslation. In the
New Testament, the original Greek word doesn't mean *homosexual*."

"That sounds suspicious," Steve said. "What does it mean then?"

"I'm not sure how to pronounce it but the word is *arsenokoitai*.
Scholars confess it's meaning is obscure because it was rarely used in
Greek literature. Literally it means 'male beds' and many conclude it
has something to do with sexual exploitation by men. It can't mean
homosexuality in general—it is not about lesbianism at all, for example. The King James translates it as a strange phrase. Something like
'abusers of themselves with mankind.'"

"Okay, but maybe the general sense is the same," Steve objected.
"It must have still referred to what we call homosexuality. Biblical
translators must have had a good reason for putting it in there."

"That's a huge assumption," I said. "You have to take into
account what was common in that time period. For example, when
Paul addresses homosexuality, he's not talking of every instance of

homoerotic behavior. In Romans he's speaking in the context of idolatry. The preponderance of evidence points to him referring to shrine prostitution. In other passages he's using ambiguous Greek words and is more likely referring to the common practice of pederasty and possibly homosexual rape. Paul did not address the morality of mutual, loving homosexual relationships."

Steve didn't buy it. "You are obviously reading too many of those liberal scholars influenced by gay activists."

"No, I'm not," I replied. "Actually, many of the Bible commentators who study this are from an evangelical background, like Jack Rogers and Lewis Smedes."[273]

"Look," Steve leaned closer to me to emphasize what he was about to say. "The proof that the Bible refers to all homosexuality as sinful is the verse in Genesis where God says he made humans male and female and a man should leave his parents to be united to his wife. There is no reference to homosexual couplings at all, nor examples of them anywhere in Scripture. You're being deceived, Mike!"

I really didn't want to get in an argument with Steve, but I had to make another point. "Steve, I think that view is reading into Scripture something that is not there. Sure, the Bible talks about heterosexual relationships in Genesis because that was the only way to propagate the human race. I mean, that verse doesn't even mention homosexuality. What if the Bible only condemns some forms of homosexuality? You know, relationships that are exploitive or integrated with worshiping idols, stuff like that. I find no evidence that homosexuals can change their orientation. Therefore, love and reason demand they be accepted. Biblically, their only limitations are the same limitations for heterosexuals: you know, love one another, treat each other kindly, be responsible."

"But, Mike, homosexuals can change," Steve said. "There are many ministries for gays and scores of testimonies about people being delivered from it."

"I used to think that, too, but it's really a half truth." A flood of memories entered my mind: my conversation with Jake when I learned Don was gay, reading Mel White's book, and about another friend of mine, Grant. "Have you heard of Mel White?"

"I don't think so."

"He's a gay evangelical writer who for years tried to live as a heterosexual. He tried everything but eventually concluded God accepted him as a gay man. He wrote a book about it. I have two friends who have similar stories. My friend Don grew up in a strong evangelical home and finally concluded it was wrong for him to pretend he was straight. I have this other friend named Grant I worked with in Malawi. He was married for years and had two kids. When we worked together I didn't even realize he struggled with homosexuality. He fully expected God to deliver him. It didn't happen. In fact, once when he joined an Exodus group to rid himself of being gay, the leader actually hit on him!"

"Those stories are probably few and far between," Steve said.

"With all the other stories I read on the Internet, I don't think so. Then there's the claim that gays and lesbians come from a sexually abusive past. Although some were abused as children or came from broken homes, many weren't and didn't. My friend Don and Mel White, for example. They have no such background. Troubled childhoods can't explain their homosexuality. Many heterosexuals come from such backgrounds as well, so clearly upbringing is not a cause, but a weak correlation at best."

"Again, you're probably ignoring other research on this," Steve claimed.

"I could say the same about you," I countered. "Look, claiming all homosexuality is sinful creates an enormous pastoral problem for the church. Most people cannot change. God doesn't take away their homosexual drives. Even John Stossel's independent research demonstrates this."[274]

Steve placed his hands on his head, put his head down, and sighed. Looking up, he continued, "Listen, Mike. People can change their behavior. Sure, they will still have urges, temptations. But that doesn't give them license to act on them. Heterosexuals are tempted to have sex outside of marriage, but they are still called to be faithful. If a drug addict or pedophile still struggles to change after asking God for help, do we tell them they can go ahead and abuse themselves and others? Of course not!"

"Yeah, but Steve, those analogies are not the same," I responded. "Marital unfaithfulness, whether sexual or non-sexual, is wrong because it hurts people. Addictive behavior harms the addict, and, well, pedophilia devastates the psyche of children. If homosexual relationships are mutual and loving, they harm no one. They don't violate the law of love."

"Yeah, but they violate Scripture!" Steve raised his voice, catching the attention of those seated near us.

"But, Steve, they really don't. The Bible doesn't say responsible homosexual relationships *are* a sin! The church keeps saying homosexuality is sinful, period, but that's not what the passages really mean. The authors weren't condemning loving gay relationships."

"Well, I think you're twisting Scripture," Steve responded. "Look, if homosexuals think they can't become heterosexual, then they should remain celibate. I don't buy your revisionist take on the Bible. The church has always condemned homosexual behavior. If their urges remain, they shouldn't act on them."

"That's like telling a heterosexual who doesn't have the gift of celibacy to become a monk, Steve. What gives us the right to order a class of people to not express themselves sexually?"

We were in a stalemate. It became obvious that neither of us was going to convince the other. Right then, Dan leaned over, tapped my hand, and pointed to the flat screen. The Celtics had held on to their lead and won the game.

"All right!" I declared. My tall mug of ale was about half full. Same with Steve's. For a minute or so we all stared at the screen watching the post-game commentary. Then Steve spoke again.

"I suppose you support gay marriage too."

"Well, yeah, I do. I would prefer calling them civil unions, but yes. I think it should be allowed and in some cases encouraged, because marriage tends to foster long-term, responsible relationships. What about you, are you worried that gay marriage will undermine traditional marriage?"

"Yes, absolutely. It changes the definition of marriage."

"Hmm. Frankly, I never understood why we evangelicals are so concerned that heterosexual marriage will crumble if gay marriage is allowed."

"It opens the door to look at marriage as something foreign to what God intended," Steve said.

By now, my fervor to share my views had subsided. It had been an emotionally charged and draining conversation. I wanted to tell Steve more. I wanted him to hear some of the stories of gay Christians I had read on *anythingbutstraight.com* or *beyondexgay.com*. It would be great for him to listen to the late Lewis Smedes, a respected evangelical author and professor at Fuller Seminary, share how he changed his view on homosexuality.[275] Or, see the powerful and provocative documentary *For the Bible Tells Me So*, which traces several families as they react to news of their son or daughter's homosexual orientation. Some parents grew to affirm their child's homosexuality after learning the biblical and psychological evidence. One mother who learned too late had to endure estrangement and tragedy. Her daughter eventually committed suicide.

Or perhaps he could see the video on YouTube of Jennifer Knapp, acclaimed contemporary Christian musician, when she came out as a lesbian on national television in an interview with Larry King.[276] She courageously stood up to two other guests, a conservative evangelical pastor and the disgraced former mega-church pastor, Ted Haggard. In the face of Knapp's convictions and story, the pastor came across as legalistic and judgmental. Haggard's remarks danced around King's pointed questions, avoiding straight answers to questions like, "Will someone like Jennifer go to hell?" Despite my desire for Steve to hear all this, it seemed time to give it a rest. Even though Steve was theologically conservative, I still respected him for his convictions.

It wasn't so long ago that I felt exactly the same way. For an awkward moment Steve and I sat quietly sipping our beers.

"Sounded like you were talking about the gay rights chapter," Dan said, breaking the silence.

"Yes," Steve sighed. "We didn't exactly agree on that topic either." I knew Dan would have been more open to my position. Nevertheless, I told myself we should change the subject. As the silence continued among all of us, I wondered how I get myself into such controversy. All I want is to get as close to the truth as I can.

I remembered another area where I attempted to do that: the polarized creation/evolution debate. Over the course of many years I had tried, through study, to reconcile my faith with the science of origins. That journey had taken me to a position few people have espoused. Although I knew I'd have some common ground with both Dan and Steve, I wasn't sure how much. Would we end up talking about it? What did Dan think of my chapter on this subject? What would Steve say? What would they think of the six key discoveries I made?

INTELLIGENT DEBATE

"Faith is the great cop-out, the great excuse to evade the need to think and evaluate evidence."[277]

– *Orthodox Evolutionist Richard Dawkins*

"When science and the Bible differ, science has obviously misinterpreted its data."[278]

– *Creationist Henry Morris*

"Dogmas and taboos may be suitable for religion, but they have no place in science."[279]

– *Unorthodox Evolutionist James A. Shapiro*

When we humans ponder our blue celestial home teeming with life, we are filled with fascination and wonder. Spinning in outer space, planet Earth orbits a massive fireball—a blazing star energized by nuclear fusion—residing in a vast solar system within a galaxy made up of billions of other fiery stars. Up to 200 billion of these galaxies occupy our known universe. These facts inspire us to ask daunting cosmic questions: How did we get here? For what purpose?

Are we alone? And the real stumper: why on Earth are there no television commercials for *quality* beer?

As a microbrew enthusiast, I believe this last question provides a good illustration for the topic at hand.

In America, the best beers are not promoted on television. This is an outrage. An unsuspecting foreigner only exposed to the media would conclude Americans only drink Budweiser, Miller, Coors, and Michelob. And maybe Sam Adams on special occasions. Authentic, fiercely independent, and superior craft brews—the Alaskan Ambers, Fat Tires, and Mac & Jack's of our land, representing almost 1,500 microbreweries in the United States—are under the radar.

In similar fashion, the best arguments that answer the ultimate Great Question of Life—*How did we get here?*—are also under the radar. People hear explanations for this question largely filtered through the mainstream media or expounded by dogmatic Biblicists. One rarely hears a *quality-beer* answer, despite the fact that the question is one of the greatest challenges to reconciling faith and reason.

During my years of searching, I uncovered authentic answers—not necessarily <u>the</u> answer—to the ultimate Great Question, first as a young evangelical and later as a wayfaring iconoclast. They came by carefully examining the arguments in the evolution vs. creation debate. The best way to do this, I found, was to approach the issue like a *whodunit* detective mystery.

THE SUSPECTS

"In the beginning, God created the heavens and the earth." This is the first sentence I read when I sat down to read the Bible from cover to cover as a twenty-two-year-old evangelical. At its face, I saw no contradiction between this simple statement and science. Faith is acknowledging a Creator God who is the source of the universe and life. Science is the study of how the universe and life operates— possibly how this God put it all together. In this sense, although it would be naïve to label people as such, logic dictates that anyone who believes in God is a *creationist*, even if he or she believes in evolution.

I had to admit in my experience in college academia, my science, history, and philosophy professors rarely put it in those terms. They never said, "Okay, science class, this semester you'll learn how God knit the world together." More common was a prevailing attitude that faith in a miraculous Creator God was simplistic and did not square with the findings of history or science.

"Jesus of Nazareth arose as a Jewish religious figure in the first century and attracted a following among the poor and uneducated," my stodgy Environmental History professor declared. "Most historians agree that later followers of Jesus fabricated the miracles and Messianic claims attributed to him. He was merely a wise teacher, not the Son of God."

"Biological evolution explains the origin of life on earth without the need to appeal to a miraculous creator," my Botany teacher confidently asserted.

Although there were some exceptions, these voices were common and revealed that Christianity or faith in God was frequently belittled among academians. Faith was a non-thinking phenomenon that the ignorant masses held on to for hope; only science was willing to evaluate hard facts and evidence. Richard Dawkins said it best: Faith is the great cop-out.

Professors and authors with this view gave the standard scientific answer to the first great question of life. How did we get here? We were not created. We evolved. We descended with modification from a common ancestor from the ancient past, going back to the first form of life several hundred million years ago on an earth that is four billion years old. The mechanism through which we evolved was natural selection acting on random mutations of DNA. The operative word is "random," meaning the process was undirected, as Darwin's theory argues. The evolution of life was unguided and purposeless, so that living things, although they sometimes may have the appearance of being designed,[280] are not. This view is best described as materialistic evolution and formed the intellectual basis for atheism. It also argues the abiogenesis explanation for the origin of the first life forms—that life arose from inorganic matter purely by natural processes.

I confess that until recently I was prejudiced toward atheists. I bought into the typical attitude in evangelical churches. Atheists deny a Creator to avoid accountability with a moral God and to justify their sinful lifestyles, went the reasoning. Then I discovered there were two types of atheists. One, those who have an axe to grind, who doggedly stick to their ideological position, regardless of the data and its implications. And two, intellectually honest atheists, who stick to the Socratic principle: go where the evidence leads. I eventually developed a deep respect for the latter.

Today, it's obvious to me that these two personalities among atheists are also present among people holding other philosophical positions. In investigating this issue, it's important for the detective to recognize the axe-to-grind personality, whether within the camps of biblical creationism, materialistic evolution, or something in between. Axe-to-grind people typically won't be willing to go where the evidence leads. Thus, one of my key discoveries:

(1) Intellectual honesty has the moral high ground, whatever one believes about life origins.

There were a few occasions in my early quest for answers when I encountered professors or science authors who were theistic evolutionists—those who believe in God *and* evolution. They would largely argue that God only created the universe and then the first form of life; thereafter, God allowed evolution to take its course, somehow mysteriously involved in knowing the outcome, although it was still a purely random, undirected process. In fact, most people I met as friends and colleagues outside the evangelical church seemed to be theistic evolutionists, although most of them wouldn't go so far as to say that the process of evolution was totally undirected. Perhaps this is because theistic evolution that strictly follows orthodox evolutionary theory—meaning the process is random—is problematic. How can an omniscient God allow for a truly random process? Omniscience means all knowing in terms of outcomes. But orthodox science says evolution knows nothing of outcomes. It has no end in mind.

I suppose this is why your average evolution-adhering theist on the street believes God guided evolution—that it wasn't random. In fact, this was my position before I became involved in the evangelical church and was exposed to the "biblical" view. Again, in this broader perspective and at the risk of being simplistic, theistic evolutionists are technically creationists. Regardless of the specifics, God is the source of life.

Theistic evolution, at least the non-random variety, has always struck me as a perfectly reasonable position. It acknowledges the need for a supernatural transcendental Being to create life, sustain it, and cause it to evolve. It denies that life can originate from non-life and complete randomness. Yet I have no recollection of meeting an evangelical believer who was a theistic evolutionist. Not to say there are none, I just don't remember meeting any. The reason for this was the church taught that evolution contradicted the clear teaching of the Bible. When one reads Scripture literally, this appears to be true.

In opposition to these views on evolution, in my new life inside the evangelical community, I was taught the Bible had the answers to *all* great questions of life, and science would only confirm what the Bible said. One day at UMass Amherst, I heard about biblical creationism for the first time. I was in a conversation with fellow evangelicals.

"Life did not evolve. God created the universe and then the earth and all living things probably less than 10,000 years ago as an act of special creation," a fellow believer confidently affirmed. "The universe, earth, and all of biological life was created in six 24-hour days as described in Genesis."

I learned this was the young-earth creationist view—extremely popular in the 1980s among evangelicals because of the widespread trend to take the Bible literally as the inerrant Word of God. Its roots grew in 1970, when Henry Morris, an engineer and evangelical apologist, founded the Institute for Creation Research (ICR), to promote what was coined creation science, or scientific creationism—the notion that the Genesis account of creation and any other pronouncements in the Bible concerning origins or the history of life (e.g., Noah's worldwide flood) are literally true and challenge modern scientific theories on the antiquity of the universe, geology, and evolution. Staunch supporters of creation science, such as Morris, often argue that the teaching of evolution is satanic and at least partially responsible for the moral decline of America.

As a new believer who was excited about my new relationship with God, I initially accepted the creation science position as legitimate. After all, the Bible did say God created the universe, Earth, and the first humans in six days. It seemed reasonable at first that the Earth was relatively young, based on the genealogies in Genesis. As I discussed in Confession 5, without a more careful examination of the original language of the Bible and inherent translation problems, it's easy to come to this conclusion if one believes in biblical inerrancy. But the detective in me always asks more questions when things don't line up. I soon learned about some of the problematic assertions of creation science.

First was the way it made the Bible trump scientific evidence. Folks who believed in inerrancy were asking questions like, *What if the Bible and science contradicted each other? Which one would be more reliable?* Their answer, and those of almost all of the churches, college ministries, and evangelical books I was reading, was that the Bible is the more reliable. The position could be summed up as "When science and the Bible differ, science has obviously misinterpreted its data."[281] But after initially accepting creation science, I changed my view when I learned that there was a third answer to that question. Not that the Bible was necessarily wrong (in this case Genesis) or that science had misinterpreted data, but that the church had misinter-preted Genesis and its purpose. In other words, the original meaning and intent of the Bible is often misunderstood, mistranslated, *or* the Bible was never meant to be the source of precise scientific assertions. This was part of my discovery of Bible abuse.

Creation science does not allow for the mistranslation, misinter-pretation, and misuse of the Bible. It insists on *uncritically* examining the biblical text. For instance, the Hebrew word translated *day* in the first chapter of Genesis is *yom,* a word that can mean anything from a 12-hour period to an unspecified period of time.[282] Creation science insists this word can only mean a 24-hour day. But this is patently false. In fact, the word is translated into many other words in other places in the Old Testament, including *year, time, age, season,* and even *forever*![283] Experts in Hebrew say the arguments that creation scientists give as to why the Genesis passage has to mean 24-hour days are not supported by common Hebrew grammatical rules.[284]

Moreover, reading the first chapter of Genesis carefully, one finds that the sun wasn't created until the fourth day. How could there be 24-hour solar days before the sun was even created? Conclusion: this word *yom* can easily refer to a period of thousands or millions of years, depending on its context.[285]

Creation science refuses to acknowledge such points. It ignores all evidence contrary to its a priori religious beliefs. Another example is its explanation of the data about the age of the universe and the earth. My scientific creationist friends at UMass Amherst insisted there must be flaws with scientific dating techniques, or possibly, that God created the universe with only the appearance that stars were billions of light years away, and therefore stars only seemed to be of an astronomical age. Of course, the scientific data—and even the biblical and theological data—doesn't support this view. The antiq-uity of the universe (14 billion years old) and earth (four billion plus years old) is well established by proven scientific dating techniques. Genesis doesn't assert that acts of creation occurred in 24-hour days.

Moreover, God's character seemed inconsistent with making celestial bodies appear old when they are not.

A final example is the insistence by creation science that Noah's flood depicted in Genesis was a worldwide flood based on a literal interpretation of the biblical narrative. I learned that scientific consensus in geology, physics, chemistry, archeology, and paleontology, contradicts even the possibility of a worldwide global flood. So is the Bible wrong? Again, the evidence pointed to the fact that the Bible narrative on the flood is misinterpreted and even mistranslated. For instance, the Hebrew word, *erets*, translated *earth* in the aforementioned passage (as in "the flood waters covered the earth") is also translated *ground*, *land*, and *country* in other places in the Old Testament.[286] Abraham was told to get out of his *country* [*erets*] into a *land* [erets] God would show him (Genesis 12:1). Obviously, the Hebrew word *erets* should not be translated *earth* regarding Abraham's sojourn. So why so in the flood narrative? It made more sense that the Genesis flood account was referring to a local flood, given these truths, and in light of the fact that people living in antiquity had no concept of a global planet. To them, the *whole earth* was the geographical region known to them.

Consequently, I quickly became an old-earth creationist—still believing that God created the universe, earth, life, and first humans essentially the way Genesis described, but within the general time frames that scientific evidence had established. My newest position was based on this next key discovery:

(2) Creation science is based on uncritical, literalist interpretations of the Bible and a pre-conceived notion about the Bible's purpose.

But my new view was not necessarily on the fringe. The evangelical church was divided on this issue. It appeared that perhaps two thirds of us were young-earth creationists, like the friends

I had conversations with in college, and one third of us were old-earth creationists.[287] Moreover, there were very few, if any, theistic evolutionists, among our ranks. It also seemed that most of us were obsessed with insisting that the one true Christian position was to reject *any form* of evolution. Dogmatism ruled the day.

THE PLOT THICKENS

I learned much about the creation vs. evolution controversy my first years as an evangelical—who the major players were (young-earth creationists, old-earth creationists, theistic evolutionists, materialistic evolutionists, atheists) and the resultant likely suspects in the mystery. As I delved into the study of evolution, I discovered the same thing was true of the theory of evolution as was true with evangelicals' creationist theories on the Bible. Scientists don't always agree on how to interpret the data. There were several theories within the theory. One of those theories got me thinking about how to approach the issue.

One day I sat down in the geology library at UMass Amherst and cracked open a book that referred to a paper written by famous paleontologists Niles Eldredge and Stephen J. Gould. I was doing research for an unusual science elective called Popular Anthropology. The class investigated instances of pseudoscience, such as the work of Erich von Daniken and the claims of evidence for extraterrestrials he presented in his book *Chariots of the Gods?* I was gathering material for a paper on creationism. I wanted to make a case that, although much of what creationists teach is pseudoscience, *some* of their arguments aren't.[288]

I began reading how Eldredge and Gould developed a controversial theory that challenged the prevailing Darwinian view of evolution. They proposed that all reproducing species underwent little or no evolutionary change during extended periods of stasis or evolutionary stagnation. When evolution occurred, it was rare and happened in rapid bursts during much shorter periods of geologic time. Gould coined this theory *punctuated equilibrium*. Both authors initially were accused of being anti-Darwinist.

What piqued my interest was the evidence that the theory is based on. Eldredge and Gould were admitting one of the problems with Darwinian evolution. "The absence of fossil evidence for inter-mediary stages between major transitions in organic design, indeed our inability, even in our imagination, to construct functional inter-mediates in many cases, has been a persistent and nagging problem for gradualistic accounts of evolution."[289] More recently, Eldredge reflected on the reactions of the day. "Darwin... enjoined us to expect evolution for the most part to be slow, steady, and gradual—whereas to me the fossil record screams loudly that such, for the most part, is not the case."[290]

These paleontologists were saying the fossil record does not support the common view that evolution generally occurs uniformly by a steady and gradual transformation—a view attributed to Darwin himself. Traditional evolutionists would argue that we don't see a steady transformation because the fossil record is imperfect, i.e., we don't have a full picture of what happened from fossils because there were times when fossilization didn't occur. But Gould, Eldredge, and others were saying otherwise. "Evolutionary biologists can no longer ignore the fossil record on the ground that it is imperfect."[291] They argued the evidence supported that species in the fossil record remained essentially the same for long periods of time (millions of years) and then in a short geologic time span (at the most 50,000 years[292]) new species appeared.

As I read these accounts, a lingering question began to form in my mind: Is there fossil evidence that evolution occurred during these short time spans, or do the new species simply occur in the fossil record without any precedents? In other words, during these short periods, do the fossils reveal a rapid burst of evolutionary sequences with a succession of increasingly advanced species? I continued read-ing and uncovered the answer: there is little if any fossil evidence for evolutionary bursts, only claims that it is supported by population genetics. The Cambrian Explosion—the rapid appearance of most major phyla in the fossil record around 530 million years ago—is a classic example of this. Prior to this period, most organisms were simple, made up of individual cells organized in colonies. It was like evolution didn't occur and then suddenly (geologically speaking), major animal types appeared. *Punctuated equilibrium* is a way of making sense of things like the Cambrian Explosion by explaining that evolution must have occurred very rapidly after long periods of stasis. According to the theory, the time taken for speciation to occur was so short it was insufficient for the concentrated transitional forms to be fossilized, which is why so few of them have been discovered. It was a way of explaining evolution, not based on the preponderance of fossil evidence, but rather based on the lack of fossil evidence for intermediates.

When it comes to gradualism, Eldridge and Gould would take issue with the phrase "an absence of evidence is not evidence of absence." In fact, Eldridge said "the fossil record [the absence of enough intermediary fossils] screams loudly" that gradualistic evolution did not occur. Hoping, expecting, assuming, interpolating, and imagining major fossil transitions in organic design doesn't make it true. Absence may not rule out future discoveries, but it does mean claims to the probable presence of intermediates are speculation.

Shortly after this, I went to my undergraduate geology professor and shared my misgivings about the evidence for evolution, particularly gradualism, and to my surprise he gave me more ammunition. "These critics have a point," he said. "Evolution still has the support of much evidence, but where the fossil record is particularly problematic is among the marine invertebrates. They show up with virtually no sign of prior ancestors."

Two things struck me. First, there was dissent in the house of evolution. Second, the fossil evidence for gradualistic evolution was lacking, and the competing theory did not have widespread acceptance. In later years, Richard Dawkins criticized punctuated equilibrium and called it an "interesting but minor wrinkle on the surface of neo-Darwinian theory."[293]

These initial studies of mine about creationism and evolution were in the early 1980s. Since then I discovered other voices of variance at odds with orthodox theories of evolution. In 1997, a bacterial geneticist at the University of Chicago, James A. Shapiro, first expressed his views, based on his research in genetics, that there was "a third way" in evolution between neo-Darwinian orthodoxy and creationism. He lamented the fact that, despite growing, new, and revolutionary knowledge of "molecular details and biological organization," open-minded discussion among scientists about the impact of these discoveries on evolutionary theory is exceedingly rare. "The possibility of a non-Darwinian, scientific theory of evolution is virtually never considered,"[294] he states.

In his article, *A Third Way*, Shapiro laid out four areas of new discoveries that open up new ways of thinking about evolutionary processes: (1) *Genome Organization,* in which he concluded, "Localized random mutation...and gradual modification of individual functions are unable to provide satisfactory explanations for the molecular data, no matter how much time for change is assumed." (2) *Cellular Repair Capabilities*, where he concluded, "It has been a surprise to learn how thoroughly cells protect themselves against precisely the kinds of accidental genetic change that, according to conventional theory [neo-Darwinism], are the source of evolutionary variability. (3) *Natural Genetic Engineering*, about which he stated, "genetic change can be massive and non-random." And (4) *Cellular Information Processing,* where he advanced the notion that a cellular repair system is "a molecular computation network demonstrating biologically useful properties of self-awareness and decision-making."

Despite these new revelations, Darwinian evolutionary theory rules the scientific world. Shapiro states, "...neo-Darwinist writers like Dawkins continue to ignore or trivialize the new knowledge and insist on gradualism as the only path for evolutionary change."[295] Shapiro claimed the reason why neo-Darwinists resist revising evolutionary theory is ideological, not scientific. He expects religious creationists to do such, but not his fellow scientists, who should have "a more open spirit of inquiry." Fundamentalists are on both sides of the Creationist-Darwinist debate, he says. What does Shapiro want? To address the central question *scientifically* that these new discoveries reveal: "Is there any guiding intelligence at work in the origin of species displaying exquisite adaptations...?"[296] Shapiro continues to expound his views today in his writing and teaching with titles such as *A 21ˢᵗ Century View of Evolution*, where he promotes viewing evolution as a systems engineering process.

In researching this chapter of the book, I learned of another renegade evolutionist, who happens to be from my alma mater, UMass Amherst (having taught there after I attended). Known for her unorthodox theory (at the time) of the origin of eukaryotic cells, Lynn Margulis (former wife of the late Carl Sagan) rejects neo-Darwinian evolution as an explanation of the diversity of life. She calls the reigning paradigm of evolutionary biology a "quaint, but potentially dangerous aberration," conceding that speciation solely due to "random mutation and differential survival" has yet to be proven.[297] In an article about her in *Science*,[298] the author tells us Margulis thinks neo-Darwinism "needs to be tossed out in order for science to answer 'basic questions' like why stasis is so prevalent in the fossil record, and how one species can evolve from another." She later formulated a theory to answer those questions that proposes that symbiotic relationships between organisms drive evolution.

The core of these alternative views on evolution brought me to two more realizations:

(3) There are fundamentalists on both sides of the Evolution-Creation debate.

(4) Darwinian explanations for evolution (natural selection acting on a gradual accumulation of random genetic change) do not square with the scientific evidence.

Still, philosophically I was not opposed to the concept of evolution. Maybe there was a non-Darwinian way to explain it, as Gould, Shapiro, and Margulis said. In fact, the man who was credited as the co-discoverer of natural selection along with Charles Darwin, Alfred Russel Wallace, did not believe materialistic mechanisms explain all of evolution. In his writings and book, *World of Life*, he argued the limits of natural selection and theorized *intelligent evolution* (IE).[299] My openness to evolution and such ideas as Wallace's didn't fit within the evangelical paradigm.

The church was couching the issue in black and white. Evolution was evil, and creationism, particularly the brand of it that a particular church or denomination espoused, was the only answer. Even though it wasn't until the late 1990s that I began to dive into the issue again and learn some important distinctions and some fascinating facts, I was hooked on following the debate.

DENYING DARWIN

In early 1998, my father, also an avid follower of the origins controversy, sent me a video copy of the recent *Firing Line* "Creation-Evolution Debate." I sat down to watch a most entertaining and engrossing spectacle as eight highly intelligent debaters sparred for two hours over the topic, "Resolved: The Evolutionists Should Acknowledge Creation." Not Creationism, but rather a form of "creation" that had to be at the root of the complexity and diversity of life. Moderated by a most witty Michael Kinsley, what struck me almost immediately were the personalities involved.

Many would have assumed the team arguing the affirmative were stock-in-trade scientific creationists from conservative Christian colleges, such as Henry Morris and another famous creationist named Duane Gish. But the affirmative team was far from your run-of-the-mill Bible thumpers. They included the hyper-intellectual, conservative-libertarian-hybrid William F. Buckley, a law professor from U.C. Berkeley named Phillip Johnson, a biochemist from Lehigh University named Michael Behe—an intelligent design (ID) theorist (ID is the notion that certain features in nature are best explained by an intelligent cause, not an undirected process such as natural selection) who makes the case that some organisms are irreducibly complex (the notion that there are some biological molecular machines, e.g., bacteria flagellum, that defy evolving through natural selection because all their parts are required to be fully present to function)—and the most fascinating of all the debaters, a mathematician and avowed agnostic, David Berlinski.

"Is William F. Buckley descended from monkeys?" Kinsley began. "That's one question we face in tonight's special *Firing Line* debate."

What the hell is someone like Berlinski doing arguing the creation side as an agnostic? I remember thinking after realizing who he was. *Could he be a true irreligious iconoclast on evolution?*

I soon learned I was correct. Berlinski, a secular Jew, had recently written a piece for *Commentary* called "The Deniable Darwin." If there ever was someone who could critique evolution and still claim he wasn't religiously motivated, it was Berlinski.

"My interest in divine creation is negligible," he confessed. In fact, when a debater on the other side assumed Berlinski advocates for intelligent design (ID), he simply said, "I don't." He's not even an ID theorist. I had to listen to what he had to say.

It was also interesting that the others on Berlinski's team were something other than the stereotype. Buckley, although Catholic, certainly wasn't known for being a fundamentalist on the lunatic fringe. Johnson taught at Berkeley, not exactly a bastion for conservative evangelicals. And Behe was a tenured biochemistry professor from another secular institution, Lehigh University.

Arguing in opposition of the resolution was an equally eclectic group of debaters. Ken Miller, a biologist from Brown University, was a theistic evolutionist who defended Darwinism. Michael Ruse, a philosopher of science at the University of Guelph near Toronto, was an atheist. Eugenie Scott was the director of the National Center for Science Education, and Barry Lynn, a lawyer and minister with the United Church of Christ, was the director of Americans United for Separation of Church and State.

What a group of unlikely cohorts. Agnostics and atheists arguing side by side with theists both for and against evolutionary theory!

I was enthralled with Berlinski from his opening lines.

"Darwin's theory of evolution is the last of the great 19th century mystery religions. And as we speak, it is now following Freudianism and Marxism into the nether regions, and I'm quite sure that Freud, Marx, and Darwin are commiserating one with the other, in the dark dungeon where discarded gods gather."

The crowd of spectators at Rutgers University chuckled. *You can't stereotype this guy,* I thought.

Halfway into the debate Berlinski argued that major transitions between species are missing from the fossil record—meaning there are major gaps between animal types where you would expect an intermediary evolutionary ancestor to bridge the two—in other words the same argument Eldredge and Gould made against gradualism.

When his opponents claimed there were in fact transitional fossils in the record at various levels, Berlinski didn't disagree, but wondered how significant they were in light of what Darwin's model of evolution required. He and his colleagues had been acknowledging the evidence for microevolution—when biological changes occur naturally within species or closely related species—as opposed to macroevolution—when biological changes result in the development of whole new classifications of organisms and animals, e.g., a new genus, family, order, class, or phylum, with new major bodily innovations. I had learned this distinction earlier and recalled it.

Microevolution, or as some call it, horizontal evolution, occurs when small-scale changes happen in gene frequencies in a population over a few generations usually on the level of a species. An example is when crop pests develop a resistance to pesticide. These changes can be easily observed, and no radically different species emerge.

Macroevolution, on the other hand, or as some call it, vertical evolution, is exceedingly more dramatic. It's when large-scale changes occur in organisms over a geologic period of time. An example is the evolutionary horse sequence where fox-sized animals developed into the modern horse and other related animals or the more dramatic land-mammal-to-whale sequence. These changes include the development of new species but have never been observed. Macroevolution supposedly occurs when natural selection, acting on random genetic variations, results in whole new body structures being formed. Since these changes have never been observed, the lineage is surmised from the data, not empirically confirmed. Not only is it not observed, but the mechanism of random mutations in DNA is problematic, since advantageous mutations are exceedingly rare or non-existent. Mutations are generally destructive.

Berlinski and his team were accusing their opponents of trying to bolster the theory of macroevolution with evidence that only proved microevolution.

At one point Berlinski asked, "What's your best estimate of the number of morphological changes required to take a dog-like animal to a sea-going whale?"

He was making the point that there were only three or four intermediate animals in the fossil record that could link the evolution of a land animal to a whale (the prevailing evolutionary theory on where whales came from), but the Darwinian theory required many more than that to reflect the physiological gradation that supposedly occurred.

I was fascinated how two of his opponents, Eugenie Scott and Ken Miller, evaded answering the question. Scott refused to answer it entirely, to which Berlinski asked, "Then how on earth can you commend the mechanism, if you are unsure whether it's adequate to the result?" Finally, Miller acknowledged the number of changes wouldn't be as high as 100,000, but Berlinski could never pin him down for a concrete figure. He only said it would be a "very, very large" number of changes.

I was starting to see Berlinski's point. Even if it was one tenth or even one hundredth of 100,000, say between 1,000 and 10,000 morphological changes, that implied the need for at least a similar number of transitional forms of animals to lead from a land creature to a gargantuan ocean-living mammal. Where is the evidence for that? Later I learned just how incredible the physical changes would need to be to transform a dog-like mammal into a whale. The lung and body capacities of whales are astounding. Sperm whales can dive over 6,000 feet and withstand enormous pressure and temperature changes. All whales carry nitrogen internally to prevent the bends. They retain a large volume of extra oxygen, store additional oxygen in muscle tissues, block blood from non-critical organs when oxygen is low, and use their flexible ribs to collapse their lungs at extreme pressures. They can communicate over thousands of miles, have a huge triangular tail for propulsion, have a breathe-blow hole on the top of their head, and an anus in the lower front of their body rather than the rear.[300] Each one of these physiological attributes would have had to evolve from radically different forms in a land mammal.

How could a handful of transitionals be adequate to demonstrate that a whale evolved into its present form? How did a breath/blow hole evolve from a nose and move to the top of their head? How did an anus in front derive from an anus in the rear? One may be able to envision how it happened, but where are the intermediate animals that demonstrate it? How did lungs and oxygen-carrying-and-preserving capacity evolve, and which fossilized animals support this? Are these types of physiological changes required for the whale's evolution only surmised and not observed? Could the mechanism of natural selection acting over time on random variations of DNA bring about these phenomenal morphological transformations? How is this substantiated? The looming questions behind Berlinski's initial question only grew.

The opposition kept hammering at Berlinski and the others that they were never satisfied with the number of transitionals that they would cite, which apparently were between three and 16, depending on the evolutionary sequence. But Berlinski would remind them that each sequence they named was also questioned in scientific literature by other evolutionists. They were often lateral transitions—evidence for microevolution at most, not evolution of major groups—or in the case of the horse sequence, they showed dozens of species that enter the record suddenly and then depart suddenly. In other words, there is no clear line to the modern horse. "We do not really know whether the modern horse has ancestral patterns with the dozens of other species that we find in the fossil record," he concluded.

I was fascinated with David Berlinski more than any of the other debaters because he seemed the most objective of all. He was neither religiously nor academically motivated. Although he wasn't an ID theorist, he believed that ID warrants serious consideration. He wasn't arguing against evolution per se, but against the self-assured arguments of orthodox Darwinists. In many ways, it was not unlike how Gould, Eldredge, Shapiro, and Margulis take on evolutionary purists. He acknowledged there are several well-documented transitional sequences in the fossil record but argued they represent a scant number of intermediate animals compared to the morphological changes that occur in each sequence. He took nothing for granted and questioned everything. It appeared that he just wanted to go where the evidence led. The quintessential skeptic. He must be a distant cousin of mine.

Over the next year or so after hearing this debate, I began reading more of the literature. I read Richard Dawkins' *The Blind Watchmaker* to learn more how evolutionists countered these types of critics. Dawkins is a brilliant defender of evolution, but he stayed clear of giving credibility to any of the critics of gradualistic evolution, such as Eldridge and Gould. In his world, there was complete uniformity. Some of his arguments against non-evolutionist theories were sound, but some appeared to be based on conjecture and had an audacious air to them. The attitude was, "Silly critics say this, but it's easy to *imagine* it could happen like this." His reasons weren't always based on empirical evidence.

I read microbiologist Michael Denton's *Evolution: A Theory in Crisis—How New Developments in Science Challenge Orthodox Darwinism*. He made forceful arguments that there is little support for Darwinian macroevolution from the fossil record and from his own field of molecular biology.

These findings solidified another conclusion:

(5) Although Darwinian theory [orthodox evolutionary dogma] adequately accounts for microevolution, it's a poor explanation for macroevolution.

NEW CRITICS AND INTELLIGENT DESIGN

The *Firing Line* debate opened my eyes to the new emerging critics of orthodox evolution of our day and the early stages of the ID movement. I learned that Philip Johnson, author of *Darwin on Trial*, was one of its founders, as was Michael Behe, who developed the concept of the *irreducible complexity* in certain organisms, e.g., bacteria flagellum. He also theorizes that ID can be detected in such complex systems.

Although many of these critics were obviously Christians (evangelical Philip Johnson and Catholic Michael Behe), they were moderates and a far cry from the dogmatic biblical literalists I had read a decade earlier like Henry Morris. They were not quoting Scripture in their arguments, they believed in the antiquity of the earth and universe, and they came from prestigious secular universities. Another is molecular and cell biologist Jonathan Wells (Ph.D. from UC Berkeley) whom I've had several conversations with, since he lives in my current hometown. He wrote *Icons of Evolution: Science or Myth?* and *The Politically Incorrect Guide to Darwinism and Intelligent Design*. Finally, Stephen C. Meyer would fall into the same category (a moderate evangelical). He is the Director of the Center for Science and Culture at the Discovery Institute in Seattle,

Washington, and wrote *Signature in the Cell: DNA and the Evidence for Intelligent Design,* a persuasive argument for the scientific validity of ID.

Not only did these critics not wear their faith on their sleeve, they held another important distinction. They welcomed the likes of David Berlinski as an ally—and as a senior fellow at the Discovery Institute—despite his agnosticism and his refusal to call himself an ID theorist. These critics, particularly Berlinski, are closer to the positions of Gould, Eldridge, Shapiro, and Margulis than purists care to admit. In recent years, when I read Berlinski's works in *The Deniable Darwin & Other Essays,* where he responds to his critics, I realized what a skilled polemicist he is. And how comical it is when critics assume he supports the doctrine of creationism. "I have never expressed support for theories of intelligent design, much less for creationism, and my essay, far from representing a change of mind—no bad thing, in any case—does nothing more than amplify objections I have long held and often voiced."[301]

Accepting Berlinski is not typical behavior for religious conservatives. No, I concluded this movement was a different animal from creation science, despite the claims by most evolutionists that its supporters are a bastion of backward-thinking Biblicists hiding under the cloak of ID.

A brief aside will illustrate this point and reveal how most evolutionists tend to stereotype their adversaries. With my interest in this subject and living in Seattle, I have attended several Discovery Institute briefings. At one of them in 2009, I had several interesting encounters.

"You seem to know a lot about the background and history of the intelligent design movement," a fellow attendee said, after cornering me in the food line during lunch. We had sat through the first morning's sessions and heard from the likes of Stephen Meyer and William Dembski (another leading ID theorist). "Maybe you could help me understand something," he added. "What is an 'evangelical Christian?'"

I was dumbfounded! How could he not know what an *evangelical* is? With the knee-jerk reaction that most people have to equate anything to do with ID theory with right-wing conservative Christianity (and the antiquated ideas of the Dark Ages, for that matter), I was curious how this guy got into a Discovery Institute event without at least knowing what kind of animal an evangelical is. He soon told me he was an American citizen who had lived in England for twelve years, where I knew evangelicals are more of a minority. He was a member of the Institute, having following the ID movement for several years. Later, another attendee I talked to described himself as a secular Jew, similar to Berlinski. Although it's true most supporters of the Discovery Institute tend to be religious conservatives, this is peripheral. At its core it is a non-sectarian organization.

And there are more critics of unguided evolution. I've already mentioned Michael Denton. In 1998 he wrote *Nature's Destiny: How the Laws of Biology Reveal Purpose in the Universe*, wherein he laid out the evidence the universe is biometrically fine-tuned for life. "...the cosmos is optimally adapted for life so that every constituent of the cell and every law of nature is uniquely and ideally fashioned to that end."[302] Denton still affirms biological evolution. What he rejects is natural selection as the driving force of macroevolution (although acknowledging it drives microevolution) and also creationist intervention theories and natural mysticism. Like Berlinski, Denton is no religiously motivated critic.

Another in the same vein is Richard Sternberg, who was highlighted in Ben Stein's movie, *Expelled: No Intelligence Allowed*. A former scientist at the Smithsonian Institute with a Ph.D. in molecular evolution, Sternberg is known for overseeing the review of an article advocating intelligent design (written by Stephen Meyer) published in a peer-reviewed journal, *Proceedings of the Biological Society of Washington*, of which Sternberg was the managing editor. As he relates in Stein's movie, the journal pressured him to resign, despite the fact that Smithsonian officials determined he did nothing wrong in the publication process.[303] Sternberg is critical of mainstream evolutionary biology for refusing to even consider alternatives to pure neo-Darwinism. When I spoke to him once at a Discovery Institute event he told me he was "agnostic" toward evolution.

Then there is the late Antony Flew, the former most renowned atheist in the world, who wrote *There is a God: How the World's Most Notorious Atheist Changed His Mind*. Although not a scientist, Flew was a brilliant philosopher who criticized the materialistic theory of abiogenesis.[304] He announced to a shocked world that he now believed some form of intelligent design must have been involved in the origin of the coded chemistry in DNA.[305] "How can a universe of mindless matter produce beings with intrinsic ends, self-replication capabilities, and 'coded chemistry?'"[306] he asked. Reading his story, I found myself developing a deep respect for this man, not because he became a believer (the deist variety, not an evangelical), but because all along his journey as an atheist, he was committed to follow the arguments wherever they lead. His intellectual honesty was refreshing. As was his lack of hostility; something that was all too prevalent among what some call the "militant atheists," such as Richard Dawkins, Sam Harris, and Christopher Hitchens. Flew reinforced to me that atheists, as much as theists, can have sound morals.

Finally, I mention Michael Behe again. In his most recent book, *The Edge of Evolution: The Search for the Limits of Darwinism*, he affirms his belief in common descent.[307] Behe turns out to be a theistic evolutionist who advocates for ID theory. All of these personalities and their scientific viewpoints reinforced another lesson for me:

(6) Evolution is not the enemy. In fact, it is compatible with intelligent design theory.

Stephen Meyer and other ID theorists openly acknowledge that ID is not incompatible with evolution. It's only incompatible with *Darwinian* or *orthodox* evolution. This is why Michael Behe still supports certain aspects of evolutionary theory. And Michael

Denton affirms an unorthodox version of biological evolution. And I suppose Richard Sternberg hasn't ruled it out. And let's not forget Alfred Russel Wallace, respected contemporary of Charles Darwin, who postulated an alternate theory to natural selection called *intelligent evolution* (IE).

Having said this, I don't want to leave the impression that ID isn't without its scientific and theological problems. Many claim it is not a verifiable scientific theory. Yet as an *idea*, I find it a compelling explanation for the existence of complex life forms. Others point out its internal inconsistencies. For example, how can this supposed design be intelligent given the problems with human anatomy? For instance, the difficulty of childbirth or the existence of ectopic pregnancies—when a fertilized egg implants in the fallopian tube, cervix, or ovary, and not in the uterus, and, without surgery, results in the death of the mother, baby, or both. Another example is the existence of congenital diseases and genetic disorders such as Huntington's Disease. These appear to be instances of bad design. How can they be intelligent? One answer is that the theory does not require optimal design, only evidence for the necessity of intelligence. Human engineers design both superior and inferior automobiles—BMWs and Gremlins. The fact that some are poorly designed in no way proves that intelligent beings did not create them or that they emerged from natural causes.

Then again, if an omnipotent all-loving God is the designer—which theists like me claim—then why aren't *all* its designs superior? But this is really a theological question, not a scientific one, a question that need not be solved on scientific grounds, since ID theory does not identify who the designer is or to what level of sophistication its designs must be. It merely claims, for the development of certain organisms, an intelligent cause is a better explanation than natural selection via random mutations. What's more, the problem of a flawed creation pales in comparison to the overall grandeur of life in which, as Michael Denton quoted earlier said, "every constituent of the cell and every law of nature is uniquely and ideally fashioned to [life's] end" producing "beings with intrinsic ends, self-replication capabilities, and 'coded chemistry.'" Besides, there is a theological answer to these flaws, one that appeals to the concept of a fallen world waiting for an optimum renewal of all things—perhaps a type of optimum design. In Romans,[308] Paul describes the yearning of creation to be liberated from its bondage to decay and brought into glory, and also how the present suffering in the world can't be compared to the glory that will be revealed.

ORIGINS IN THE PUB

In the midst of my musings, Dan saved the day. He changed the subject. After we had watched a bit of the post-game commentary, he dived into the next topic in the book. "Maybe you two would have more in common if you talked about the chapter on creation. I learned a lot when I read it."

Dan seems positive about the chapter, I thought.

"Okay," said Steve. "What's your take on that? I suppose you believe in evolution."

"Well, it's not so simple. In fact one of the problems with this topic is how the media positions the debate in black-and-white with no shades of gray. Evolution is explained as one substantiated, uniform theory, completely accepted by the scientific establishment. Debates between evolutionists—orthodox vs. unorthodox evolutionists—over gradualism and natural selection are virtually ignored, let alone taught in classrooms. On the other side, most evangelicals portray evolution as a diabolical, evil idea, with no consideration for some form of theistic evolution."

"Yeah, but don't you think evolution is hard to reconcile with Scripture?" Steve asked. "I mean, there's no indication of anything like it in the Bible."

"Sure, if you take everything literally and expect the Bible to be a science text book," I said.

"It would be easier for you to understand that," Dan said to Steve, "if you read his material on how to handle the Bible. I agree with Mike it doesn't have to be a black and white issue." Dan mentioned to Steve the book by Francis Collins, *The Language of God*, and suggested it was a good example of how evolution can fit into a biblical worldview. Collins, former head of the Human Genome Project, is one of the rare "gray" voices among evangelicals that has helped frame this debate. A theistic orthodox Darwinian evolutionist, Collins argues that modern science and faith in God and the Bible are in harmony, when one acknowledges the Bible need not be taken literally. As Dan explained this, I was thinking how rare people like Collins are in the evangelical world. In my experience, I don't remember ever meeting anyone in the church like him; someone who reconciles mainstream theories of evolution with faith.

"I've heard of that book," Steve said. "I might consider that he makes a good case for reconciling science and faith, but still, that doesn't mean his take on evolution is true."

"But isn't evolution pretty much settled scientifically?" Dan asked.

"Well, from what I've read," I told Dan, "Despite what the media and purists say, much of Darwin's idea of how evolution worked is not settled. The mechanism he theorized—a gradual succession of natural selection acting on random mutations—is problematic."

I suspected Dan was a theistic evolutionist like Francis Collins—believing in Darwinian evolution. I wanted to balance things out, so I finished my point. "The other thing the media does is disparage intelligent design theory as unscientific—biblical creationism in disguise—you know, on par with the claims of the Flat Earth Society. I don't think the facts support this."

Steve acknowledged this point, but I didn't think Dan was sure, since he seemed to accept Collins' position. "Hmm... I don't know enough about ID to know if that's true," he said.

I explained how most people don't differentiate between intelligent design as an *idea* and intelligent design as a *doctrine* based on a literalist approach to the Bible. There's a huge difference. In fact, evolutionist James Shapiro entertains the idea of a "guiding intelligence" behind the origin of biological life. Renegade evolutionist Michael Denton forcefully argues that purpose and intelligence are behind the laws of biology. What's more, ID theorist Michael Behe is an evolutionist, albeit an unorthodox one. I briefly mentioned these examples, then lost my train of thought.

"Hmm... where was I going with this?" I said as I looked up.

"Brews will do that to you," Dan said laughing.

"Originally, you were on the point of the media being black and white," Steve said.

"Oh, yeah, that's it. I think there's fundamentalist thinking on both sides. Like their fundamentalist cousins in evangelicalism, fundamentalist Darwinists can't think outside the box."

"Wait a minute, Mike," Steve said. "Not all evangelicals are fundamentalist. You know that."

"What I mean is the mindset on this issue. On the conservative religious side they say evolution is a godless idea, and on the orthodox evolution side they say ID is a fundamentalist Christian wolf in sheep's clothing. Both sides can't see the forest for the trees."

Dan nodded, but the wheels seemed to be turning in his head.

I went on with an example on the evolution side. "Academic ID sympathizers and theorists are tenured professors from major secular universities. Some are agnostics, even atheists. Orthodox evolutionists dismiss this. When they are forced to address it, they cry foul." I explained what happened to Richard Sternberg—the scientist and editor who published a pro-ID article in a peer-reviewed journal and was promptly corrected and forced to resign—and how purists can't bring themselves to take ID seriously.

"I didn't realize there were non-religious folks among ID supporters," Dan said. He then brought up an example on the creationism side. "Young-earth creationists don't take scientific research seriously. They dismiss anything—like the four-billion-year-old age of the earth—that doesn't fit their narrow interpretation of the Bible."

"So, where are you going with this, Mike?" Steve asked. "You believe in both evolution and intelligent design?"

"Actually, I guess I'm more of an agnostic on this. I have problems with the two typical sides' ways of thinking—you know, materialism and biblical creationism—but yes, I'm open to the combination of ID and evolution. Call it *intelligent evolution*. I'm also open to some kind of progressive creation combined with microevolution, or what some call horizontal evolution. But if evolution is true, I think the evidence is against the random, undirected variety, whether it's defended by purists or Francis Collins."

"So what is it that Collins says that you don't agree with?" Dan asked.

I then began a long explanation about Collins' argument. Dan and Steve let me go on. I told them how Collins paints a persuasive picture of theism that squares with modern science, first by citing breakthroughs in astronomy that reinforce the Anthropic Principle—the notion that the universe is finely tuned to give rise to biological life on earth, and one I think fits the evidence.[309] Then he shows how physics, chemistry, biology, and evolution are compatible with the Divine.

"To me," I said, "Collins didn't carefully look at the evidence for intelligent design. He dismissed ID out of hand. Although he admitted it's compelling, he rejected it because most biologists haven't embraced it. But maybe that's because the renegade evolutionists are right. Many biologists are wed to evolutionary *ideology*, not pure science. My personal studies support this claim."

"Actually, I can see how that can happen," said Dan. "I mean, really, what does the majority opinion have to do with it? Good science is not decided by a majority but by how worthy the evidence and arguments are."

Even Steve agreed. "Sure, there have been lots of scientific discoveries in history that weren't accepted initially by most scientists."

"That's one of the points I make in my book," I said to Steve. "It's true, not only for scientific discoveries but also for religious discoveries. In science and in the church, a majority opinion does not settle an argument. We should not appeal to the majority but to the merits of a case. In this origins debate, for me, it's not about finding a few detractors to hang my belief on, but about examining the evidence for myself. The same way I rejected biblical inerrancy, even though a majority of evangelicals affirmed it, I came to reject orthodox evolution after careful investigation."

"That's something I should do," Dan said. "Look at this more carefully."

"I think you should. Collins' explanation for how to reconcile the doctrine of randomness in Darwinian theory with an intelligent Creator could easily fit into an ID argument. As Collins states, the creation of life looks undirected, but it's not. An intelligent God is behind the seemingly random mutations that drive evolution. His notion, that mutations aren't really random but are mysteriously directed, is not incompatible with ID. If they aren't really random, then why call them random? Why not call them intelligent?"

"I see your point," Dan responded. "In a way, it's semantics. I guess Collins' mysteriously guided evolution could just as easily be what you called intelligent evolution."

"What's more," I added, "Collins' take is actually at odds with what Richard Dawkins says. In Dawkin's world, life appears to be designed or directed, but it's not. It's random. In Collins' world, it appears to be random, but it's not. It's directed."

"That's an interesting observation I never thought of," Dan said. "You know I was thinking, back to what you said about being agnostic-but-open. That may be a good way to look beyond the culture wars and our differences."

"Well, I think there's a Christian way to look at origins, and we have to be careful that whatever we believe squares with Scripture," Steve said. "If God created the world through evolutionary means, I think it would be in the Bible, and it's not."

I didn't want to get into the "how to interpret Scripture" debate again. I let Steve's comment pass. But Dan made an important point that actually was one of my flagship ideas.

"It may be more important, Steve, to go where the evidence leads," he said. "I think God also speaks to us through scientific discovery."

"Go where the evidence leads." I repeated. "That's a huge lesson I learned. But to pursue it, it takes an open mind free from bias. And without it, following the evidence can rock your world."

Dan, Steve, and I wound down our conversation on origins and drank the rest of our brews. Although we disagreed on much, we did have some things in common. Our talk had reminded me again of where I'd come. I had had many paradigm shifts in my life. Early on, I doubted God could act on a personal level—that supernatural events were possible. My experiences told me I was wrong. I thought I had found the answer to all of life's questions in the evangelical movement, but discovered that was a fallacy. I secretly mocked *all* agnostics and atheists as dishonest deniers of truth. But I was prejudicial in my assessment. Today, I respect those doubters who exhibit intellectual honesty, e.g., David Berlinski, Ayaan Hirsi Ali, and the late Antony Flew. There's also Camille Paglia, who concedes that any secular society with contempt for faith sinks into materialism and self-absorption.[310]

Another atheist to add to that list is Bradley Monton, an analytical philosopher and Associate Professor of Philosophy at the University of Colorado, Boulder. Why? Because of his willingness to investigate intelligent design with an open mind. In his book, *Seeking God in Science: An Atheist Defends Intelligent Design*, Monton argues ID deserves serious consideration as a scientific theory. Wonders never cease.

Similar to Dan's and my thoughts on not taking an entrenched position on origins, Monton refuses to participate in the culture wars. He objectively and fairly evaluates intelligent design. His conclusion? ID theory is legitimate science.[311] There is some plausible evidence for it. It makes him less certain of his atheism, but it's not enough evidence to cause him to stop being an atheist. (He also recognizes the theory isn't inherently theistic). He sees the strongest evidence for it in the fine-tuning argument for physics, the cosmological argument regarding the features of the universe, the argument for the origin of life, and what he calls the simulation argument.

Due to his support of the theory of a spatially infinite universe,[312] he doesn't think the arguments based on evolution that I've reviewed in this chapter are persuasive. No matter how unlikely it is for a series of random mutations to result in a new life form (which Monton concedes to be true), in a spatially *infinite* universe with other worlds like ours, it becomes likely, he argues. Finally, he concludes it would be beneficial for students to hear arguments for and against intelligent design theory in the classroom, but only if individual teachers choose to pursue it.

What a refreshing attitude, I thought, when reading his book.

My journey to answer the ultimate Great Question *(how did we get here?)*, led me to a nuanced perspective. I rejected materialistic orthodox evolution—the gradual, random, undirected neo-Darwinism model—but was open to an intelligent design hypothesis, combined or not with evolution. I had to admit that perhaps Alfred Russel Wallace's notion of *intelligent evolution* (IE) made the most sense. The man who independently proposed an evolutionary theory by natural selection that spurred Darwin to publish his own theory believed the "unseen universe of Spirit" had intervened in evolution at least three times. First at the creation of life from inorganic matter, second when consciousness developed in higher animals, and third, at the development of superior mental faculties in humans.[313] At any rate, evolution was no longer the enemy. My openness to it puts me at odds with most evangelicals—with the exception of the rare Francis Collins variety—and my defense of the *idea* of intelligent design puts me at odds with most evolutionists. It's a wonderful thing to think for oneself.

Steve got up and left for the restroom. Dan leaned over to me, "I meant to ask you, how did Steve react to your view of homosexuality?"

"He got pretty defensive," I said. "It turned into quite the debate."

"I'm not surprised," said Dan.

I knew Dan would agree with me on that issue for the most part. He was a rare breed in the church. Dan's question reminded me of what I wanted to say about Jennifer Knapp appearing on Larry King. I remembered Ted Haggard's inability to say a Christian like Knapp *wasn't* going to hell. That was another topic in which I had changed my view dramatically. In the last few years the amazing discoveries I made about the traditional concept of hell and the church's view of salvation had solved a long-standing mystery in my mind. That story elicited similar reactions from my evangelical friends as my progressive views on homosexuality did. In many ways, my new views on hell and salvation were even more controversial than my views on homosexuality.

I planned on bringing them up, first to Dan, but wanted to collect my thoughts a bit. The beer was making me very relaxed. I remembered being on the ferry talking to another friend, who told me about a conservative-turned-universalist pastor.

Confession #12
Universal Life

"...I bid you cheer, from a heathen and a pagan
on the side of the rebel Jesus."

– *Jackson Browne*

"Love never fails."

– *The Apostle Paul*

Seattle, 2008

Helen, a woman in her late fifties with short gray hair, had an illuminating story to tell as she sat across from me in a booth on the 7:05 ferry to Seattle. I was on my daily commute working for a Microsoft partner, having quit working for evangelical aid agencies five years earlier.

Thirty feet away out the window, the Puget Sound glistened in the morning sunrise with speckles of silver and gold dancing on the waves. In the distance above the water line delineating earth and sky rose massive Mt. Rainier, 14,000-plus feet in elevation, its commanding presence towering above the foothills. Magnificent. White on deep blue with thin orange blazes highlighting its snow-covered slopes. I sat mesmerized. How often its looming majesty unexpectedly enters into view, especially after hidden for days behind clouds, and dominates one's whole perspective. This morning, it took my breath away. I could barely keep my eyes off of it as Helen began to talk.

"I gotta tell you about this show I saw last night," Helen said.

I motioned for Helen to turn and look at Rainier. She gasped. "Incredible. Puts a different spin on your day, huh?" she said. For a few seconds we both took it in, and then she turned back.

"The show," she continued. "I was flipping channels and just happen to catch it. It fits perfectly with what you said about the concept of universal love."

Helen's eyes were bright with excitement. I was no longer distracted by the splendor of Rainier. She had my full attention. She leaned forward slightly, looked me straight in the eye, and began to tell me about the interview she saw on a re-run of NBC's *Dateline*.

Pentecostal pastor and Christian mega-star Carlton Pearson, whose Tulsa, Oklahoma, church drew 5,000 people weekly, shared a shocking revelation—at least shocking for his church member-ship and his mentor, evangelist Oral Roberts, she told me. After an encounter with God while watching a television special on Rwanda, Pearson began rethinking his concept of hell. One day he announced to his church he no longer believed that God would condemn the majority of humankind to a place of eternal torment. "Because of the sacrifice of Christ, the whole world is already saved—everyone in all religions and even non-believers. They just don't know it yet," he had explained. His peers soon declared him a heretic. Ultimately, he lost most of his congregation and pastorate.

"It wasn't his revelation that struck me," Helen said after she finished sharing what transpired on the show. "As a spiritual inde-pendent, I have a similar view. No, it was the timing. Just recently, you had told me about your research for your book and the misguided traditional view of hell. Remember when you also told me God's created universe is an expression of inclusive love? And then soon after that I see this guy on television. Is that serendipitous or what?"

"That's incredible!" I said. "That's just the kind of material I need. I'll look for a recording of the show on the Internet." Hearing Helen share about Pearson confirmed to me that others within conservative churches were discovering the same revelations. I wasn't alone.

A few days later, not only did I find and watch the show, I bought Pearson's book, *The Gospel of Inclusion*, and added it to an arsenal of research I had already done on this subject.[314] My view of the nature of salvation was slowly changing, and the more questions I asked, the more answers I got from unlikely sources. Helen had helped me find another one.

THE HELL HOLE

Years earlier I had confronted what I thought were problematic verses in the Bible where Jesus and other New Testament writers seem to teach that those who don't embrace Christ or do the will of God in their life will face everlasting damnation in a place called hell. Since only 33 percent of the world's population is Christian, and evangelicals claim that a much smaller percentage are "true" Christians, that meant God supposedly consigns the overwhelming majority of the human race to an eternal painful demise. How can this be? I could not ignore that looming question.

Over the years, I had kept wondering. Particularly about the Somali and Ethiopian Muslim refugees and the Malawian Muslims I knew. They were warm, hospitable, and sincerely following the religion of their forefathers—even if I found it intrinsically legalistic—and whose entrenched culture put up enormous barriers between Islam and Christianity. In their world, converts to Christ are considered infidels and typically disowned by their family. Anyone who leaves Islam is subject to harassment by his or her clan members, which sometimes includes death threats. Converts to Christianity pay an enormous price. With barriers like these, according to conservative theology, what hope do Muslims have, let alone Jews, Buddhists, Hindus, and Animists?

My conclusion back in 1983, that God is inherently inclusive and that salvation is possible (although not inevitable) outside Christendom, was comforting, even though it didn't fit neatly into my tidy evangelical box. Still, that meant *some people* would go to hell and experience its finality. This idea, supposedly taught in Scripture, was another thorn in my flesh. Whenever I dwelt on the never-ending, cruel-sounding nature of it, I felt uneasy. Over the years, I tried to work out the dilemmas that the doctrine created. Hell was a hell of a problem.

What about those who will never have a chance to hear the Bible's message of salvation? *God will take that into account and judge them differently.*

That's what I concluded. This is what people like Billy Graham had said—despite the fact that most evangelicals avoided teaching it. But even if that is the case, what about the times that people do go to hell? How can a loving God consign souls—however resistant to His will—to untold torment?

Some evangelicals are honest enough to ask these types of questions and dig a little deeper into the Bible, or their own hearts, to find answers. For instance, evangelicals concede that children who die (before some mysterious age of accountability), all go to heaven. This concession is remarkable because Augustine, one of the most revered church fathers even among evangelicals, taught that because of God's furious wrath, eternal hell was the default destiny of all—even unbaptized babies! So why can't evangelicals brand Augustine a heretic for that kind of asinine theology? For one, they are largely ignorant of such historical facts.

My search continued. I heard some commentators minimize the horror of hell.

"Hell is not a torture chamber."[315]

This is what New Testament scholars like J. P. Moreland say. Moreland's take is that the references to unquenchable fire in hell were figures of speech. After all, it was also described as a place of darkness. It could not be full of fire *and* darkness. These types of arguments made the case that hell was fundamentally a place of separation from God. Separation from the Creator is a terrible thing, so the reasoning went, but it's not a tortuous dungeon.

This made the doctrine more palatable and soothed my objections. At least for a while. Eventually, another important question arose. Why would God separate Himself from the objects of His love for eternity?

Because in a sense, they choose the separation. This was another answer I heard from some commentators. Due to the fact that their soul rejects God's love, they would feel extremely uncomfortable in heaven. They would rather be in hell.

C.S. Lewis and his clever fictional account of heaven and hell, called *The Great Divorce*, had helped me see this concept. Inhabitants of hell—a dreary community of selfish and bitter souls—travel to heaven on a bus and are given the opportunity to remain there. Not one of them chooses to stay. They consider childish the forgiving, accepting attitudes of heaven dwellers and dutifully climb back on the bus back to hell.

Again, perhaps more reasoned, but it still left other questions unanswered. I could see an unrepentant serial killer feeling out of place in heaven and choosing to go to hell (if hell was at its core a separation from a good God), but why the assumption that everyone who winds up in hell has no capacity to turn? Moreover, why only one bus ride? Why doesn't God allow evil people the *ongoing* opportunity to reflect on their actions and change, let alone misguided souls steeped in destructive behavior often connected to childhood trauma? Why the painful finality of hell? Why would God leave open the possibility of redemption and change in this life but not in the hereafter?

According to evangelical theology, why would serial killer, sex offender, and torturer Jeffrey Dahmer be saved because he "accepted Jesus" before his execution, but Mahatma Gandhi wouldn't because he was a Hindu? If *God* is *unfailing love,*[316] desires all people to be saved,[317] does not show favoritism,[318] and declares His purposes will be fulfilled,[319] then why isn't all of humankind ultimately made complete in God? Not because God forces people, but because His love is irresistible in the end?

Without realizing it, I was questioning an array of theological positions developed over the centuries that tried to reconcile the character of God with what the Scriptures taught. This included Calvinism[320]—the theological grid that questions free will and states God preordains who will be saved. When I looked at Calvinism closely, I found it incredibly problematic. It asserts that God chooses to save some and not others. Not exactly my idea of the epitome of love. Can you imagine a parent who chooses to love and protect one of his or her children but not another? Yet Calvinism wasn't the only problem. *Every* traditional view I encountered was not adequately answering my questions.

The theology in opposition to Calvinism—Arminianism—had its own inconsistencies. Despite individuals choosing their fate so to speak, Arminianists still claimed God consigned people who resisted His grace to hell, with no possibility of future pardon. But this was incongruent. The question remained: How could a God—as expressed through the person of Christ—known for unconditional, unfailing love and radical forgiveness in this life, send resistant souls to a place of cosmic punishment in the afterlife, with no offer of future redemption? If true, upon death, God's love for people becomes conditional and ultimately fails. This also flew in the face of my own powerful personal experiences with the indiscriminate love of God. Two of those experiences had left an indelible mark on my soul.

The first one happened in 1984 during a time in my spiritual walk when I was desperate. I had recently returned from my first stint in Africa. A renewed spiritual hunger had formed deep inside me. Today I can see the source of that hunger was a false image of God. I had been steeped in evangelical *religion* for the previous five years. As a "depraved sinner," I needed Christ to help me overcome sin. Not necessarily a bad idea if one's "sin" was alcoholism, meth addiction, sexual abuse, rape, or a perverse attraction to violently hurting others. Maybe even if the sin was only judgmentalism or hypocrisy. But in the churches I attended and in the evangelical material I read, just being human is bad enough. Literal interpretations of Bible verses had made their legalistic impression on my sensitive conscience. And the moralistic teachings of ALCC—my experiment in a cutting-edge Christian community in Pasadena, California—had taken their toll. The list of sins I believed myself guilty of were numerous due to the influence of these religious voices.

One, I had committed adultery in my heart—perhaps a million times—by lusting after attractive women, even though I wasn't married. Never mind that every breathing man in the church did, too, according to the way the church defined "lust."[321]

Two, I was battling temptation to pursue deeper relationships with single women. For I had bought into the notion that it was not God's will for me to date women, let alone be sexually active with them. I was to wait patiently for God to show me whom to marry, and then, and only then, would I pursue a relationship. I had kissed dating goodbye before the book was even written.[322] I wasn't exactly joyfully obeying this directive. Never mind that this was a radical morality not remotely spelled out in the Bible but read into specific passages with no consideration for ancient culture.

Three, I was guilty of the sin of masturbation. Never mind most people on the planet were. Despite the Bible's lack of references to this "sin," numerous pulpits and moralistic books expounded its dangers. Hello, Guilt, my old friend. Have you come to visit me again?

Four, I was not consistent in maintaining spiritual disciplines— daily personal prayer, Bible reading, and attending church prayer meetings (I had church attendance mastered at this time, thank you). As we have learned, never mind that these religious practices are optional and have nothing to do with genuine faith most beautifully expressed though loving others.

And five, I wasn't adequately obeying the Great Commission—to make disciples of the lost—despite the fact I had already lived two years abroad as a development missionary! Some argued my contribution wasn't sufficiently evangelistic. If it were, it would entail *church planting*. Never mind that the church's way of interpreting and practicing evangelism is extremely narrow and often alienates people. Not to mention that God is not dependent on Western missionaries and their missiological strategies to save lost people.

So, one day, I got down on my knees and prayed. Really hard. That meant I was earnest. I wanted God to communicate something to me I could grasp, so I would be set free from paralyzing guilt. I thought that might come in the form of God's transforming me into some super spiritual giant: someone who would rise from his knees after a whole night in prayer with the fortitude and strength to resist every sinful temptation. And thereafter, to awaken at 5:00 a.m. every morning to pray as Jesus did, boldly share his testimony with every non-believer he came in contact with, and perhaps become a Protestant male version of Mother Theresa, albeit one who could get married. (I wasn't sold on celibacy.) That didn't happen. What did blew me away.

After a half hour of praying, it started. Like a cool summer breeze arriving unexpectedly on a stifling hot day, a spiritual presence entered my room. It blew across my body, now prostrate on the floor at the edge of my bed. It flowed into my chest and pulsated through my arms and legs.

Then a fountain of joy began. A succession of jubilant waves of energy entered my frame, as if pounding incessantly on a sandy shore. Energy, joy, a quiet lull, then more energy and joy. Was this what they told me about at church? Was I being filled with the Holy Spirit? ALCC, remember, was a charismatic church. They said everyone needed to be "baptized in the Holy Spirit" and preferably speak in tongues. It wasn't uncommon for pastors or leaders to pray for people after church, to "lay hands" on them and wait for them to be filled with the Spirit. I was the recipient of such prayers on a few occasions but never seemed to have that spiritual breakthrough. Alone in my room, I was having better luck.

The experience intensified. "Thank you, Jesus. Praise you, God," I voiced what I had learned to be words of worship. The feeling of euphoria grew and became more than a physical stimulation. It began to encompass my mind with thoughts of compassion, kindness, comfort, empathy, and concern. Was this the love of God? I felt an infilling Presence. Five years earlier I had felt the spirit of Christ next to me. Today, I was engulfed in Divine love. Yet I was still in complete control of my faculties.

I climbed up on the bed and sat upright, arms out front with the palms of my hands pointed heavenward as if to receive. I continued to shake intermittently. The thoughts of caring first centered on me. I was the object of an outrageously loving Being. Like an artist who creates and nurtures his or her masterpiece and then stands back to admire the work with pride, a Presence was doling love over me! Yet humility was called for. I was loved, but I was aware of the immensity of the Being's created order. I was one of billions.

I began to think of my acquaintances, friends, and family in a way I never had before. The same care, concern, and empathy I sensed for myself, I began having for them. It had nothing to do with what they did, but everything to do with who they were. Each was a treasured part of a vast interconnected Creation. No matter whom I thought of, an unimaginable feeling of love sprang forth from deep within. Was I thinking the very thoughts of a loving God? With every thought, came yearning for more. With every yearning came more compassion. Electrifying Love dominated my whole perspective. Its intensity continued to grow, until...

Lord, I don't know if I can handle this, I thought. *Can you turn it down a bit?* It worked. Soon the feeling began to gradually subside, and I was left with my own energy. I was at peace but overwhelmed with what had just happened.

I wondered, *have I been searching for the wrong thing? It has nothing to do with keeping in line with religious expectations, but receiving and giving Divine love.*

No sermon could teach such a lesson so effectively. Unfortunately, in the long run the lesson didn't entirely stick. Eventually it was filtered through the teachings of the ALCC church and other churches. In so many evangelical circles, the simple biblical formula of "love God and love your neighbor" becomes a set of commands to be obeyed. To truly love God, according to them, one has to get hyper-involved in a Bible-based church, accept "orthodox" doctrines, believe the whole Bible, pray right prayers, speak acceptable words, write appropriate books, sing approved songs, think pure thoughts, and behave the evangelical way. Nevertheless, through the ensuing years, my Holy Spirit experience—a kind of euphoric Divine love trip—came to mind many times as I grappled with the concept of hell.

The second experience happened in 1995 after returning from Malawi in what charismatic evangelicals called The Toronto Blessing—named after the Vineyard church in Toronto where the phenomenon developed. Once I attended a conference in Toronto and had a gripping experience with a loving Presence. A few months later, at someone's home, I experienced a powerful dose of "laughing in the Spirit." Two women friends from my church and I sat in a corner and laughed hysterically for an hour. For me, I was overwhelmed with the accepting nature of God. To think I feared Gods' displeasure struck me as hilarious.

These two experiences had an impact on my psyche that led me to search deeper for answers about the afterlife. My personal experience with God was inconsistent with what the church taught and what Scripture supposedly said. Why? Was the church wrong? Was the Bible incorrect? Was my bleeding heart misinterpreting God's character and attributing to the Divine more grace than was warranted? If that were true, did I want to serve such a God?

THE TRUTH WILL SET YOU FREE

"I am reading a fascinating book on an evangelical case for Universalism," I confessed to a fellow believer.

"Why would you want to do that?" was the response. "Universalism isn't biblical."

Another evangelical put it more bluntly. "I think it's a load of crap."

Once, when I shared with my church home group some of the reasons why I thought we evangelicals have misinterpreted verses regarding hell, I was met with blank stares and even laughter. "You gotta be kidding, Mike. The Bible is clear. Besides, if you claim there is no eternal punishment, then neither is there eternal life." Despite my attempts to explain why that is not true based on the definition of the original Greek word for eternal, the whole concept was rebuffed.

Dan and Gina were the only ones out of my evangelical friends who were open to the idea. Dan was excited about the things I discovered that supported universal reconciliation.

"I've been struggling with what the church taught for years," he told me. After reading a book I recommended called *The Inescapable Love of God,* he shared what he learned with his Bible study group.

"Gina was the only one who supported me," he later divulged. "Another man actually gave me a stern warning. 'I would be careful studying such a doctrine. It can be dangerous,' he said."

"It can give people false hope," another person added.

Dan and I were flabbergasted. Part of us thought most people would welcome such a possibility. We figured they would have had the same concerns we had about believing in a God who on the one hand claims to love everyone equally, making provision through Christ to forgive all wrongdoing for those who seek it, but on the other hand appears malevolent by handing nonbelievers a final judgment and eternal penalty in the hereafter.

We thought people would be glad there was a way around this incongruity and the Scriptures that appear to support it. There is no longer reason to despair over a family member or friend who has died "without Christ." The dilemma of how one can enjoy paradise in Heaven while loved ones suffer in hell is solved. We need not needlessly lament about the eternal destiny of "unreached peoples" of the world who never come to Christian faith. In fact, the good news is better than we ever thought. No one is excluded. God's love is inescapable. Even for recalcitrant souls, judgment may be terrible—as it should be for the most evil among us—but temporary, not forever. Irresistible love will win. Moreover, perhaps some skeptics would be more open to faith because there is no longer a reason to be repulsed by the doctrine of hell and a wrathful God.

But part of us understood the resistance evangelicals have. Universalism is considered a false teaching. We realized evangelicals are gripped by fear—afraid of not being true to the Scriptures, frightened of being branded a liberal, heretic, or New Age adherent, or that everything they believed over the years is really not true and they have lived a lie. Or maybe they are terrified of hell itself. It's better to believe in hell and be wrong than not believe it and possibly lead others down a path to everlasting destruction.

Another objection was based on a misunderstanding. To us evangelicals, Universalists believed one could live a life of sin and not be held accountable in the end. There was no need for an immoral or evil person to repent. Of course, this is a gross misreading of the doctrine. The brand of Universalism I was studying still taught that evildoers face a judgment. Not eternal torment, but, as a good parent would subject his or her child to correction, a loving discipline in the hereafter. Not by a vindictive Deity, but by a merciful God. It also taught that more often corrective punishment for genuine sin (not sin contrived from legalistic interpretations and twisting of Scripture) is revealed through painful consequences in this life. There may be exceptions, but most of us reap what we sow before we die.

Despite objections by our evangelical friends, Dan, Gina, and I continued to investigate the position of Universalism. For me, I was taking a final step in overcoming my propensity to seek approval for my own decisions. I didn't care what others thought anymore. I wanted to follow wherever the evidence led. As I did, I clearly began to see the lie of hell. That was a truth that set me free.

THE CASE FOR UNIVERSALISM

There were three revelations about Universalism that turned my evangelical worldview upside down. The discoveries themselves didn't shock me. They are rational and solved many disconnects I had about the character of God and what the Bible supposedly taught. What shocked me were the looming questions that the revelations raised: Given the evangelical claim to know the truth about God, why aren't these facts taught in evangelical seminaries and churches? Why didn't I ever hear of these facts in my evangelical experience? Why are they hidden? And, perhaps most importantly, why do they seem to threaten people of conservative faith?

(1) The Bible Does Not Support the Doctrine of Eternal Punishment:

The doctrine of everlasting punishment is not derived from a fair exegetical reading of the Bible but rather the theology of Augustine, who, not being a native speaker of Greek (he wrote in Latin), seriously misunderstood the original language of the New Testament.[323]

There are three words in Greek translated as *hell* in modern Bibles: *hades, Gehenna,* and *tartarus.* First, *hades* is simply a translation of the Hebrew word *sheol,* which for the Jews was the place or state following death for departed souls, whether righteous or unrighteous. It was not a place of eternal punishment. Later translations like the *New International Version* more correctly translate *hades* as "grave" or "death."

Second, *Gehenna* is a word used by Jesus only four times as recorded in the Gospels. *Gehenna* refers to the Valley of Hinnom in southwest Jerusalem. It was a place of pagan worship where

Ahaz, king of Judah in Jerusalem around 700 B.C.E, had instituted worship of the god Molech, to whom children were sacrificed in fires according to 2 Chronicles 28:2-4. To Jews it became a symbol of an accursed place and was turned into a public incinerator—an ongoing smoldering garbage dump.

Jesus uses the term *Gehenna* to warn people that true adherence to God's law must begin in one's heart. For example, "You have heard that it was said to the people long ago, 'You shall not murder, and anyone who murders will be subject to judgment.' But I tell you that anyone who is angry with a brother or sister will be subject to judgment. Again, anyone who says to a brother or sister, 'Raca,' is answerable to the court. And anyone who says, 'You fool!' will be in danger of *Gehenna*."[324] [emphasis mine]. Modern Bibles have translated "Gehenna" as *the fire of hell* and our cultural understanding has read into that phrase the idea of everlasting torment. This was one of those problem passages that gnawed at my soul. When read like that, the moral quandary is obvious. How could God even consider sending people to hell who are merely angry with someone?

But there was another way to parse this, given what *Gehenna* meant. In referring to *Gehenna*, Jesus was using a metaphor for *judgment*, not hell. There is no indication it will be an everlasting judgment. In the spirit of Oriental languages with their hyperboles, metaphors, and imagery, Jesus, speaking in Aramaic—the native language of Palestine in the first century—warns the spiritually shallow that just because they haven't committed murder, doesn't mean they are pure as the driven snow. He was simply saying that sins of the heart, such as harsh anger, hatred, bigotry, and the like, are subject to judgment. In every instance where an English Bible refers to hell in this section of Matthew, Jesus is using the word *Gehenna*.

Gehenna wasn't the only metaphor for judgment Jesus used in this passage. Another one that is equivalent to *Gehenna,* because it expands on the warning of calling someone 'You fool!' and serves the same teaching purpose, is the word *prison*. Jesus warns that if people don't attempt to make relationships right, their adversary might hand them over to the courts, and they might be thrown in prison. "Truly I tell you, you will not get out until you have paid the last penny."[325] This prison is a temporary judgment, *until* the offenders have paid their debt. Clearly, he doesn't have everlasting punishment in mind. Moreover, use of Eastern poetic metaphorical language should not be hardened into an enshrined dogma.

The final word mistranslated *hell* in some translations is *tartarus*. It is only cited once in 2 Peter 2:4 and describes a type of purgatory for fallen angels before judgment. There is no basis for translating it as hell, with the eternal nature the word brings to our Western mind. In fact, the modern English word hell is derived from Old English and the Anglo-Saxon heathen concept of the world of the dead. Thus, it has pagan origins.

Another misunderstood teaching of Jesus that conjures up the concept of everlasting hell in our minds is in Matthew 25:46, where Jesus, supposedly speaking about the final judgment, states, "Then [the unrighteous] will go away to eternal punishment, but the righteous to eternal life."

In this parable called The Sheep and the Goats, it's interesting that the unrighteous are not defined as those who "didn't accept" Jesus as Lord, but rather those who didn't help Jesus in his time of need, when he was hungry, a stranger, sick, or in prison—meaning Christ identifies with the poor and oppressed. Those who fail to help them fail to help Jesus. Neither are the righteous defined as those who "accept" Christ, but rather those who helped the poor and oppressed, and in so doing helped Jesus. Neither group realizes they have either abandoned Jesus or helped Jesus in their actions. But this point is supplemental to our topic.

Was Jesus speaking of hell when he stated the phrase "eternal punishment"? The key to understanding what he really meant, I discovered, was in knowing the meaning of two Greek terms represented by that phrase.

The word translated *eternal*, and in other instances *everlasting* or *forever*, is the Greek adjective *aionios*, derived from the root *aion*, which is similar to our word *eon* or *age*. *Aionios* is a relative term for which there is no corresponding word in English. It derives its character and duration from the subject to which it refers. Although most English Bibles translate it *eternal* when Jesus uses it in Matthew, there is a nearly impenetrable case that this is an incorrect translation and that it should be translated *age-abiding* or *pertaining to an age*, for that is its literal sense.[326] Some scholars have warned that it's a grave error to constantly translate *aion* or *aionion* as eternal, for it never literally means never ending.[327] In fact, there are four Bible translations that don't use the word *everlasting* at all in The Sheep and the Goats passage in Matthew, but say "age-abiding correction," "punishment of the age," or something similar.[328]

Another consideration is that *aionios* is used in the Septuagint (the Greek translation of the Hebrew Scriptures) in numerous passages in ways that show it cannot mean eternal or forever. For example, Jonah was in the belly of the whale [*aionios*] until he was spat out,[329] a Moabite is forbidden to enter the Lord's house [*aionios*] until the tenth generation,[330] and God lives in Solomon's temple [*aionios*] until it is destroyed.[331] These terms can't mean *forever* because they are specific to a particular circumstance. Scholars of ancient Greek literature conclude that the concepts of infinity or time-everlasting are not intrinsic in the terms *aion* in Greek, its equivalent in Hebrew (*olam*), or in the biblical usage.[332]

When I made these points at a Bible study I attended, people had the objection I shared earlier that if *aionios* doesn't mean forever when describing punishment, then it can't mean forever when describing eternal life. But this is a misunderstanding of the meaning of the term. *Aionos* is not a term that denotes a set duration, but its duration depends on what it is associated with. It typically means different durations, as it does in Romans 16:25-26: "The message about Christ is the secret that was hidden for long ages past [*aionios*] but is now made known. It has been made clear through the writings of the prophets. And by the command of the eternal [*aionios*] God..." In this passage the same term is limited in duration in the first instance. In the second instance it is translated *eternal* because it is referring to God. If it is referring to life in God, one could argue it should be eternal because God is always alive, but if it is referring to a human time frame or a particular punishment, it depends on the nature of that punishment. "True, the age to come is everlasting, but that does not necessitate that the punishment of the age to come lasts for the duration of the age, simply that it occurs during that age and is appropriate for that age."[333]

As I studied some of the books I have cited, I encountered another important point I had never considered. The Greek word translated "punishment" is *kolasis,* which has a specific meaning. It refers to *remedial* punishment, a corrective discipline, as its root is derived from the concept of pruning trees to improve their growth for bearing fruit. One Greek scholar stated "...in all Greek secular literature, *kolasis* is never used for anything but remedial punishment."[334] Corrective punishment has an end and results in a renewed and redeemed individual. A punishment that lasts forever cannot be remedial but can only be described as retributive.

Yet still there was another angle. I had learned from scholar N.T. Wright that all the apocalyptic language of the New Testament, including Jesus' teaching on *Gehenna* and his parables of his coming again and the "punishment of the age to come," was not speaking of a period outside our space-time universe—in a hereafter—but rather a divine judgment in our world coming upon the corrupt religionists of the Jewish Temple,[335] a judgment and period of trials that would occur within one generation and would culminate in the destruction of Jerusalem in 70 A.D. My research on the "end times" applies here. The evidence is strong that Jesus wasn't even speaking of post-mortem judgment in most of these passages, and therefore couldn't be speaking of hell. Believe me, this stuff is not remotely part of Evangelicalism 101. But as I put all these points together like constructing a puzzle, a more logical image began to form.

(2) Universalism Was Common in the Early Church and Throughout History:

Probably one of the most fascinating secrets hidden from evangelicals is the fact that according to some of the most revered personalities in church history, Universalism is not a dirty word. Take the 19th century author and minister, George MacDonald. Famous for his fantasy novels and his influence on such Christian icons as J. R. R. Tolkien, G. K. Chesterton, and C. S. Lewis (all favorites among modern evangelicals), MacDonald's books are sold by the boatload at evangelical bookstores and have been for years. C. S. Lewis said of him, "I know hardly any other writer who seems to be closer, or more continually close, to the Spirit of Christ Himself."[336] Avid readers among fundamentalists and evangelicals eat up his innovative fantasies but are largely unaware he was a staunch Universalist who detested Calvinistic theology, rejected the doctrine of substitutionary atonement,[337] and passionately argued for the universal reconciliation of humankind. When I discovered this I was shocked. Why hadn't I heard this before? How can Universalism be so detested among us when one of those we revere promoted it?

The early church fathers are another example. The way most evangelical churches insist that Universalism is an obscure false teaching, one would think the historical record would support this position. Think again. This quote below that I discovered in my research was provocative and earth-shattering. It forced me to revisit my whole Christian worldview.

> In these early centuries those holding the doctrine of eternal punishment were in the minority and no one was counted unorthodox who believed in restitution and the ultimate and complete victory of Christ [that all would be reconciled to God].[338]

People who believed in hell were a minority in the early church? Why isn't this information disseminated? Frankly, I felt cheated. Deceived even. We evangelicals supposedly have all the answers. To

us, anyone who believed or taught universal reconciliation was denying the Bible—the very teachings of Jesus. But now I was hearing this
isn't true. As I studied more, it became clear the preponderance of
evidence is just the opposite. More likely, anyone who teaches eternal
punishment is denying the original intention of the New Testament
writers.

"His [Augustine's] influence probably more than that of any
of the other Church Fathers brought forward and emphasized
the doctrine of never ending punishment."[389]

Could Augustine have been wrong? There were many who
believed he was. Even Augustine admitted that much when he said,
"There are many in our day, who though not denying the Holy
Scriptures, do not believe in endless torments."[340] It turns out the
"many" Augustine referred to among the church fathers was a very
impressive list. The most noteworthy were Clement of Alexandria,
Gregory of Nyssa, and Origen.[341] Clement and Gregory were pillars.
As for Origen, some people discredit his universalism because he
was later condemned for other supposed false doctrines during the
stage of the Roman Church when heretics were sought under every
rock. Yet he was never condemned for his belief in universal salvation. In addition, another revered church father named Irenaeus
wrote a book in the 2nd century called *Against Heresies*. In it he
never mentions universalism as heretical. Other Universalist early
church leaders included Gregory Nazianzen, Jerome, Hillary, Titus,
Diodorus, Theodore of Mopsuestia, Saint Macrina the Younger (a
nun), Cyril of Alexandria, Theodoret, and Ambrose (who converted
Augustine).[342] Most of these pre-dated Augustine, who began
pushing an endless hell around 420 A.D. and taught it at the theological school he founded. In fact, out of the six major schools of
Christianity founded in Mediterranean region, four of them taught
Universalism. The two schools that didn't were in the Latin-speaking
(Roman) world, from which Western Christianity derived.

Despite these voices throughout the second to the fourth

centuries, Augustine's powerful influence ultimately resulted in the doctrine of eternal punishment's becoming predominant in the Western Church. It wasn't until 543 A.D. that Emperor Justinian anathematized the doctrine of the deliverance from post-mortem punishment. Later, in 553 when the Fifth Ecumenical Council in Constantinople (don't think "ecumenical" the way we moderns think of it!) issued fifteen condemnations against universal-like teachings, the fate of orthodox Universalism was sealed. But not entirely.

Throughout the history of the church there have been noteworthy Universalists, despite the risk of being labeled a heretic. Medieval mystics like Lady Julian of Norwich held a Universalist position in her book, *The Revelations of Divine Love*. From the sixteenth to the twentieth centuries there was a mini-revival of Universalism in the Western Church. The reformer Martin Luther was at the very least sympathetic to Universalism when he said, "God forbid that I should limit the time for acquiring faith to the present life. In the depth of the Divine mercy, there may be opportunity to win it in the future."[343] Some Protestant movements, including Anabaptists, Moravians, Methodists, and Quakers,[344] had many Universalists among their leaders. The denomination, the Universalist Church of America, was a strong *orthodox* Christian movement before it became heavily influenced by secular thought in the mid 1800s and finally, in 1961, when it merged with the Unitarians and became the Unitarian Universalist Church.

Notable Universalists of history include John and Abigail Adams, Thomas Jefferson, Benjamin Rush (signer of the Declaration of Independence), John Quincy Adams, Clara Barton, Florence Nightingale, Charles Dickens, Abraham Lincoln, and Susan B. Anthony. Lincoln wrote an essay in 1833 in which he argued for "predestinated universal salvation in criticism of the orthodox doctrine of endless punishment."[345] In the modern era, besides George MacDonald, more notable Universalists included Hannah Whitall Smith, Jacques Ellul, Karl Barth, Hans Kung, and possibly Pope John Paul II,[346] known for conciliatory gestures and improving

Catholic Church relations with Judaism, Islam, Buddhism, and the Eastern Orthodox Church.

(3) Both Old and New Testament Passages Support Universalism:

Earlier we had pinpointed one phenomenon of literalist ways of thinking within evangelicalism as *selective literalism*. Even for literalists, it's hard to be consistently literal. In order to solve that problem, literalists will consciously or unconsciously select the passages in the Bible they take literally. The other ones, they explain away, conveniently ignore, or simply let them go over their head. Literalists accuse people like me of doing the same thing. It's a fair challenge. Yet it's one thing to explain away an interpretation based on evidence from history, culture, original language of the Bible, literary style, biblical scholarship, and evaluation of manuscript authenticity, and quite another to explain it away because of a preconceived bias. In truth, all are susceptible to personal bias when they read a book like the Bible, myself included. But what of evangelicals on the idea of Universalism? Their bias against it is self-evident, given the facts I have revealed.

What if I told you the Bible teaches the universal reconciliation of humankind? A conservative Christian might say with a sarcastic tone, "Right. That's ridiculous. I read the Bible every day, and I've never seen it." I essentially thought the same way for years. Without a new set of eyes, the verses below glide over the head of people steeped in traditional views.

"Therefore just as one man's trespass [Adam] led to condemnation [death] for all, so one man's act of righteousness [Christ], leads to justification and life for all" (Romans 5:18).

Thomas Talbott, being careful to not take this verse out of context to the surrounding passage and argument Paul makes in Romans, picks apart the common objections to this universalistic verse. Detractors say "all" doesn't really mean *all* humankind. Talbott

308 CONFESSIONS OF A BIBLE THUMPER

persuasively argues that it does and wonders how outraged we would be if someone tried to argue that "all men are created equal" didn't literally mean *all* people.[347]

Talbott shows how Paul uses parallel structure in arguing his logic. For instance, in the verse above the first concept determines the extent of the second. Its use here clearly stipulates, since Adam's fall led to death for *all* humankind (which no conservative would deny), Christ's act leads to life for *all* humankind. Paul makes similar statements throughout his letters.

"For God has imprisoned all in disobedience, so He may be merciful to all" (Romans 11:32).

"For as all die in Adam, so all will be made alive in Christ" (I Corinthians 15:22).

The parallel structure of these verses insists the second concept be the same scope as the first. Hence, God is merciful to *all* <u>and</u> *all* will live in Christ. Paul makes many other statements that either imply or explicitly teach the concept of universal salvation.

"At the name of Jesus, every knee should bend, in heaven and on earth and under the earth, and every tongue confess that Jesus Christ is Lord" (Philippians 2:10-11).

As I have alluded to elsewhere, it would be wrong to assume this verse above means one has to become a Christian to be right with God. Rather, the verse merely states Paul's position, that ultimately everyone will revere Jesus as Lord[348]—meaning God anointed Jesus to be the means of reconciling human beings to God. Non-Christians may object to this, but the point is that this is the teaching of Paul, that everyone *eventually* will honor Christ.

With my experience with spiritually open-minded non-Christians, to me, this really isn't far-fetched. When non-believers see a genuine Jesus, stripped of right-wing politics, church-imposed legalistic caricatures, and misunderstood hard sayings about hell, divorce, adultery, etc., he is surprisingly progressive. He is a counter-cultural

rebel, condemning religion, legalism, hypocrisy, greed, and materialism and teaching freedom, inclusivity, and love. He is a magnet for
progressive thinkers.

Nevertheless, the evangelical lens implanted over the eyes of the
church tells people that this verse doesn't mean everyone will be
saved. Some people say "Jesus is Lord" against their will, goes the
argument. But of course, coerced reverence is not genuine reverence.
It also is interesting that the verse that Paul alludes to in the Old
Testament, Isaiah 45:23-24 ("Before me every knee will bow; by me
every tongue will swear. They will say of me, 'In the LORD alone
are deliverance and strength.'"), uses a verb that denotes praise and
thanksgiving.[349] That means it's a genuine confession.

Another verse is:

"...and through him [Christ], God reconciles to himself
all things, whether things on earth or things in heaven..."
Colossians 1:20

Again, here is Paul's theme that God reconciles *all*—not some or
only the elect—through Jesus. In fact, as this idea began to sink in, I
recollected many other verses that reinforced a Universalist theology.
When John the Baptist saw Jesus for the first time he said, "Behold,
the Lamb of God, who takes away [forgives] the sins of the world."[350]
Not the sins of the elect, but *the world* (*kosmos*). When the angels
announced the birth of Christ, they said, "I bring you good news of
great joy that will be for all people."[351] Not for some or the elect, but
all. "Mercy triumphs over judgment."[352] Mercy doesn't compete with
judgment. It *triumphs*. Jesus said "For I did not to come to judge the
world, but to save the world."[353] The writer of I Timothy declares,
"[God] wants all people to be saved and come to a knowledge of the
truth [the good news]."[354] Not some, but *all*. And finally, "He died in
our place to take away our sins, and not only our sins but the sins of
all people"[355] [emphasis mine].

These declarations were a theme, also apparent in the Old
Testament. "His [God's] mercy endures forever,"[356] is a phrase

repeated 41 times. A more obscure verse says, "Like water spilled on the ground, which cannot be recovered, so we must die. But that is not what God desires; rather, he devises ways so that a banished person does not remain banished from him."[357] And finally, the proclamation that God will bless all the families of the earth through Abraham: "I will bless all nations [tribes of the earth] through you."[358]

When the rationale for rejecting the doctrine of hell or eternal damnation sank in, I began to notice how a Universalist theme illuminates the Bible. As Mt Rainier's towering presence captivates ferry riders on the Puget Sound as it did Helen and me that arresting moment, the universal love of God began to dominate my entire perspective. Suddenly, the whole concept of universal harmony—ultimate oneness of humankind with a God of unhindered affection for *all*—and its corollary, that the essential expression of the universe is inclusive love, was one of the most beautiful things I ever pondered.

But it wasn't evangelical theology. My transformation had culminated. I could no longer call myself an evangelical. But then what was I?

SAVED IN THE PUB

When Steve returned from the restroom, I had stopped ruminating about my spiritual sojourn and Dan and I were talking about Rob Bell's new book, *Love Wins: A Book about Heaven, Hell, and the Fate of Every Person Who Ever Lived*. In it, Bell, a fringe evangelical and emergent church leader, defends the possibility of universal reconciliation. It caused quite a firestorm in the evangelical world and even got Bell written up in *Time* magazine with the thought-provoking question "What if there's no hell?" gracing the cover. I was pleasantly surprised that Dan was very positive about the book, another one I recommended to him, and what I wrote in my manuscript. We knew

Steve's negative view on Universalism but wanted to ask him what he thought of Bell's book. Dan was the one who probed him.

"What do you think of the notion that love wins in the end?"

Before he could answer, Brenda interjected. "It's last call guys. What'll you have?"

"Already?" I said. "Wow, time flies. I'll just nurse this one." Dan agreed, since we had already had three tall mugs by now. Steve ordered a second one but made it a short glass.

"You must have a chapter in your book about this," Steve said. "I haven't read Bell's book, but I've read commentary about it on the Internet. I have several problems with Universalism—or whatever Bell calls it. One, I don't see it in Scripture. Two, if taught, it can give people false hope—you know, that an unrepentant person will think they are right with God when they aren't, and three, it would undercut the motivation for missions. If everyone is saved in the end, why bother evangelizing? Why follow Christ for that matter?"

"Bell's book goes into some of that and also that book I talked about at our small group, *The Inescapable Love of God*," Dan said. "There are really good answers to your concerns. Like the Scripture question. It's there in Scripture, but because of mistranslations and bias, it's easy to miss."

"It's back to that other problem I told Mike," Steve replied. "Universalists claim the church was wrong all these centuries about what it taught about hell. That's outrageous."

"Again," I began, "remember the church has been wrong before—on slavery, for example. And, the historical record tells us the church didn't always teach a traditional hell. It didn't start until three or four centuries after Christ. *And* many church fathers believed in Universalism."

"I know this is hard to fathom," added Dan. "I felt the same way when I first encountered it. But if you take the time to study the it, it's a strong case."

"You haven't convinced me," Steve added, but he seemed to have a slightly softer position than the last time one of us talked to him about it.

"Your third problem is a good question," I said. "The risk of undermining motivation for missions. It's part of a larger question—if Universalism is true, how does that change the way we engage the culture?" I paused to gather my thoughts. It *was* getting late. And I was enjoying my beer buzz.

"I think the question about missions reveals how far off the church has gone from the original message," I began again. "I mean, why do we need an everlasting hell as a default destination to motivate us to love others and spread good news? Isn't doing the right thing enough? You ask, why follow Christ? Well, because he meets spiritual needs. Following his example of love will change the world—and it has when you filter out the evil done in his name. I think a more accurate way of looking at the afterlife shows us we don't need to be saved from eternal hell but from our own fears, selfishness, and prejudice."

"Yeah, but all this sounds like you're saying all roads lead to heaven," Steve said. "People can't be right with God unless they give their hearts to Christ."

"We talked about this before," Dan offered. "Mike and I don't see salvation as an event or formula anymore, you know, formally pray to receive or 'accept' Christ. It's more of a process. And we think that's a more biblical way of looking at it. If God is reconciling the whole world to himself, then he's working in ways we can't see—like when we see a person genuinely express love, whatever their religion—that's God, and maybe Christ, working in them. I think the traditional way to evangelize often alienates people, because it's like we're saying, you're not the right religion, you need to experience God our way—which is the only way. You're not good enough for heaven unless you act more like us, and that's treating people as inferiors, like there's no way God or Christ can save someone apart from them fitting into a Christian box."

Wow! Dan's gets it, I thought. Earlier I didn't realize how far along he'd come. "So, I guess to answer your question about evange-lizing," I jumped in, "a Univeralist would still do it, but the attitude and the message would change. The right thing to do is to love others. The message wouldn't be 'repent and accept Christ because you're separated from God and on the way to hell,' but rather 'turn and choose love because God is making us all one.' And 'choose to make the world a better place because that's God's agenda.'"

"And because it's an exciting and rewarding journey to be in on God's plans," Dan added.

"Sounds like a watered down gospel to me," Steve responded. "You wouldn't even invite people to follow Jesus?"

"Well yeah, but what do you mean by 'follow Jesus'? Follow Jesus *or* follow the way of Jesus? Meaning love." I countered. "Jesus didn't found an organized religion, Steve, he founded a new way of spiri-tual life. Perhaps one can follow Jesus—his way of love—and not be formally a Christian. You know, like Gandhi did."

We didn't get much farther than that. Steve thought the idea loony.

"You can't be a Christian and a Muslim or Hindu at the same time," he responded, his voice rising slightly. "That's impossible!"

Dan and I were emotionally exhausted. I no longer wanted to counter what Steve said. It had been a long night, and it was finally drawing to a close. Discussing every element of my book had been revealing. It made me see myself more clearly and how far *I* had come. Since my days as a young evangelical, I had radically transformed. This latest conversation was a good example of how much. Still, in other ways, I was the same.

I had to admit that on the subject of salvation, what Dan and I were saying was a whole new paradigm. But to me, it was the only one that made sense. I think Gandhi, as a progressive Hindu—one who rejected the caste system for instance—had the spirit of Christ in him; but in a mysterious non-Christian way. I think Shukria Barakzai,[359] an Afghan woman and devout Muslim, who stood up to the Taliban and began a movement to secretly educate young girls, has accepted Jesus' message of *love over law*, even though she doesn't call it that. I think God transcends religion, reaches countless people we don't realize, and will ultimately reconcile everyone. Sure, people will be held accountable for their actions, but by a loving God bent on remedial correction that transforms, not everlasting punishment that dooms. Some will need a firmer judgment—either in this life or the next—to finally wake up to the love message. On the other hand, maybe I'm wrong. We really can't know anything with absolute certainty. But I had made a decision to bank on the truth of this one phrase: *Love never fails.*

In 1972, inside the universe of the evangelical Jesus Movement, I doubted that beers and Jesus mixed. Tonight was different. My time with friends discussing our spiritual journeys, while drinking tall mugs of Ridgetop Red, Pumpkin Ale, and Belgium Blonde, was a divine occasion. God was in the pub.

EPILOGUE

"Love the Lord your God with all your heart
and with all your soul and with all your mind...
And...love your neighbor as yourself.
All the Law and the Prophets hang
on these two commandments."

"So in everything, do to others
what you would have them do to you,
for this sums up the Law and the Prophets."

– Jesus Christ

My controversial revelations about the nature of the Bible and specific evangelical dogma cleared up major contradictions in my faith. Things came to a head in the mid 2000s. I left the church, rethought how to approach the Bible, began showing solidarity for gays and lesbians, and became a Christian Universalist. Ironically, my faith grew stronger. After all, the overwhelming majority of those nagging doubts had dissolved. Much of the Bible, stripped of biased translations, misguided misinterpretations, and disputed texts—the stuff of *religion*—contains a progressive, inclusive message. As for the rest, I was free to evaluate it with my heart *and* mind, rather than be bound to a literalist approach.

In 2010 Dan, my fellow microbrew enthusiast, told me he wanted to form a progressive Christian home group to explore any aspect of faith without feeling judged. I was delighted. We recruited three others and began studying emergent/progressive themes. Gina has grown in her pursuit of truth and now considers herself a Christian Universalist. When her mind was in an evangelical vein, she agonized over the destiny of her bitter, "unsaved" mother. The very day Rob Bell's *Love Wins* book arrived on Gina's doorstep, her mom passed away. She devoured its pages in one evening, and its assertion that love melts away all resistance—as well as the case for universal reconciliation argued in other books she had read—encouraged her that her mother was in gracious Hands.

Dan and Gina recently told me they aren't passionate about church these days. Not because they feel the act of attending is legalistic, but because the church was limiting their propensity to ask the tough questions and pursue a faith outside the box. Neither of them, nor I, have found an alternative church home. Our organic home group is our Christian fellowship—as are our gatherings at Silver City and other local microbreweries and restaurants. I have found others who think the same way. Recently, I met a man who organized what he called Church on Tap. Once a month, twelve guys talk life and theology over brews. Fellowship in the pub lives on.

Steve is still resistant to most of my "crazy" ideas. I have many other evangelical friends and family, including my wife Lori, who don't agree with the major themes of this book. We are all learning to agree to disagree and live at peace with one another.

During the writing process, I was amazed how much the issues I addressed unfolded in the larger culture. Time and again I made my own discoveries and then learned I wasn't the only one coming to the same conclusions. My misgivings about the institutional church were validated in Frank Viola's updated book, *Pagan Christianity* and also the organic church movement. My extensive research on the Bible led me to meet historian Garry Wills and read his exegetically sound guides to biblical interpretation in *What Jesus Meant*, *What Paul Meant*, and *What the Gospels Meant*. My conclusions

MICHAEL CAMP   317

about homosexuality and the Bible were confirmed countless times, as when I heard the late Lewis Smedes, a popular evangelical author, biblically defend gay Christians on Mel White's website and more recently when evangelical musician Jennifer Knapp publicly announced she was a lesbian on Larry King.

My leaving evangelicalism was an agonizing decision complicated by a cloud of accusatory voices from my past. Frank Schaeffer's memoir on his exodus out of the movement, *Crazy for God*, was published in the nick of time—right when I thought I might be going berserk, it reassured me I was sane. At least relatively so. His later work, *Patience with God: Faith for People Who Don't Like Religion (or Atheism)*, proved a therapeutic balm for my wandering soul.

My suspicion that God shines His love through people of other faiths and philosophies (even atheists) was reinforced through several sources: the dauntless fight for women's rights of Somali Muslim-turned-atheist Ayaan Hirsi Ali, the faith in Love's supremacy of Muslim, Buddhist, Hindu, Bahai, and Christian leaders as expressed in the documentary *Beyond Our Differences*, and the spiritual epiphanies of former skeptic Jessica Maxwell as told in *Roll Around Heaven*, to name a few. After I uncovered the facts surrounding the doctrine of eternal punishment, a slew of books surfaced that verified my findings, including Carlton Pearson's *The Gospel of Inclusion*, *The Evangelical Universalist*, and Rob Bell's *Love Wins*. Then in 2011 my newfound friend and co-seeker-of-original-biblical-meaning, author Julie Ferwerda, published *Raising Hell: Christianity's Most Controversial Doctrine Put Under Fire*. Julie is no stranger to conservative Christianity. Her book is courageous as much as it is persuasive. As Dan said, "It's like a revival of progressive Christian thought!" Most of these universalist-themed books—written by current or ex-evangelicals—were not available ten years ago.

Moreover, I began to meet a new Christian breed that was serious about following Christ—and His way of love—but was operating in a non-evangelical paradigm. Like my friend Jason, who became a believer after reading Marcus Borg's *The Heart of Christianity*.

(His conversion is particularly astounding to people from a religious conservative background since Borg is a member of the Jesus Seminar). Over a microbrew one evening, Jason told me the story of how he came to appreciate God's grace—by watching a video of a gay audience spontaneously wash Carlton Pearson's feet after he spoke on the inclusive gospel.

In 2011, I learned of a new progressive Christian movement that had begun a to-be-annual event called the Wild Goose Festival in North Carolina—a festival of justice, spirituality, music, and the arts (the wild goose is a Celtic metaphor for the Holy Spirit). Despite my inability to attend, I was touched by the lineup of speakers, activists, and musicians who represented a new kind of Christian spirituality—from gay rights activist Peterson Toscano to emergent leader Brian McLaren to social justice advocate Jim Wallis to former evangelical Frank Schaeffer. Organizers encouraged attendees to embrace the creative and open nature of their faith in order to re-build relationships with each other and the larger culture—and perhaps build bridges across "our country's current cynical, religious, and political divide." These folks weren't constructing a parallel, religiously acceptable, Christian universe. I liked that. When I read accounts of the event later (and learned they had a beer tent—this was conspicuously missing at Explo '72 and the Jesus Festivals of my youth!), it was confirmed. Although there were complaints that Wild Goose didn't take a stand on things like gay rights, which I think they should, at least they were open to alternative theologies. It appeared I had missed a watershed event and I vowed to attend in 2012.

Even attending the U2 360 Tour concert in Seattle and hearing Bono sing and subtly muse about Christ and ways to fight for social justice was a spiritual experience. *Our God is too small*, I thought, after I heard him highlight Amnesty International's 50th anniversary and saw Burmese activist Aung San Suu Kyi speak on the giant overhead screen. Just seven months earlier I spearheaded two Amnesty write-a-thons, a gathering of people to write letters protesting the holding of prisoners of conscience. I knew Bono and U2, despite their drinking, smoking, and swearing, were leading voices of social activism and a more open faith in Christ, but didn't realize they supported Amnesty. Years earlier, as a dedicated young evangelical, I never dreamed God could be this big—or broad minded.

My journey out of a conservative Christian worldview has ended, but my spiritual sojourn is far from over. Whether you're a believer or not, I hope the same is true for you. Like a child chasing a wild goose, may we follow the Spirit and remember to question institutionalized religion, embrace grace, and pursue faith in ways that align with our sense of reason. In the end, I believe we are only called to focus on two mandates: love God with all our heart, soul, and mind, and love our neighbors as ourselves—including our global neighbors. And to do it in ways that genuinely bring social justice to the world, protect the weak, empower the poor, and nurture planet earth. I'll raise a microbrew to that. Will you join me?

NOTES

AN INVITATION

1 The emergent or emerging church is a progressive arm of evangelicalism and other Christian movements disillusioned with conservatism and the traditional church. They focus more on social activism, a missional lifestyle, and a new monasticism, which encourages contemplative and communal living and outreach to the poor. They attempt to transcend "modernist" labels such as conservative and liberal and live their faith in a "post-modern" society. Some in this movement consider themselves evangelicals or post-evangelicals, and others don't consider themselves evangelicals at all. Leaders include Brian McClaren, Phylis Tickle, and Rob Bell.

2 Although there have been many reforming evangelical currents within the movement, e.g. Tony Campolo, Mark Noll, Ron Sider, and Myron Augsburger (a Mennonite who considers himself an evangelical), in my experience today's prevailing evangelical view is entrenched in conservative religion the way I define it. During the 19th century, there were stronger progressive elements of the movement; for example, leading British abolitionist William Wilberforce and the American abolitionists in the North.

3 I use the term "progressive" loosely, not as a new ideology or orthodoxy, but a way to describe my new paradigm within faith in Christ juxtaposed to my conservative past.

CONFESSION 1

4 Anne Lamott, *Bird by Bird: Some Instructions on Writing and Life,* (New York: Anchor Books, 1995).

CONFESSION 2

5 John Marks, *Reasons to Believe: One Man's Journey Among the Evangelicals and the Faith He Left Behind* (New York: HarperCollins Publishers, 2008), 219.

6 Stephen King, *On Writing* (New York: Simon and Schuster, 2000)

7 "Evangelism is Most Effective Among Kids," Barna.org, 2004: http://www.barna.org/barna-update/article/5-barna-update/196-evangelism-is-most-effective-among-kids (accessed July 2010).

8 In *The Shack*, a Christian novel by William P. Young, God the Father takes the form of an African American woman called both Elouisa and Papa.

CONFESSION 3

9 E. Stanley Jones, *Mahatma Gandhi: An Interpretation* (Abingdon-Cokesbury Press, 1963), 8.

10 Matthew 28:18-20

11 Liberal Protestant or Roman Catholic churches did not count. Their members were supposedly not saved.

12 For example, see Matthew 19:21.

13 The second of the two greatest commandments: Love your neighbor. See Matthew 22:34-40.

14 United Nations High Commissioner for Refugees (UNHCR) was the umbrella entity for myriad aid agencies working in Somalia in the 1980s, including a handful of evangelical aid organizations.

15 John 14:6

16 I Timothy 2:5

17 I Timothy 2:3

18 William Lane Craig, as quoted by Thomas Talbot, *The Inescapable Love of God*, (Universal Publishers, 1999, rev. 2002), 83.

19 I John 4:8

20 II Peter 3:9

21 Gregory MacDonald, *The Evangelical Universalist,* (Eugene, Oregon: Wipf & Stock Publishers, 2006), 1.

22 C. S. Lewis, *The Problem of Pain* (New York: Macmillan, 1944), 127.

23 Tony Campolo, *Speaking My Mind* (Nashville: W Publishing Group, 2004), 77

24 "Accelerating the Fulfillment of the Great Commission in our Generation,"

GNMS.net, 2010: http://www.gnms.net/envisioning.html (accessed December 2010).

25 John and Anna Travis, "Insider Movements." Mission Frontiers, September-October 2005.

26 Some evangelicals will object to such statements and say that their mission is not to convert people to a religious institution but to help people develop a relationship with God. But in my experience this is just a mask to avoid saying the obvious. Mission-minded evangelicals insist that the spread of the gospel message be done through organized church institutions; hence the widespread focus on church planting. Although some are more careful than others to attempt to plant churches or congregations of believers that are culturally relevant to the indigenous people and not a Western structure, the fact remains that if someone is not a part of a Christian church, however contextualized to culture it is, and if someone does not convert to a recognizable orthodox Christian view, then that person is suspect at best and considered unsaved at worst.

27 This American Baptist church was conservative theologically but not considered fundamentalist. Nevertheless, they did not accept women for nomination as elders or pastors, based on literal interpretations of Paul's writing in the New Testament. As a result, only I, and not my wife, was eligible to be ordained.

28 In the Muslim chiefdom where we lived, we called our place of worship the Chiyao word for mosque rather than church. But everyone knew it was a Christian "mosque," not Muslim.

29 More open-minded evangelical missionaries concerned with reaching as many Muslims as possible with the message of Christ (often due to the missionary syndrome) have advocated a range of "contextualized" strategies. The most controversial is the "C5" approach that recognizes the possibility there can be Muslims who follow Christ—and from their point of view, they are not "Christians." They still attend mosque, pray five times a day, and may even acknowledge Mohammed as God's prophet. The difference is they also "accept" or "follow" Jesus. In this way, they can remain in their Muslim community to reach others, whereas typical converts to Christ are ostracized and usually must flee their communities. Still, C5 advocates would typically believe that one must "accept" Christ to receive salvation. A Muslim who doesn't decide to follow Jesus in this life would not be "saved."

30 See *Infidel*, by Ayaan Hirsi Ali, and *The Trouble with Islam Today*, by Irshad Manji for two examples of a Muslim call for reform.

31 "Pilgrim's Progress." Newsweek Magazine, August 14, 2006.

32 John 14:6

33 Hebrews 9:27

CONFESSION 4

34 Psalm 119:105

35 "Einstein and Faith." Time Magazine, April 16, 2007, 46.

36 I Samuel 15:1-3, Deuteronomy 2:31-37, Numbers 31:7-18, and Joshua 6:20-21

37 Genesis 1:1-31

38 Leviticus 20:9-13 and Exodus 31:14

39 Matthew 5:32 and 19:9

40 Matthew 5:22

41 Matthew 12:31-32

42 Matthew 18:21-22

43 I Corinthians 14:33-35

44 N.T. Wright, *The Last Word: Beyond the Bible Wars to a New Understanding of the Authority of Scripture* (New York: Harper SanFrancisco), 106–110.

45 According to Merriam-Webster, inerrant means "free from error," and infallible means "incapable of error."

46 2 Timothy 3:16 states "All ScriptureScripture is God-breathed and is useful for teaching, rebuking, correcting and training in righteousness..."

47 Written in 1968, Francis Schaeffer's book, *Pollution and the Death of Man*, was way ahead of its time even for environmentalists.

48 Frank Schaeffer, *Crazy for God: How I Grew Up as One of the Elect, Helped Found the Religious Right, and Lived to Take All (or Almost All) of It Back* (Cambridge, MA: Carroll and Graf Publishers, 2007), 210-211.

49 Francis was one of the signers of the Chicago Statement of Biblical Inerrancy, a 1978 document formulated by 200 evangelical leaders.

50 Years later, I learned the details of this from books like Misquoting Jesus,

by Bart Ehrman. Since we don't have the originals, establishing which biblical texts are closest to the originals is not always a simple matter. The vast majority of biblical manuscript copies we have were produced hundreds of years after the originals and copied from much later copies.

51 The only exception I could find was when there was a contradiction regarding a number. That kind of inconsistently was usually explained as a copyist error.

52 Laura Engelhardt, "The Problem with Eyewitness Testimony," Stanford Journal of Legal Studies: http://agora.stanford.edu/sjls/Issue%20One/fisher&tversky.htm (accessed June 2011).

53 L. William Countryman, *Biblical Authority or Biblical Tyranny? Scripture and the Christian Pilgrimage* (Harrisburg, PA: Trinity Press International, 1994), 8.

54 (Countryman), 21.

55 Ibid (Frank Schaeffer), 310.

56 "Countering Bible Contradictions," Bible Contradictions Answered: http://www.bringyou.to/apologetics/bible.htm#INDEX (accessed May 2009).

57 L. William Countryman, *Biblical Authority or Biblical Tyranny? Scripture and the Christian Pilgrimage* (Harrisburg, PA: Trinity Press International, 1994), 16-17.

58 Here are three more examples: Matthew and Mark say that John the Baptist baptized Jesus. Luke says that John was already in prison when Jesus was baptized. In Mark, Jesus cites an Old Testament story (when King David ate the bread of the priests on the Sabbath) and says "when Abiathar was the high priest." But the story in I Samuel says Abiathar's father, Ahimelech, was the high priest, not Abiathar. In Mark Chapter One, he states Isaiah wrote the quote that follows but the first part of the quotation is from Malachi, not Isaiah.

CONFESSION 5

59 Steve Brown, *A Scandalous Freedom* (West Monroe, LA: Howard Publishing Co., Inc., 2004), 11.

60 Frank Viola and George Barna, *Pagan Christianity: Exploring the Roots of Our Church Practices* (Tyndale House Publishers, 2008), xix.

61 Garry Wills, *What Jesus Meant* (London: Penguin Group, 2006), 78.

62 Frank Viola and George Barna, *Pagan Christianity: Exploring the Roots of Our Church Practices* (Tyndale House Publishers, 2008), 1-8.

63 Revival is typically explained as a great outpouring of the Holy Spirit that results in mass conversion and moral cleansing in society, as occurred in The Great Awakening of the early 1700s under the leadership of Jonathan Edwards or the Second Awakening of the 1800s under the influence of preachers like Charles Finney. In the early 1980s, charismatic church leaders and musicians like Keith Green were calling for nothing less than a modernist version of historical American revival.

64 From *I Want to Be a Clone*, 1983, the debut album of Steve Taylor.

65 Hebrews 13:17

66 A prophetic word is what someone addresses to the church, supposedly under the direction of the Holy Spirit, giving an encouraging, or challenging, or predictive message.

67 Mike Yaconelli, in Dave Tomlinson, *The Post Evangelical* (Grand Rapids, Michigan: Zondervan, 2003), 28.

68 Donald Miller, *Blue Like Jazz: Nonreligious Thoughts on Christian Spirituality* (Nashville: Thomas Nelson Publishers, 2003), 214.

69 Gregory R. Frizzell, *Returning to Holiness: A Personal and Churchwide Journey to Revival* (Memphis, Tennessee: The Master Design, 2000), x.

70 A notion of holiness that claims you aren't measuring up as a Christian unless you thoroughly clean up your thought life, give thanks for all things at all times, set aside all of Sunday for God, take communion with deep examination of personal sin, never complain to those in authority, engage in prayer at least 30 minutes a day, keep a list of people to pray for, distribute evangelistic tracts, enroll in a witnessing strategy, fast on a regular basis, and my personal favorite, refrain from the use of slang, based on a twisted interpretation of something Jesus said! (Matthew 5:37). Ibid (Frizzell), 32.

71 Tithing is the practice of giving ten percent of one's income to the church, before taxes. If you do it after taxes, you are supposedly cheating God.

72 Malachi 3:6-12

73 See Confession 7, and Frank Viola and George Barna, *Pagan Christianity: Exploring the Roots of our Christian Practices* (Tyndale House Publishers,

2008), 172-178, and Matthew E. Narramore, Tithing: Low-Realm, Obsolete, and Defunct (Tekoa Publishing, 2004).

74 I Corinthians 6:12

75 Galatians 3:25

76 Romans 2:13

77 Romans 7:6

78 Romans 10:4

79 See Bart D. Ehrman, *Misquoting Jesus: The Story Behind Who Changed the Bible and Why*, (New York: HarperOne, 2005).

80 "Jesus, Christians and the Law," UKapologetics.net: http://www.ukapologetics.net/Jesusandthelaw.html (accessed June 2011).

81 Jacques Ellul, *The Subversion of Christianity* (Wm. B. Eerdmans Publishing Company, 1986), 37.

82 Ibid (Ellul), 43.

83 To their credit, my former pastors at ALCC, Che Ahn and Lou Engle, broke from PDI/SGM in the early 90s because of disagreements they had with controlling "apostolic" leaders. On the other hand, the new church they started still practiced what I call churchianity.

84 Garry Wills, *What Paul Meant* (London: Penguin Group, 2006), 180-181.

85 Frank Viola and George Barna, *Pagan Christianity: Exploring the Roots of Our Church Practices* (Tyndale House Publishers, 2008).

86 Dave Tomlinson, *The Post Evangelical* (Grand Rapids, MI: Zondervan, 2003), 31.

87 Matthew 18:20

88 Matthew 25:31-46

89 Ayaan Hirsi Ali, Infidel (New York: Free Press, 2007).

CONFESSION 6
90 Bernard N. Nathanson, M.D. with Richard N. Ostling, *Aborting America*, (Toronto: Life Cycle Books, 1979), 259.

91 Philip Yancey, *What's So Amazing About Grace* (Grand Rapids, MI: Zondervan, 1997), 231.

92 Frank Schaeffer, *Crazy for God: How I Grew Up as One of the Elect, Helped Found the Religious Right, and Lived to Take All (or Almost All) of It Back* (Cambridge, MA: Carroll and Graf Publishers, 2007), 347.

93 Mark A. Noll, Nathan O. Hatch, and George M. Marsden, *The Search for Christian America* (Colorado Springs: Helmers & Howard, 1989), 17.

94 Ibid (Noll, Hatch, and Marsden), 36.

95 Randall Ballmer, *Thy Kingdom Come: How the Religious Right Distorts the Faith and Threatens America* (New York: Perseus Books Group, 2006), 42.

96 Ibid (Noll, Hatch, and Marsden), 72.

97 Cal Thomas and Ed Dobson, *Blinded by Might: Why the Religious Right Can't Save America* (Grand Rapids, Michigan: Zondervan Publishing House, 1999), 54.

98 Harvey Cox, *When Jesus Came to Harvard: Making Moral Choices Today* (Boston: Houghton Mifflin Company, 2004).

99 Gregory A. Boyd, *The Myth of a Christian Nation: How the Quest for Political Power is Destroying the Church* (Grand Rapids, MI: Zondervan, 2005).

100 Randall Ballmer, *Thy Kingdom Come: How the Religious Right Distorts the Faith and Threatens America* (New York: Perseus Books Group, 2006), 42.

CONFESSION 7

101 Matthew 24:1-51, Mark 13:1-37, and Luke 21:5-36

102 R.C. Sproul, *The Last Days According to Jesus* (Grand Rapids, MI: Baker Books, 1998), 158.

103 Mel White, *Religion Gone Bad: The Hidden Dangers of the Christian Right* (New York: Penguin Group, Inc., 2006), 183.

104 Thatcher, Adrian, *The Savage Text: The Use and Abuse of the Bible* (West Sussex, UK: Wiley-Blackwell, 2008), 4.

105 L. William Countryman, *Biblical Authority or Biblical Tyranny? ScriptureScripture and the Christian Pilgrimage* (Harrisburg, Pennsylvania: Trinity Press International, 1994), 85-89.

106 Bart D. Ehrman, *Misquoting Jesus: The Story Behind Who Changed the Bible and Why*, (New York: HarperOne, 2005).

107 The story of Onan in Genesis 38:8-10 is often claimed to refer to

masturbation, but a careful study of the passage reveals it is about Onan's failure to obey the Leverite Law and fulfill his duty to impregnate his deceased brother's wife. He wasn't condemned for masturbation or even birth control per se, but for refusal to provide offspring for his brother.

108 See Confession 9, "The Sex God."

109 Fee's book, *How to Read the Bible for All Its Worth*, and other commentaries.

110 Jacques Ellul, *The Subversion of Christianity* (Wm. B. Eerdmans Publishing Company, 1986), 24.

111 Gregory MacDonald, *The Evangelical Universalist*, (Eugene, Oregon: Wipf & Stock Publishers, 2006), 35.

112 Gordon Fee and Douglas Stuart, *How to Read the Bible for All It's Worth*, (Grand Rapids, Michigan: Zondervan, 1981 and 1993), 36.

113 Garry Wills, *What Paul Meant* (London: Penguin Group, 2006), 177.

114 The chapter and verse denotations in modern Bibles were not part of the original Hebrew or Greek text.

115 Frank Schaeffer, *Crazy for God: How I Grew Up as One of the Elect, Helped Found the Religious Right, and Lived to Take All (or Almost All) of It Back* (Cambridge, Massachusetts: Carroll and Graf Publishers, 2007), 309.

116 N.T. Wright, "How Can the Bible be Authoritative?" Vox Evangelica, Volume 21, 1991.

117 For example, I Timothy 3:16 states the ScriptureScriptures of the day (the Old Testament) are "God-breathed" or "inspired." It is referring only to the Hebrew ScriptureScriptures and does not say they are infallible.

118 John, Chapter 1, says that the "Word" was God and the "Word" became flesh in the person of Jesus. The Greek term Logos, translated "Word," also means "reason" and "rationality," according to L. William Countryman (Biblical Authority or Biblical Tyranny, page 90). Perhaps it's not Jesus' literal words in the Bible that are authoritative, but his reasoning, which can only be understood in their historical, cultural context.

119 Ironically, in Jesus' day, the word Scripture included the Apocrypha, a portion of the Bible not recognized by modern evangelicals or other Protestants. The New Testament writers quoted the Septuagint, the Greek translation of the Hebrew Scriptures, which included the Apocrypha.

120 Thatcher, Adrian, *The Savage Text: The Use and Abuse of the Bible* (West Sussex, UK: Wiley-Blackwell, 2008), 4.

121 There are exceptions to this as when some NIV translators were willing to make English translation changes due to respect for textual criticism.

122 For an introduction to how to do this, read historian Garry Wills' treatment of Scripture that expertly separates fact from fiction in *What Jesus Meant, What Paul Meant,* and *What the Gospels Meant.*

123 Mark 16:9-20

124 John 7:53-8:11

125 I John 5:7 in older English versions said: "For there are three that testify in heaven, the Father, the Word, and the Holy Spirit, and these three are one." This verse was not found in any Greek manuscript before the 16th century.

126 Garry Wills, *What Paul Meant* (London: Penguin Group, 2006), 15-16.

127 Ehrman, Bart, *Misquoting Jesus, The Story Behind Who Changed the Bible and Why*, pages 210-211.

128 N Matthew E. Narramore, *Tithing: Low-Realm, Obsolete, and Defunct* (Tekoa Publishing, 2004).

129 Malachi 3:6-12

130 Matthew 23:23

131 David Instone-Brewer, "What God Has Joined," Christianity Today, October 2007.

132 David Instone-Brewer, *Divorce and Remarriage in the Church: Biblical Solutions for Pastoral Realities* (Downers Grove, IL: InterVarsity Press, 2003).

133 *Keriythuwth* in Hebrew and *apostasion* in Greek mean to execute a legal divorce by giving a certificate of divorce to a woman.

134 *Shalach* in Hebrew and *apoluo* in Greek both mean "to put away" a woman without giving her a bill of divorcement.

135 Malachi 2:16

136 Walter Callison, *Divorce: A Gift of God's Love* (Leawood, KS: Leathers Publishing, 2002), 4-5.

137 Wendy Francisco, "Does God Hate Divorce?" http://www.rockymountainministries.org/Articles/ChristianityAndDivorce/godhatesdivorce.html (accessed July 2011).

138 Rob Bell, *Love Wins: A Book About Heaven, Hell, and the Fate of Every Person Who Ever Lived*, (New York: HarperOne, 2011), 42.

139 N. T. Wright, *Jesus and the Victory of God* (Minneapolis, MN: Fortress Press, 1996), 202.

140 Garry Wills, *What Jesus Meant* (London: Penguin Group, 2006), 84.

141 Garry Wills, *What Jesus Meant* (London: Penguin Group, 2006), xxv.

142 Garry Wills, *What Paul Meant* (London: Penguin Group, 2006), 90.

143 Ibid. (Wills), 99.

144 Gordon Fee, *The First Epistle to the Corinthians* (Grand Rapids, MI: Wm. B. Eerdmans Publishing Co., 1987).

145 1 Timothy 2:11-12 says "I do not permit a woman to teach or have authority over a man; she must be silent."

146 1 Corinthians 11:6 says "If a woman does not cover her head, she should have her hair cut off; and if it is a disgrace for a woman to have her hair cut or shaved off, she should cover her head."

147 3 John 1:2, says "Beloved, I pray that in all respects you may prosper and be in good health, just as your soul prospers."

148 Bishop Carlton Pearson, *The Gospel of Inclusion: Reaching Beyond Religious Fundamentalism to the True Love of God* (Azusa Press International, 2006), 175.

149 Dr. Henry Cloud and Dr. John Townsend, *12 "Christian" Beliefs That Can Drive You Crazy: Relief from False Assumptions* (Grand Rapids, MI: Zondervan Publishing House, 1995), 9.

CONFESSION 8

150 Quoted in Mark A. Noll, *The Scandal of the Evangelical Mind* (Grand Rapids, Michigan: Wm. B. Eerdmans Publishing Co., 1994), 174.

151 This notion comes from Jesus describing what the "time of the end" will be like: "...then there will be great distress, unequaled from the beginning of the world until now" (Matthew 24:21).

152 In high school, I remember reading a comic book on the subject, probably a short version of Lindsey's book written for children and youth, with an image of people, in 70s-style clothing, rising into the sky with glorious smiles

on their faces going to be with Jesus. It looked like a Marvel comic with super heroes flying through the sky.

153 Dr. David Jeremiah, *What in the World is Going On? 10 Prophetic Clues You Cannot Afford to Ignore* (Nashville, Tennessee: Thomas Nelson, 2008), 97.

154 Gary DeMar, *Last Days Madness: Obsession of the Modern Church* (Smyrna, Georgia: American Vision, Inc., 1997), 193-218.

155 N.T. Wright, *Surprised by Hope: Rethinking Heaven, the Resurrection, and the Mission of the Church* (New York, New York: HarperOne, 2008), 133.

156 See R.C. Sproul's, *The Last Days According to Jesus*, or Richard Perry's The *Complete Idiot's Guide to the Last Days*, for an overview of the major views and doctrines.

157 Matthew 24:1-3

158 Lindsey strongly implied the end would come by 1988 based on his theory that end-times Bible prophesies would happen within a generation (40 years) of the creation of Israel in 1948. This "theory" was commonly espoused among fundamentalists and evangelicals, often to entice unbelievers to repent and accept Jesus, until... well, 1989!

159 2 Thessalonians 2:3 (KJV)

160 Frank Schaeffer, *Crazy for God: How I Grew Up as One of the Elect, Helped Found the Religious Right, and Lived to Take All (or Almost All) of It Back* (Cambridge, MA: Carroll and Graf Publishers, 2007), 299.

161 Gary DeMar, *Last Days Madness: Obsession of the Modern Church* (Smyrna, Georgia: American Vision, Inc., 1997), 7-13.

162 Bart D. Ehrman, *Misquoting Jesus: The Story Behind Who Changed the Bible and Why*, (New York: HarperOne, 2005), 109-110.

163 Kenneth L. Gentry, *Before Jerusalem Fell: Dating the Book of Revelation* (Atlanta: American Vision, 1998), 9

164 Matthew Chapter 24.

165 Gary DeMar, *Last Days Madness: Obsession of the Modern Church* (Smyrna, Georgia: American Vision, Inc., 1997), 45.

166 Ibid (Gary DeMar), 166.

167 Matthew 24:14

168 Ibid (Gary DeMar), 65-66.

169 Colossians 1:23

170 Ibid (Gary DeMar), 44.

171 *The Quest Study Bible: New International Version* (Grand Rapids, Michigan: Zondervan Publishing House, 1994), 1369-1370.

172 Gary DeMar, *Last Days Madness: Obsession of the Modern Church* (Smyrna, Georgia: American Vision, Inc., 1997), 39-66

173 R.C. Sproul, *The Last Days According to Jesus* (Grand Rapids, Michigan: Baker Books, 1998), 158.

174 Russell, J. Stuart, *The Parousia,* (1887; reprint, Grand Rapids, Michigan: Baker Books, 1983), 366.

175 Isaiah 19:1

176 Psalms 104:3

177 Ezekiel 30:3

178 Mark 14:62

179 The root is *erchomai.* See Gerhard Kittel and Gerhard Friedrich, Editors; abridged by Geoffrey W. Bromiley, *Theological Dictionary of the New Testament* (Grand Rapids, Michigan: William B. Eerdmans Publishing Company, 1985), 257.

180 N.T. Wright, *Surprised by Hope: Rethinking Heaven, the Resurrection, and the Mission of the Church* (New York, New York: HarperOne, 2008), 125-126.

181 Gary DeMar, *Last Days Madness: Obsession of the Modern Church* (Smyrna, Georgia: American Vision, Inc., 1997), pages 159-165.

182 N.T. Wright, *Surprised by Hope: Rethinking Heaven, the Resurrection, and the Mission of the Church* (New York, New York: HarperOne, 2008), 127. Wright also argues during his earthly ministry, Jesus said nothing about his return to earth but rather spoke of his vindication and spiritual coming (going) into God's presence.

183 R.C. Sproul, *The Last Days According to Jesus* (Grand Rapids, Michigan: Baker Books, 1998), 208.

CONFESSION 9

184 Slavery in Old Testament times was rampant in all cultures and not associated with a particular race. Slaves were typically prisoners of war or those

who couldn't pay off their debt. Although the Bible does not disapprove of the institution, at times it does regulate it humanely. For instance, Hebrew slaves were to be released after six years; all aliens, including slaves, were not to be oppressed; and in the New Testament, masters are told to treat their slaves kindly. Nevertheless, the absence of a verdict against the institution is an intrinsic problem in the Bible and led to its justification by Christians in some societies.

185 Philo Thelos, *Divine Sex: Liberating Sex from Religious Tradition* (Victoria, British Columbia: Trafford Publishing, 2002), 54-64.

186 This law found in Deuteronomy 25:5-10 is sometimes called the Levirate Law.

187 Deuteronomy 21:15-17

188 2 Samuel 12:8

189 Song of Solomon 7:1-8

190 Song of Solomon 5:11-16

191 Song of Solomon 4:10-13

192 Song of Solomon 5:1

193 Genesis 38:1-30.

194 Judges 16:1

195 Deuteronomy 23:17

196 Rodney Stark, *Cities of God: The Real Story of How Christianity Became an Urban Movement and Conquered Rome* (New York: HarperSanFrancisco, 2006), 50 and 92.

197 Acts 15:1-35 commonly known as The Council at Jerusalem

198 John Bloom, "Ole Anthony and the God Thing," The Wittenburg Door: http://www.wittenburgdoor.com/?q=node/76 (accessed November 2009).

199 One example is *The Gift of Sex*, by Clifford and Joyce Penner. In 1997, erotic writer Susie Bright acknowledged much of the wisdom of such authors in her Salon article "Let Jesus Be Your Sex Therapist." On the other hand, she disagreed with their across-the-board condemnation of pornography, erotic literature, and fantasies, making the case that supporting each other's erotic imagination could be a gift to a marriage.

200 *Philo Thelos*, Divine Sex, L. William Countryman, *Dirt, Greed, and Sex,*

Raymond J. Lawrence, Jr., *The Poisoning of Eros*, and Raymond J. Lawrence, Jr., *Sexual Liberation: The Scandal of Christendom*

201 Raymond J. Lawrence, Jr., *The Poisoning of Eros: Sexual Values in Conflict* (New York: Augustine Moore Press, 1989), 11.

202 Ibid. (Raymond J. Lawrence, Jr.), 1-30.

203 Ibid. (Raymond J. Lawrence, Jr.), 1.

204 Ibid. (Raymond J. Lawrence, Jr.), 2.

205 I Corinthians 6:18

206 L. William Countryman, *Dirt, Greed, and Sex: Sexual Ethics in the New Testament and Their Implications for Today* (Philadelphia: Fortress Press, 1988), 73.

207 For example, as referenced earlier, the Temple of Aphrodite in Corinth at one point had 1000 sacred female prostitutes.

208 Marty Klein, Ph.D., *America's War on Sex: The Attack on Law, Lust, and Liberty* (Westport, Connecticut: Praeger, 2008), 1.

209 Matthew 5:28

210 Gerhard Kittel and Gerhard Friedrich, Editors; abridged by Geoffrey W. Bromiley, *Theological Dictionary of the New Testament* (Grand Rapids, Michigan: William B. Eerdmans Publishing Company, 1985), 134 and L. William Countryman, *Dirt, Greed, and Sex: Sexual Ethics in the New Testament and Their Implications for Today* (Philadelphia: Fortress Press, 1988), 151.

211 Ibid. (L. William Countryman), 177.

212 Philo Thelos, *Divine Sex: Liberating Sex from Religious Tradition* (Victoria, British Columbia: Trafford Publishing, 2002), 127.

213 John White, *Eros Defiled: The Christian and Sexual Sin* (Downers Grove, Illinois: Inter-Varsity Press, 1977), 22.

214 L. William Countryman, *Dirt, Greed, and Sex: Sexual Ethics in the New Testament and Their Implications for Today* (Philadelphia: Fortress Press, 1988), 264.

215 Coincidentally, Josh Harris later became the senior pastor of Covenant Life Church in Gaithersburg, Maryland, the founding church of the PDI/SGM denomination of which I was a part.

216 I Corinthians 7:9

217 Rob Stein, "Premarital Abstinence Pledges Ineffective, Study Finds," Washington Post, December 29, 2008: http://www.washingtonpost.com/wp-dyn/content/article/2008/12/28/AR2008122801588.html   (accessed April 2010).

218 See Amy Kreger, "Evangelicals: Why Do We Have the Highest Divorce Rate?" Associated Content, 2007:   http://www.associatedcontent.com/article/137829/evangelicals_why_do_we_have_the_highest.html   (accessed April 2010).

219 Song of Solomon 5:14 translated the correct way with a dynamic equivalent.

220 Song of Solomon 7:2 translated the correct way with a dynamic equivalent.

221 For a discussion on the meaning of biblical prohibitions against male homosexuality, see Confession 10.

222 Particularly erotica that couples can mutually enjoy and educational material, e.g. the Better Sex Video Series by the Sinclair Institute.

223 Walter Wink, "Homosexuality and the Bible," SoulForce: http://www.soulforce.org/article/homosexuality-bible-walter-wink (accessed May 2010).

224 Garry Wills, What Paul Meant (London: Penguin Group, 2006), 175.

225 L. William Countryman, Dirt, Greed, and Sex: Sexual Ethics in the New Testament and Their Implications for Today (Philadelphia: Fortress Press, 1988), 159.

226 Genesis 2:24

227 Deuteronomy 21:15

228 Galatians 3:28

229 For example, as described in Hirsi Ali, Ayaan, Infidel, and in Mormon-based polygamous cults that condone men's marrying young girls.

230 John Stossel, Myths, Lies, and Downright Stupidity, (New York: Hyperion, 2006), 46-48.

231 Wangari Maathai, Unbowed, (New York: Anchor Books, 2007), 18. Maathai describes the polygamous homestead of her childhood, where her mother, "younger mothers," and "older mothers" were free from jealousy and hatred.

232 Paraphrase of 2 Timothy 3:16

233 Romans 7:6

234 Galatians 3:25

235 Fil Anderson, *Breaking the Rules: Trading Performance for Intimacy with God* (Downers Grove, Illinois, InterVarsity Press, 2010).

236 Romans 13:10

237 Matthew 22: 34-40

238 Addison Taylor, "1 in 2 Young People Will Get an STD by Age 25," KVAL.com: http://www.kval.com/news/national/42831487.html (accessed January 2011).

239 Sex education in Sweden is sex-positive and geared toward youth making intelligent, responsible choices. They have fewer unwanted pregnancies and STDs than American teenagers. Finnish teens receive a similar education and on average, begin intercourse a year later than their American counterparts. See Dr. Roger W. Libby, *The Naked Truth About Sex* (Topanga, California: Freedom Press, 2006), 26.

CONFESSION 10

240 Genesis 1-2 (Creation account that does not specifically mention homosexuality), Genesis 19:1-19 (Sodom account), Leviticus 18:22 and 20:13 (Holiness Code), and Romans 1:24-27, I Corinthians 6:9, and I Timothy 1:10 (Letters of Paul).

241 Other translations say "abomination."

242 See Confession 7. The phrases "Kingdom of God" and "Kingdom of Heaven" do not refer to a place of paradise in the afterlife.

243 *Sex, Lies, and Life on the Evangelical Edge, an interview of Philip Yancey* by Jim Wallis, Sojourners.

244 Philo Thelos, *God is Not a Homophobe* (Victoria, British Columbia: Trafford Publishing, 2004), 7.

245 I discovered liberal authors weren't the diabolical demons I had imagined. Many of them both critiqued conservative theology while defending the Bible as relevant. On this and other subjects, four examples are William Countryman, Jack Rogers, Bart Ehrman, and Garry Wills. While Countryman critiques literalist, inerrant views of the Bible, he recognizes powerful lessons in Scripture and the general historicity of Jesus and the Gospels. Rogers is actually an evangelical Presbyterian with a high view of Scripture who changed his view on homosexuality. Although Ehrman

exposes the human elements of composing the Bible, including copyist errors (and ultimately became an agnostic for other reasons), he maintains this helps one make more sense of the Bible. Historian Wills reveals the Bible is not altogether historically accurate but fully believes the reality and power of the life and message of Jesus.

246 Found primarily in the book of Leviticus.

247 Leviticus 13:12-13

248 L. William Countryman, *Dirt, Greed, and Sex: Sexual Ethics in the New Testament and Their Implications for Today* (Philadelphia: Fortress Press, 1988), 25-26.

249 Ibid. (Countryman), 27.

250 Leviticus 18: 19, 26, 29

251 Leviticus 11:4-45

252 Jack Rogers, *Jesus, the Bible, and Homosexuality: Explode the Myths, Heal the Church* (Louisville, Kentucky: Westminster John Knox Press, 2006), 72.

253 Mark 7:19

254 Romans 7:6

255 Romans 10:4

256 Romans 7:6 and Romans 8

257 Philo Thelos, *God is Not a Homophobe* (Victoria, British Columbia: Trafford Publishing, 2004), 28.

258 Particularly in I and II Kings

259 Justin R. Cannon, *The Bible, Christianity, and Homosexuality,* (Justin R. Cannon, 2009), 12.

260 Rodney Stark, *Cities of God* (San Francisco: HarperSanFrancisco, 2006), 50.

261 Ibid (Rodney Stark), 92.

262 Philo Thelos, *God is Not a Homophobe* (Victoria, British Columbia: Trafford Publishing, 2004), 58.

263 Some conservatives claim the story of Sodom addresses homosexuality, hence the popular notion that the term "sodomy" refers to anal intercourse. See L. William Countryman, Dirt, Greed and Sex, page 31 to learn why this is not the case.

264 Tony Campolo, *Speaking My Mind* (Nashville: W Publishing Group, 2004), 67 and Jack Rogers, *Jesus, the Bible, and Homosexuality: Explode the Myths, Heal the Church* (Louisville, Kentucky: Westminster John Knox Press, 2006), 73-74.

265 Ibid. (Jack Rogers), 74.

266 Justin R. Cannon, *The Bible, Christianity, and Homosexuality,* (Justin R. Cannon, 2009)

267 Philo Thelos, *God is Not a Homophobe* (Victoria, British Columbia: Trafford Publishing, 2004), 62.

268 Ibid (Philo Thelos), 85-87.

269 Justin R. Cannon, *The Bible, Christianity, and Homosexuality,* (Justin R. Cannon, 2009). 4-6.

270 Daniel A. Helminiak, Ph.D., *What the Bible Really Says About Homosexuality, Millennium Edition* (New Mexico: Alamo Square Press, 2008), 23.

271 I Kings 14, 15, and 22 and Hosea 4:14

272 I Corinthians 14:34

273 Former professor at Fuller Seminary and famous author, the late Lewis Smedes speaks on his new understanding of Romans and homosexuality here: http://www.soulforce.org/article/lewis-smedes-video

274 John Stossel, Myths, Lies, and Downright Stupidity: Get Out the Shovel—Why Everything You Know is Wrong, (New York: Hyperion, 2006), 185.

275 "There's a Wideness in God's Mercy," Video Interview with Dr. Lewis Smedes on Romans 1: http://www.soulforce.org/article/lewis-smedes-video (accessed October 2011).

276 Larry King Live, April 23, 2010.

CONFESSION 11

277 Francis S. Collins, *The Language of God: A Scientist Presents Evidence for Belief* (New York: Free Press, 2006), 4.

278 Ibid (Collins), 5.

279 James A. Shapiro, "A Third Way," Boston Review, February/March 1997.

280 Richard Dawkins, *The Blind Watchmaker: Why the Evidence of Evolution Reveals a Universe Without Design* (New York: W. W. Norton & Company, 1996), 1.

281 Henry Morris, Famous-Quotes.com, Gledhill Enterprises, 2011:

http://www.1-famous-quotes.com/quote/758260 (accessed September 2011).

282 Similar to the way we use the word day to mean a solar day or an age or epoch of time. See "Old Earth Creation Science," Word Study Yom: http://www.answersincreation.org/word_study_yom.htm (accessed June 2011).

283 Ibid ("Old Earth Creation Science").

284 Ibid ("Old Earth Creation Science").

285 "The Great Debate on Science and the Bible," The John Ankerberg Show (DVD).

286 Donald Hochner, "Noah's Flood: Global or Local?" http://www.angel-fire.com/ca/DeafPreterist/noah.html (accessed June 2011).

287 The old-earth creationist position is best defended by Hugh Ross, an evangelical astrophysicist who wrote *A Matter of Days: Resolving a Creation Controversy.*

288 Some of the arguments made in A.E. Wilder-Smith's, *The Creation of Life: A Cybernetic Approach to Evolution.*

289 Gould, Stephen J., "Is a New and General Theory of Evolution Emerging?" Paleobiology, vol 6 (1), p. 119-130 (1980).

290 Niles Eldredge, "Confessions of a Darwinist," The Virginia Quarterly Review, Spring 2006.

291 David S. Woodruff, Science, p.717 (May 16, 1980).

292 Gould was quoted using this number in R. Lewin, "Evolutionary Theory Under Fire," Science Vol. 210:883-887 (November, 1980). 50,000 years is a relatively short period of geologic time.

293 Richard Dawkins, *The Blind Watchmaker: Why the Evidence of Evolution Reveals a Universe Without Design* (New York: W. W. Norton & Company, 1996), 251.

294 James A. Shapiro, "A Third Way," Boston Review, February/March 1997.

295 Ibid. (Shapiro).

296 Ibid. (Shapiro).

297 "Lynn Margulis," Lynn Margulis – Wikipedia: http://en.wikipedia.org/ wiki/Lynn_Margulis (accessed April 2011).

298 "Lynn Margulis: Science's Unruly Earth Mother," Science, 1991, Vol. 252, page 378.

299 Michael A. Flannery, *Alfred Russel Wallace's Theory of Intelligent Evolution: How Wallace's "World of Life" Challenged Darwinism* (Riesel, Texas: Erasmus Press, 2008), 1-55.

300 Geoffrey Simmons, MD, *Billions of Missing Links* (Eugene, Oregon: Harvest House Publishers, 2007), 30.

301 David Berlinski, *The Deniable Darwin & Other Essays*, (Seattle: Discovery Institute Press, 2009), 341.

302 Michael Denton, *Nature's Destiny: How the Laws of Biology Reveal Purpose in the Universe* (New York: The Free Press, 1998), 385.

303 Critics of ID say ID is not genuine science partly because ID theorists have not been able to publish their theories in peer-reviewed scientific publications. When Meyer's article was published, the editor, Richard Sternberg, was criticized and pressured to resign. So ID theorists have a Catch 22. They won't be taken seriously until they get widespread publication in peer-reviewed scientific journals, and they can't achieve widespread publication in such journals because most editors don't take them seriously. When they do—with Sternberg as a precedent—an editor risks censure and termination.

304 Abiogenesis is the theory of how biological life, including the first life on Earth, arose from inorganic matter through natural processes.

305 Antony Flew, *There is a God: How the World's Most Notorious Atheist Changed His Mind* (New York: HarperCollins, 2007), 95 and 123.

306 Ibid (Flew), 124.

307 Michael Behe, *The Edge of Evolution: The Search for the Limits of Darwinism* (New York: Free Press, 2007), 182.

308 Romans 8:18-22 states, "I consider that our present sufferings are not worth comparing with the glory that will be revealed in us. For the creation waits in eager expectation for the children of God to be revealed. For the creation was subjected to frustration, not by its own choice, but by the will of the one who subjected it, in hope that the creation itself will be liberated from its bondage to decay and brought into the freedom and glory of the children

of God. We know that the whole creation has been groaning as in the pains of childbirth right up to the present time."

309 Francis S. Collins, *The Language of God: A Scientist Presents Evidence for Belief* (New York: Free Press, 2006), 57-84. For further study on this subject, see *God and the Astronomers* by Robert Jastrow (2000), *Rare Earth: Why Complex Life Is Uncommon in the Universe*, by Peter Ward and Donald Brownlee (2000), and *The Privileged Planet: How Our Place in the Cosmos is Designed for Discovery* by Guillermo Gonzalez and Jay Richards (2004).

310 David Berlinski, *The Devil's Delusion: Atheism and its Scientific Pretensions* (New York: Crown Forum, 2008), 12.

311 Bradley Monton, *Seeking God in Science: An Atheist Defends Intelligent Design* (Peterborough, Ontario, Canada: Broadview Press, 2009), 47-74 and Stephen C. Meyer, *Signature in the Cell: DNA and the Evidence for Intelligent Design* (New York: HarperCollins, 2009), 396-415 give the best case I've found for why ID is a valid scientific theory.

312 Although Monton concedes the infinite space or multi-universes theories are speculative, he cites some evidence for them. Personally, the infinite universes explanation seems irrelevant to me since they are not proven.

313 "Alfred Russel Wallace," Alfred Russel Wallace – Wikipedia: http://en.wikipedia.org/wiki/Alfred_Russel_Wallace (accessed August 2011).

CONFESSION 12
314 "Universalism and the Bible," by Keith DeRose (http://pantheon.yale.edu/~kd47/univ.htm), Thomas Talbot, *The Inescapable Love of God*, and Gregory MacDonald, *The Evangelical Universalist.*

315 Lee Strobel, *The Case for Faith: A Journalist Investigates the Toughest Objections to Christianity* (Grand Rapids, Michigan: Zondervan, 2000), 241.

316 I John 4:16 and I Corinthians 13:8

317 I Timothy 2:3-4

318 Acts 10:34

319 Job 42:2

320 Calvinism or Reformed Theology has five pillars: (1) Humankind is totally depraved and has no ability to choose to follow God on its own accord. (2) God chooses from eternity whom to save (becoming the elect), and this choosing is in no way based on a person's own merit, virtue, or faith. (3) The

atonement derived from Christ's death was only designed to cover the sins of the elect. (4) The saving grace of God, which is irresistible and causes someone to follow God, is only applied to the elect. (5) Since God is sovereign and his will can't be frustrated, those whom He called to be the elect will continue to the end. The major opposing view of Calvinism is Arminianism—the belief that humans freely choose to follow God or not, despite the fact of their supposed depravity. The ideas of C.S. Lewis on the nature of salvation would fall under this view.

321 Earlier I offered an alternative meaning of this passage in light of the original Greek. The word translated "lust" can also be translated "covet." See Confession 9, The Sex God.

322 *I Kissed Dating Goodbye* by Josh Harris became a popular book among conservative evangelicals in the late 1990s and 2000s making the case that courtship, not traditional dating, was superior for singles.

323 "The History of Universalism," The Christian Universalist Association: http://www.christianuniversalist.org/articles/history.html (accessed January 2011).

324 Matthew 5:21-22

325 Matthew 5:26

326 See the arguments in Gerry Beauchemin, *Hope Beyond Hell: The Righteous Purpose of God's Judgment* (Olmito, Texas: Malista Press), 21-45, Gregory MacDonald, *The Evangelical Universalist*, (Eugene, OR: Wipf & Stock Publishers, 2006), 147-148, and Thomas Talbot, *The Inescapable Love of God*, (Universal Publishers, 1999, rev. 2002), 86-92.

327 Gerry Beauchemin, *Hope Beyond Hell: The Righteous Purpose of God's Judgment* (Olmito, Texas: Malista Press), 24.

328 *Young's Literal Translation*, the *Rotherham Translation*, the Weymouth Translation, and the *Concordant Literal Translation* do not translate *aionios* as everlasting but use a phrase like punishment of the age.

329 Jonah 1:17 and 2:6

330 Deuteronomy 23:3

331 2 Chronicles 7:16 and 1 Kings 8:13; 9:3

332 Gerry Beauchemin, *Hope Beyond Hell: The Righteous Purpose of God's Judgment* (Olmito, Texas: Malista Press), 25 and 45.

333 Gregory MacDonald, *The Evangelical Universalist*, (Eugene, OR: Wipf & Stock Publishers, 2006), 148.

334 Thomas Talbot, *The Inescapable Love of God*, (Universal Publishers, 1999, rev. 2002), 91.

335 N. T. Wright, *Jesus and the Victory of God* (Minneapolis, MN: Fortress Press, 1996), 320-368.

336 "George MacDonald," George MacDonald – Wikipedia: http://en.wikipedia.org/wiki/George_MacDonald (accessed March 2011).

337 Ibid. (MacDonald).

338 Charles Pridgen as quoted by Gerry Beauchemin, *Hope Beyond Hell: The Righteous Purpose of God's Judgment* (Olmito, Texas: Malista Press), 145.

339 Charles Pridgen as quoted by Gerry Beauchemin, *Hope Beyond Hell: The Righteous Purpose of God's Judgment* (Olmito, Texas: Malista Press), 146.

340 Ibid. (Beauchemin), 146.

341 Gregory MacDonald, *The Evangelical Universalist*, (Eugene, OR: Wipf & Stock Publishers, 2006), 173.

342 Gerry Beauchemin, *Hope Beyond Hell: The Righteous Purpose of God's Judgment* (Olmito, Texas: Malista Press), 229-233.

343 Martin Luther in a letter to Hanseu Von Rechenberg in 1522.

344 "The History of Universalism," The Christian Universalist Association: http://www.christianuniversalist.org/articles/history.html (accessed January 2011).

345 "The History of Universalism," The Christian Universalist Association: http://www.christianuniversalist.org/articles/history.html (accessed January 2011).

346 Gregory MacDonald, T*he Evangelical Universalist*, (Eugene, OR: Wipf & Stock Publishers, 2006), 175.

347 Thomas Talbot, *The Inescapable Love of God*, (Universal Publishers, 1999, rev. 2002), 56-60.

348 In Greek, *Kyrios*, which is a title of honor expressive of respect, with which servants greet their master.

349 Thomas Talbot, *The Inescapable Love of God*, (Universal Publishers, 1999, rev. 2002), 69.

350 John 1:29

351 Luke 2:10

352 James 2:13

353 John 12:47

354 I Timothy 2:4

355 I John 2:2 (New Century Version)

356 I Chronicles 16:41

357 2 Samuel 14:14

358 Genesis 22:18

359 Story told in *Beyond Our Differences*, PBS Home Video (2009).

CPSIA information can be obtained at www.ICGtesting.com
Printed in the USA
BVOW071141080412

287094BV00001B/1/P